"If you're tired of predictab[...]iters, check out Liz Charlotte Gra[...]o read someone who knows what language can do w[...]eash."

"Never have I read a book quite like this one. Liz Charlotte Grant opens a door to wonder and awe, drawing from science and art, history and myth, to create nuanced readings of Genesis. From dark matter to holy lightning, Grant invites us to contemplate cosmic questions and explore the unknown and unknowable. No matter where we find ourselves in faith and doubt, we are free to find something new in these pages, something quite like magic."

"This book is not like the others. In this truly fresh take on Genesis, Grant weaves together biblical scholarship, science, and Jewish midrash to introduce readers to the depth and complexity of Genesis as truly adult literature. For those who are interested enough in the Bible to not want the same old same old, here's your reintroduction to a book that has been mined for meaning for over two millennia. Let Grant be your guide."

# KNOCK AT THE SKY

Seeking God in Genesis
after Losing Faith in the Bible

**Liz Charlotte Grant**

WILLIAM B. EERDMANS PUBLISHING COMPANY
GRAND RAPIDS, MICHIGAN

Wm. B. Eerdmans Publishing Co.
4035 Park East Court SE, Grand Rapids, Michigan 49546
www.eerdmans.com

Published 2025
Printed in the United States of America

31  30  29  28  27  26  25      1  2  3  4  5  6  7

ISBN 978-0-8028-8375-9

**Library of Congress Cataloging-in-Publication Data**

A catalog record for this book is available from the Library of Congress.

*For those who wander*

# CONTENTS

# FOREWORD

"How do I learn to love my Bible again?"

It isn't an abstract philosophical question for many of us, I know. Many of us were part of an evangelical (or evangelical-adjacent/influenced) generation raised on loving, memorizing, and obeying Scripture in a deeply formative way, so it can be a profoundly disorienting experience when we find ourselves questioning the Bible, doubting the Bible, feeling resentment and anger toward the Bible, let alone falling out of love with the Bible. It feels like our whole foundation of understanding and being has shifted. Some of us find this to be freeing; others find it scary. Perhaps at best, we simply had an incomplete relationship with Scripture, but for many of us, the Bible was even actively used to oppress, marginalize, silence, or incite violence and even abuse. In the aftermath, we're left wondering, "What to do with this book? How do we read it now? Does it still matter? Should I walk away from the Bible altogether if I don't believe the same things I used to believe? Is there anything worth holding onto here?" Those are such fair questions.

I've never felt certain on how to answer the question about how to love our Bible, as that seems to me to be the work of the Spirit—and not a lady who overshares on the Internet for a living. What I can tell you is that I do love my Bible more now than ever and, yes, I believe the Spirit was at the root of that work. I spend more time with my Bible now than I ever did as an overly earnest Word of Faith kid, and it is flowing through me like wine through water at this point. The Bible still regularly disrupts me, the way light always disrupts the darkness, just as much as it comforts, strengthens, and guides me.

*Foreword*

One of the reasons that I love my Bible again is because of teachers, theologians, poets, artists, scholars, and writers like Liz Charlotte Grant who boldly reenter these pages with us, retelling the stories we think we know and widening our gaze to include more goodness and more truth. It is so important for us to embrace a curious and humble posture to learn about context, interpretation, story, politics, history, poetry, and theology all present in the text. Now, I can see the work of the Spirit in how I relearned to love my Bible by listening to people like Liz who have wrestled with, loved, and remained in conversation with the Bible too. It turns out there was more than one way to read the Bible all along.

In my early days alongside many refugees of the evangelical movement, I was a bit surprised by how many folks cited their questions about the book of Genesis as the origin point for their deconstruction experience. It seemed to consistently be the first shot across the bow signaling an imminent battle, the first block to fall in the Jenga tower, or the first thread to be pulled in the unravelling sweater. Now it makes perfect sense to me that Liz Charlotte Grant started here, where many of us first began to doubt and question how we were taught to read and understand the Bible. She has given us a fresh but rooted perspective on the text of Genesis, and even given us permission to allow the Bible to be what it actually is.

Liz is my favorite type of stubborn: the faithful kind. She won't give up her Bible just because some folks use it badly or disingenuously and ignorantly. She holds on to curiosity, imagination, and wisdom as she declares, "These stories are mine, too." (Never underestimate a Bible nerd.) Those stories are also yours. You get to wrestle with, doubt, love, challenge, and be changed by these stories, too. Much about how you read and understand the Scriptures may change, hallelujah, and this is still your story.

Whether you are arriving at this book with a semi-truck full of baggage regarding the Bible or just a few questions and curiosities, you'll find something good here. In these pages, you'll encounter insightful, spacious, wise, and even playful discussions about so many of your questions from inerrancy to methodology, authority, power, biblical interpretation, our obsession with certainty, and beyond. This isn't apologetics for progressives; it's a much needed half-step over from the tightly managed paths of your past into the wildflowers off the trail, closer to the trees, with a view on the vast horizon still ahead. There is room to breathe here.

Liz is as honest as she is compassionate. (She is also a heck of a writer.) You won't find her shying away from the difficulties and painful moments. But neither does she lose sight of the beauty, the redemption, the possibility of the good news for us either. By taking a run at one of the most contested, debated, and disruptive books of the Bible, she shows her fearlessness and her grounded humility in equal measure.

In the end, the group-project of the Bible will do what it often does: reveal God and reveal us. Liz gently turns us to curiosity, wonder, mystery, humor, collaboration, community, and holiness in these pages. As she invites us to do so beautifully, when you feel stuck behind a locked door, please keep knocking. The loving and surprising responses that open the door might surprise you, but you're always welcome. You always were.

*Sarah Bessey*

# ABBREVIATIONS

| | |
|---|---|
| ESV | English Standard Version |
| JPS | Jewish Publication Society |
| NASB | New American Standard Bible |
| NET | New English Translation |
| NIV | New International Version |
| NRSVue | New Revised Standard Version Updated Edition |

# A NOTE TO FORMER AND CURRENT EVANGELICALS

**DISCUSSED:**

*Contemporary Christian Music, Dinosaurs, The People of Certitude, The Chicago Statement on Biblical Inerrancy, Golden Calf, Faith Deconstruction, The Bible as Oral History, An Invitation to Wander*

I used to be a good evangelical. I aced every Bible class in my private Christian high school and nearly earned a minor in Bible at my prestigious Christian college. I never missed youth group, spent my summers laying bricks for the needy in Mexico, and woke up early for a regular quiet time, during which I wrote out prayer requests in a journal purchased from the Christian bookstore. I memorized contemporary Christian music lyrics and pasted the posters of CCM bands to my walls as a teenager. I even dated Jesus until meeting my husband at twenty-one, saving my first kiss for him.

Once, at age ten, I debated a neighbor's mother who was hostile to my family's religion, when she asked me on the playground, "Where are the dinosaurs in the Bible? How can it be trusted if it doesn't even mention the dinosaurs?" Her questions did not faze me. The presence or absence of dinosaurs changed nothing, and I told her so. My certainty in the Bible, Jesus, none of it weakened at her prodding. That early in my life, the conviction of those around me—parents, relatives, pastors, church volunteers—had already supplied me with complete confidence in a text that predated my oldest grandparent by millennia. Not that I knew anything about the origins of that book. I did not need to. I trusted the people who trusted the book.

Certitude is a trait of my people. We evangelicals are people of the book, the only book that matters, the Bible. There, God dwells. To find God, to find the truth, we needed only to turn to the four-pounder on our bookshelves.

Evangelicals value this text so highly because of a favorite doctrine of our fundamentalist forefathers. Inerrancy, literally meaning "without error," is a doctrine we apply exclusively to the Bible. A 1978 conference in Chicago gathered three hundred of these forefathers to hammer out what inerrancy meant as applied to the Bible. They pounded out several statements between then and 1986 that would define the behaviors and thinking of American Evangelicalism for the next fifty years. The first and most notable they called "The Chicago Statement on Biblical Inerrancy."[1] The issue at stake to these men was authority. The preface begins, "The *authority* of Scripture is a key issue for the Christian Church in this and every age. . . . Recognition of the total truth and trustworthiness of Holy Scripture is essential to a full grasp and adequate confession of its *authority*" (italics mine). In the Scriptures, the idea of authority shares space with dominion, rule, and authorship (*author*ity) and coincides with other hierarchical cultural norms within the Bible, such as monarchy, patriarchy, and slavery. However, the concept is not applied to the *law* as the Jews knew it but to *the people* who expounded it, and authority comes exclusively from God. Authority is relational, not inherent to any text.

However, the Bible does seem to assert inerrancy of a kind. In Matthew 5:18, Jesus says, "Until heaven and earth disappear, not the smallest letter, not the least stroke of a pen, will by any means disappear from the Law until everything is accomplished" (NIV). In Matthew 24:35, Jesus says, "Heaven and earth will pass away, but my words will not pass away" (NIV). In John 10:35, Jesus says, "Scripture cannot be set aside." Jesus seems to be promising that every apostrophe, verb, and footnote in the pages of the Bible would last forever and evade the corrosive effects of time, culture, catastrophe. This is how I used to interpret Jesus's words, anyway, and how the writers of the statement seem to read Jesus, too. No wonder doubting the Bible's inerrancy felt to me like calling Jesus a liar.

Yet the writers of the statement go further, claiming that the authority of Christ and the authority of the Bible are the same.[2] To be fair to the signatories of the statement, their statement only attempts to confer this level of authority to the *original* manuscripts, rather than secondary translations or interpretation—though in common practice, this distinction is irrelevant. (For example, how many of us can access the original manuscripts during our personal Bible study? For most Americans, translations and interpretations *are* the Bible.)

But a book of God, even written *by God* through a possessed inspiration, is by no means the *same* as Godself. The book and the Deity are not synonymous. Pretending God and God's book are the same only repeats the heresy of the Israelites. After Moses came down from Mount Sinai with the commandments of God inscribed in stone, they assumed the essence of God could be contained in stone tablets or even in a golden idol (Exodus 32). Yet God is beyond any created thing, including the Bible.

\* \* \*

I do not know precisely why these evangelical leaders settled on inerrancy as the one and only methodology to decipher the writings we Christians call the Bible. Still, once they had pressed the Bible into this mold, they would do their damnedest to keep it.

You could argue their aim was admirable. We evangelicals sought to make God accessible for those without theology degrees. But to create a single interpretation of this complex, ancient work of literature required ignoring much of what was true about the text and about God. We had to ignore, for example, the range of biblical interpretations that had existed across time. We had to diminish the genuine disagreement among Christians about the *right way* to understand God, the *right way* to read the book about God, and the *right way* to apply the book to our distinctive settings and personalities. And we had to refuse legitimacy to the hundreds of denominations and preferences that have marked our religious tribe since its conception. This strategy also encouraged us to read our lives in black and white, same as our text: two options only. We could allow no compromise, no third way of religious practice and interpretation. All *true believers*, we assumed, would agree with us. Unity was obvious, binary, faithful. We began to demonize disagreement itself.

In this single argument, today's contentious American Evangelicalism clarifies before our eyes. To many Americans, Evangelicalism represents an imperious tribe committed to a true-false exclusionary set of beliefs. And if you disagree? You're condemned to burn in an eternal hell. Granted, this paints a stereotype of American Evangelicalism, not the reality of every evangelical person or evangelical church community. But for those who have been raised inside and then have left (or been booted), we recognize truth within the stereotype. So, many Christians find our belief in inerrancy wavering.

In particular, the young Deconstructionists like myself have witnessed the once-steady religious institutions shift and collapse. Public falls from grace—the failings of leaders like Mark Driscoll, Ravi Zacharias, and Bill Hybels, each one a leader that shaped my own upbringing within 1990s American Evangelicalism—have intensified our doubt. In 2016, Dr. James Dobson, the leader whose tape series *Preparing for Adolescence* introduced me to the birds and bees, endorsed a presidential candidate whose immoral behaviors turned criminal in private, calling him a "baby Christian."[3] The Southern Baptist Convention, whose theology had most directly shaped the convictions of every supposedly nondenominational evangelical church community I attended in my upbringing, has ejected female pastors from their denomination despite these leaders' decades of faithful service. And the SBC's flagship seminary has only recently admitted to centuries of racism and bigotry that influenced denominational decision-making. Add in the trauma of the LGBTQ+ community, and you have a tsunami of betrayal.[4]

Power has its own gravity, a black hole allowing no light to escape. In view of these many hypocrisies, my peers and I have witnessed the humble way of Christ discarded, trampled, and exploited. And as our faith in institution and authority has collapsed, so too has our certainty. The way is narrow, Christ told us, and now we have experienced the truth of his words for ourselves.

Worse, because our leaders and institutions claimed their authority from the pages of the Bible, those harmed by Evangelicalism have increasingly mistrusted the book that we once believed unquestioningly. Some discard it entirely; others wonder whether these words that we have recited and memorized and journaled and tattooed on our forearms still contain any remnant of God. Perhaps we wonder whether they ever did. Was the whole thing a magic trick? We do not know what to believe now that our forefathers and their faulty hermeneutic have been proved suspect.

This background undoubtedly affects the way I understand truth: I no longer see the value in securing the truth with superglue as Evangelicalism seems to demand. What can human beings know? And how can we know what we know *for certain*? Nearing my forties, I resonate with the words of Ecclesiastes: "When I applied my mind to know wisdom . . . then I saw all the work of God, that no one can find out what is happening under the sun. However much they may toil in seeking, they will not find it out; even though those who are wise claim to know, they cannot find it out" (Ecclesiastes 8:16–17 NRSVue). As humans, we cannot help trying to collect knowledge, that is our occupation. Yet we know so little. I am weary of any dogmatism that becomes a tool to bludgeon the unsure.

I used to read the Bible in binary terms—inerrant versus errant, fallible versus infallible. This led me and many American Christians to believe that the whole of our spirituality could be slotted into binaries. We could read a passage either rightly or wrongly. Our interpretation could be true or false. We ourselves could be classed as good or bad, damned or redeemed, friend or enemy. Reading the Bible like this also encouraged us to believe in *one single interpretation*, an interpretation that must be the most obvious, the "plain reading," because God would not try to keep Godself from us. We flattened the Bible for the sake of simplicity.

My evangelical upbringing instilled in me a unique seriousness about my pursuit of God. And I learned to seek God in community. So I am grateful for this formation, and I take it with me into new religious spaces, even as I have left Evangelicalism behind. But I am seeking a new method to read the old text, a method more curious and capacious than the doctrine of inerrancy allows. My goal is the same as always: I want to commune with God. But I'm no longer a good evangelical.

After my certainty collapsed, I was surprised to find that American Evangelicalism is *not* Christianity at large. Nor is it the last word on God or the Bible. Christianity disagrees fervently among itself and always has. Thank God.

Three faiths have claimed the Bible, not only Christianity. I may have studied the Bible within a white American evangelical context, but these writings have a rich history (and present) that expands beyond my religious tradition, particularly within the writings of Jewish scholars.

Further, the Bible has existed long before my Christian forebears settled the notion of inerrancy. The collection of stories that would be compiled into the holy Scriptures existed earlier still. Before clergy scandals; before the horseback riding, slave-owning revivalists spread their bull horn gospel across the American West; before the European scientific revolution called faith naive; before the rebellion of Martin Luther and the genocide known as the Crusades; before the Christian church gained a state budget from the Roman emperor Constantine; before Jesus walked on our spinning globe; before a word of the Bible was ever transcribed, even then humanity's up-close encounters with God were already being told and retold.

Eventually, scribes would commit these oral histories to ink and paper. Then, across generations, readers passed these pages so that, eventually, these ancient writings would reach me in the suburbs of Denver, Colorado, theUnited States of America in the twenty-first century as the red and black arial words printed on wispy pages and bound in vinyl: the Bible on my bookshelf.

For me, and not only my ancestors, the Bible has evoked curiosity, imagination, and pathos, and my reforming faith has not changed the fact. I cannot shake the belief that I encounter something transcendent when I open the book, a narrative wider and truer than my own individual life. Does the book contain God? Do the words offer a glimmer of afterlife to the reader? Can each word, verse, and story be decoded like a cereal box prize? I do not know. But I am not ready to cede the Bible to the literalists. While some of my formerly evangelical peers prefer to ditch this often-troubling book altogether, I refuse to. These stories are mine, too.

I believe this book still deserves our attention—even when it refuses to submit to our age's demand for historicity, even if we readers leave literalism behind. Truth is not the same as fact. To refuse ourselves these stories is a death by starvation. These spiritual stories sustained our spiritual forebears; without these stories, I suggest that we cannot maintain the imagination required to nurture belief.

So, in the coming chapters, like a well-indoctrinated evangelical, I am returning to the Scriptures. (You can't take the Bible study out of the girl.) But I am reading it slant. I attend to the sky and the ground with free-ranging curiosity, comingling origin stories from science and art with the Bible's account of God's first encounters with humanity in the book of Genesis. I explore the story of how the Bible itself came to be, how we Christians came to read it as we do, and what Jewish readers of the Bible can illuminate about our too-familiar text.

Rather than flat-footed rejection, I encourage wandering. Our best questions often sound like doubts, yet I believe curiosity is the most reverent stance a human can take. Wandering itself is a spiritual discipline. Far from losing faith, I have found that wandering has allowed me to find it.

I believe the Bible does have the power to tell us what God is like, even to introduce us to the Creator. But I read the Bible differently than I used to. I move more cautiously, listening closely to a variety of careful scholars—theologians, archaeologists, philologists, linguists, and manuscript critics. I am determined to be patient and humble. I myself am a learner, not a scholar.

In this book, you too have permission to question the sacred without fearing a backslide into unbelief. Knock loudly. Listen to your gut and let your tears run. Reject answers that do not admit complication. Seek the resonance at the base of the story. The seeking is the point. Because there, in your wandering, God is.

# ON GENESIS
# AND METHODOLOGY

## DISCUSSED:

*A Brief Overview of the Book in Question, Midrash as Art, Eisegesis, The God of All/No Genders, Resisting the Urge to Make Science Out of Genesis (Because That's Boring)*

*On Genesis*

Genesis, the first book of the Christian Bible and Jewish Torah, is one of humankind's oldest texts. Fundamentalist scholars suppose that Moses authored the Torah, including Genesis, likely alongside a group of scribes who made additions and subtractions (such as describing the death of Moses) at the request of the Hebraic community and its leaders.[1] However, later scholars have agreed that the composition of the book was less tidy than our traditions supposed and that the creation of the text instead involved *many* authors, editors, redactors and commentators to compile the scroll of Genesis that we know today. (More on this to come.)

The narrative of Genesis can be split into three acts: act 1 is God's creation of a primordial cosmos and God's interactions with early humankind; act 2 is God's relationship and actions toward Israel's patriarchs; and act 3 is God's orchestration of the life of Joseph, son of the third patriarch, including the Israelites' descent to Egypt and eventual enslavement by that nation.

This book examines Genesis 1–32, the first two acts of Genesis, exploring the creation account through Jacob's wrestling match with God or an angel. I pay particular attention to the story of Abraham and his immediate family.

## On Sources, Midrash, and Textual Authority

I have written this book as an experiment in eisegesis, as in, reading life *into* the biblical text. My guides into this mode of textual criticism have been nondominant culture theologians. I rarely refer to white voices, especially white male voices—not because I do not care about the thoughts of John Calvin or Martin Luther, but because at the time of the writing, I was familiar with the thrust of white male theology already, and I was hungry for more, for different. So, I turned to scholars, creatives, and rabbis I had never read. These illuminated Genesis as I had not seen it before, including scholars such as James H. Cone, Howard Thurman, Delores S. Williams, Wilda C. Gafney, Abraham Joshua Heschel, Avivah Gottlieb Zornberg, Phyllis Trible, Simone Weil, Gustavo Gutiérrez, and Rashi. Additionally, I've highlighted premodern biblical perspectives and legends, such as those from the Christian mystics, the patristic fathers, and the rabbis.

My methodology most resembles midrash. The word "midrash" can mean "exegesis," as in the critical and academic interpretation of a text that emphasizes authorial intention and historical and linguistic context. Yet midrash can also lean into creative territory. Midrash seems to align more closely to the interpretative method of eisegesis with its emphasis on a reader's experience, stories, associations, and personal interpretations of a text. Think of exegesis as science and eisegesis as story. (Though the distinctions are not quite as clear as this metaphor paints, as we'll discuss later.)

Midrash is generally a Jewish exercise, though Catholics treasure their own expansions of the biblical canon. In the margins of the Talmud, the Jewish code of law and ethics, the rabbis argued over every part of their Bible (our Old Testament). And the rabbis often supplied extra detail and story to flesh out the parts that remained confusing, or silent, or where meaning may have been lost in translation. John C. Reeves describes this rabbinic activity as occurring in two categories: "1) *Midrash halakhah*, or halakhic midrash, wherein *explicit precepts or guidelines* for conducting one's life in accordance with God's mandates are deduced from Biblical discourse; and 2) *midrash haggadah*, or haggadic (or aggadic) midrash, wherein *explanatory comments, expansive additions, illustrative anecdotes, and legendary stories are generated from what are perceived to be pregnant, yet silent, aspects of the biblical text.* Common to both categories . . . is its bibliocentric basis . . . midrash necessarily presupposes the concept of an authoritative text."[2]

To rephrase, midrash halakhah draws laws and ethics directly from the pages of the Bible, often skimmed off the top in a plain reading, whereas midrash haggadah offers extrabiblical expansion as a way to understand confusing narratives or to refer attention to past communal interpretative storytelling.

Yet both categories of midrash consider the Bible authoritative and divinely inspired. Jews, like Christians, traditionally believe that the holy text, as compiled in its original languages, contains the words of God. However, Jewish teachers more openly admit that the Bible does seem somehow incomplete. To answer this incompleteness, they patiently meditate on the text, as if savoring a hard candy on the tongue, seeking any and all insights the text offers, welcoming hypotheses and storytelling and free association as essential modes of discovery. The midrash asserts that the Bible contains both question and answer.

Midrashic scholar Avivah Gottlieb Zornberg describes her own eisegetical scholarship in her book *The Beginning of Desire: Reflections on Genesis*: "My mode of inquiry was closer to the 'rhetorical' than to the 'methodical,' in terms of Gerald Bruns's distinction—the 'rhetorical' *having 'no greater ambition than to discover what can be said*, in any given case.' I am . . . looking to loosen the fixities, the ossifications of preconceived readings. . . . The aim of interpretation is, I suggest, not merely to domesticate, to familiarize an ancient book: it is also, and perhaps more importantly, to *'make strangeness in certain respects stranger*.'"[3]

The aim of eisegesis is not to arrive at *one clear, singular interpretation* that explains any portion of the Bible, but to muddy the waters for the purpose of disrupting incorrect readings. And eisegesis makes the complexity of the Bible more obvious for the sake of deeper and truer understanding. Eisegesis needles the idea of textual authority by making plain the fact that reading the Bible is necessarily *interpretative* and that interpreters have a context and perspective. No one reads the Bible plainly; such a reading is impossible. Evangelicals prefer to imagine the Bible to be *obvious* to interpret for everyone, but eisegesis states emphatically that this is untrue. For that reason, eisegesis has not traditionally been a popular fundamentalist interpretative mode. Yet I argue that its methodology has much to teach us who read (or once read) the Bible in binary.

### On Naming God, Gender, and Pronouns

I refer to God by many names throughout this text, some of which may feel foreign to evangelical readers. I call God the Deity, Divinity, the Voice, the Presence, the Poltergeist, the Omnipotent, the Being, and many more pseudonyms. However, I personally affirm all three historic Christian creeds. So, I mean to reference the Christian God: the "I AM" who leads and directs the Hebrews throughout the Old Testament; whose entrance into the world leads to the death, resurrection, and ascension of Jesus Christ, Godself, in the first century CE; and whose scattering occurs among the people of God at Pentecost by the same Spirit that vivifies the Christian church to this day. The names I use for God are nontraditional, but I do not mean another God.

I have also intentionally *not* assigned a single gender to God, seeing that any divine gender designation is anthropomorphic. God is a wholly other category of being that does not inhabit human binary gender categories, especially within the Old Testament. The exception is the person of Jesus who is male. Yet Jesus's male gender does not make *every* member of Godself male at all times. In fact, though many of our Christian metaphors for understanding the Trinitarian Godhead are male—father and son being the most common metaphors—this gendered picture is incomplete based on the scope of the Scriptures. God's essence is not male (or female) only.

Throughout the Bible, God expresses Godself in both genders. For example, God's *ruakh*, meaning alternately breath, wind, and Spirit, animates humankind in Genesis. When referred to individually, the Hebrew language genders *ruakh* as female. God, the female Spirit, births humankind and creation. The Hebrew prophets enhance this meaning further by using female metaphors for birthing, breastfeeding, and child rearing to refer to God's work among the Israelites.

Another example: God's *shekinah glory* leads the newly emancipated Hebrews out of Egypt to crisscross the Sinai desert as cloud and fire. Again, God's presence here is gendered female in the Hebrew language. God, the female holy Presence, protects her flock as they seek the promised land. And this *shekinah* also inhabits the temple of the Israelites, marking God's continued presence and blessing (or absence and cursing) to the people throughout the Old Testament.

Last, *Torah*, the Israelites' name for both the first five books of the Bible and the general term for *all* the teachings of the Old Testament, is gendered female in the Hebrew language. *Torah*, the feminine wisdom of God, also sees representation as the wisdom character of the Proverbs (also gendered female).[4]

Because God participates meaningfully in history and in the biblical story within both genders, both female and male, I refer to God as beyond our gender constructions throughout this book. I use neutral, nongendered pronouns for God as often as possible, including Godself, Theirself, Their, It, Itself. I also substitute nongendered pronouns within biblical quotations. The use of "It" in reference to God is not meant to convey an impersonal or unthinking created object but instead a Higher Being whose essence is—with the exception of Jesus—beyond embodied gender distinctions. In order to avoid confusion, any word or pronoun meant to refer to God will be capitalized.

## On Historical Accuracy

One question I will not address in this work—though it is an important question—is the question of Genesis's historicity. Is Genesis a transcription of the beginning of the world, a literal and factual account exactly as it happened? Or is Genesis a series of fables that its writers never meant readers to take literally? Whenever scholars examine past artifacts, scholars disagree among themselves, and the Bible is no exception. Not every part of this book can be tested and weighed on the scales of science.

But I will say, I believe that God is phenomenologically true. I believe this because I have witnessed God acting within perceptible reality, both historically and in my own lifetime. Yet God remains unprovable according to the scientific method. The Bible suffers the same fate, including the book of Genesis. I find the question "Is it historical?" to be beside the point.

What is the point? The Bible is a profound work of art that has influenced Western culture for centuries. As a student of literature, a creative writer, and a devout Christian, I work from the premise that the biblical texts have profound value, both morally and artistically.

And I have committed to study the words as they appear on the page without making a judgment about their historicity. I recognize that not all readers of the Bible can set aside this question of history, though I personally find the arguing boring and unnecessary. I refer these readers to the dedicated scholars who are, anyway, more qualified than I am to decide what to make of a text so ancient.[5] To each her own.

However, I urge readers to consider what value the Bible offers contemporary readers apart from any evidence that does or does not corroborate the details in this collection of stories, poems, history, law, and advice. What else can we find in the Bible besides fact? What does the Bible say about reality, about death, about the purposes and origins of humanity? What does the Bible reveal about God? Ask, and you will receive. Seek, and you will find. Knock, and the door will blow wide open. Thanks be to God.

# 01

# FIRST CONTACT

**DISCUSSED:**

*The Throat of God, Avivah Gottlieb Zornberg, How Soundwaves Travel, The "Murmuring Deep" (Tehom), A Cosmic Goose, Hydrophones, Frank Watlington, Johnny Cash, Humpback Whale Karaoke, St. Augustine, Translating the Septuagint, The Golden Record, Human Error, Reading the Bible While Standing on Our Heads*

**"**

*The earth was formless and desolate emptiness,*
*and darkness was over the surface of the deep, and*
*the Spirit of God was hovering over the surface of*
*the waters. Then God said. . . .*

**—GENESIS 1:2-3**
*(New American Standard Bible)*

**EVERYTHING DEPENDS UPON** the voice of God. Still or small, the thunder in the cloud or the quiet in the center of the gale, a donkey's haw or a finger tracing the wall: the Voice needs no invitation. God always seeks out first contact.

I have felt the treble resonance of God within my body. I cannot map how or where it arrived, though I believe my whole self to be attuned to the divine speech: nerves and thoughts, bone and marrow, retina and optic nerve, all parts receptive to the sound wave of God.

Occasionally, I wake at night and startle to the Presence of God in the room, as if my four-year-old has silently wandered into my bedroom at five in the morning and clicked on the light. But revelation does not have to be as subtle as a sneaking child. Revelation can arrive at decibels that rupture the eardrum and split the sky. God in the tornado that knocks flat the house, God in the sudden skid of the heart, God in the whites of the ocean.

Yet the Bible begins its account of the Divine with little exposition. Genesis 1:2 reads, "The earth was formless and desolate emptiness, and darkness was over the surface of the deep, and the Spirit of God was hovering over the surface of the waters" (NASB). God, the suspended Spirit. God, the Poltergeist who existed from *before*. God, a current of wind blowing across open water. God, floating.

This hovering Spirit God comes into focus when we attend to Its setting. The location where the Ghost appears acts as foil: the earth, without shape, empty, dark, and marked by a feature called "the deep." The Hebrew word for "the deep" is *tehom*. Other translations render it the "watery abyss" or the "murmuring deep." These secondary translations arrive nearer to the original, which connotes more than a measurement of underwater depth, more than a sounding.

According to Jewish scholar Avivah Gottlieb Zornberg, "[Rabbi] Rashi reads a human consciousness into the uncanny void, as though to say, 'If a person had been there, he would have been astounded, aghast at such absence—at so unbearable a presence of nothingness.'"[1] In other words, before creation, the existential nothingness would have been unendurable to a human witness. The setting in which God first appears is pure absence.

Yet the void is not empty. A Spirit hovers. The Spirit's appearance in the scene offers the reader an intake of breath. Here is a presence. Any second now, the exhale. And the undoing of this absence will arrive by an unexpected instrument: God's own voice.

In fact, while most theologians have counted the separation of light and dark as God's *first* creative act, my favorite retelling of the creation narrative says that God, before anything else, creates silence. The theory depends on translation—not God "hovering over the waters" but God "hovering over *the murmuring deep*." Using that translation, Zornberg writes, "God's speech actually interrupts a primal *noise*." And this "dark watery mass that God's words transfigure" has roots in the Hebrew "*hamam, hamah, hom* [which] cover meanings like *humming, murmuring, cooing, groaning, tumult, music, restlessness, stirring, panic.*" Zornberg notes, "'The murmuring deep,' a poetic translation from the Hebrew *tehom*, represents a non- or prelinguistic sound." He quotes scholar Stephen Frost, who wrote, "It is not that silence is broken, but silence itself breaks, interrupts, the continuous murmur of the Real, thus opening up a clearing in which words can be spoken." And so "speech and silence," Zornberg continues, "are created together to counteract the 'inconsolably alien' murmur of the deep."[2] Silence, then, is the setting that allows God to get to work. Silence is God setting the table.

* * *

Scientists have proven that a human's perception of sound—from eardrum to nerve to brain stem—arrives faster than our eyes perceive light.[3] Though light and sound might transpire simultaneously, humans hear before we see.

When we imagine the mechanics of speech—how a human or animal projects a sound through their body and into the air—we're talking about sound waves echoed within a throat. Fleshy cavities, teeth and cartilage, tongue and lips. We cannot conceptualize a voice apart from its container. That container explains the mechanism of the sound—vibration—but also the origin, the body behind the noise. Whatever idea or instinct motivated the sound in the first place depends on the container that made it.

Of course, God has no throat. That should make speech impossible, according to the material dynamics of the universe. Which makes the following verses in Genesis defy physics. The Deity projects its voice clearly enough to conceive *all that is*. Out of God's noise, the cosmos expands. Out of this Throat fly solar systems and species by the millions, every created bit of matter individuated from every other—continent from cloud, ant from cockroach, eye from lash. The Being without shape produces every shape.

Usually, words do not make matter. Usually, breath does not exist apart from a set of lungs. Here, they do.

Other Near Eastern peoples of the Iron Age (ancient Near Easterners)—the likely period when the stories of the Old Testament began to circulate—had their own origin myths. Like the Hebrew account, many neighboring origin myths involved speech as a means of creation. For example, the mortuary text, *The Book of the Dead*, was composed by hundreds of Egyptian priests between 2400 and 1550 BCE. Rather than inscribing these words on paper, they scratched the hieroglyphs into the walls of tombs like treasure maps to point the deceased occupant to the underworld. According to these directions, the world's beginning involved a cosmic goose laying an egg that contained the entire universe, including a creator deity and the primordial landscape. The authors named the original poultry "the Great Honker." And its "strident cry was the first sound."[4]

It's easy to guffaw at this image of a goose, an egg that holds the cosmos, and a honk that initiates sound and life. But maybe the creator as a goose makes more sense than the Creator as a Spirit—at least the Creator would have a body. A body is helpful when you're establishing worship practices. For example, a body suggests a direction to bow and feet to bathe, grapes to feed. A body provides an object and a mode for worship. A body is charisma, sweat, and sway.

Other ancient Near Eastern religions adopted embodied deities. Some myths claimed two lover gods created the world through their copulation.[5] So, why didn't Moses or the other authors of Genesis describe God with a body, too? There is a reason, has to be. Perhaps a Spirit suggests a realm beyond humanity's sight, underscoring God's transcendence, literally. God as *beyond*, God as *other*. We humans are limited by our own bodies, encased and restricted by skin, limited by a single mind within a single skull. Our Deity is not. Our Deity is spirit, breath, wind, a hovering. Our Deity is the Presence that we cannot picture. Our Deity is beyond this world.

\* \* \*

The creation poem in Genesis 1 is one way I have come to understand the otherness of God. Another way has arrived in the story of Frank Watlington.

Frank had the youthful face of the awkward young man even past age fifty. Lean and tall, his black hair thinning at the temples, his ears protruding, Frank appears in a photo from the 1960s aboard a research sailboat, shirtless and grinning. He has set out to drop a hydrophone—an underwater microphone—fifteen hundred feet into the ocean, joining a Navy team whose mission was to map the sounds of the Atlantic during the Cold War.[6] By analyzing the ocean's sounds, the Navy aimed to catch Soviets in their spying submersibles; instead, Frank caught another mystery entirely.

Come March of each year, the hydrophone picked up interference. And the interference had a pattern, one that indicated a biological source, not a technological one. So, the sound could not be a sub on a covert mission. The crew figured that a creature had entered their ocean space and was making a racket. But for years, they could not identify the source.

For Frank, the question turned personal one late night in the 1960s after he had installed a new set of speakers. His coworkers had gone home hours before. He was alone in the deserted lab. So, when he switched on the speakers and the room filled with "ghostly noises" (according to Frank's colleague, Dr. Ray McAllister), he couldn't help feeling unnerved. In the dark laboratory, he even picked up a microphone to use as a weapon, just in case, before realizing that the *speakers* had finally brought the mysterious noises into an octave his ears could hear.[7]

From that night on, the noises became a code the engineer determined to decipher. Every morning, Frank pumped up the speakers, amplifying the clicks, groans, and whines like nails on a chalkboard. His coworkers were less enthusiastic about Frank regularly tuning in, so eventually he stopped listening live and made his own unclassified recording. He carried the tape with him to play for anyone who would listen. Finally, a group of local fishermen cracked the code: "Oh, that's whales," they said.

Mystery solved: Frank and his team had been listening for years to a fin whale as it passed by Bermuda heading for its mating grounds. Which meant Frank was the first person ever to record whale song.

However, though Frank was the first, Roger Payne receives credit for making whale song famous. Payne, a marine biologist, was the first scientist to listen to Frank's recordings. And the sounds confounded him. He determined to share this discovery, and so he released a record that topped the charts in 1970, a record that was extolled by *Rolling Stone* magazine and Janis Joplin alike.[8]

The recordings changed the course of Payne's life. Payne dropped his other projects and reoriented his research around the vocalizations of the largest mammals on Earth. As he told Hal Whitehead and Luke Rendel in their book, *The Cultural Lives of Whales and Dolphins*, "It was the first time I had ever heard the abyss. Normally, you don't hear the size of the ocean when you are listening, but I heard it that night. . . .

That's what whales do; they give the ocean its voice."[9] Payne, like Frank, had witnessed a haunting, and the presence he witnessed had changed him.

\* \* \*

There is a legend about the making of the Greek Old Testament, the Septuagint, that rolls around my head like a marble. Saint Augustine, the early church father from Algeria, tells how Egyptian Pharaoh Ptolemy II Philadelphus (287–247 BCE) commissioned a translation of the scroll for the Alexandrian library. Seventy translators sit at desks, copying the words from Hebrew to Greek using a shared scroll for reference. Augustine writes in *City of God* that "without consultation [the translators] . . . translated the whole as if with one mouth."[10] In other words, according to legend, every copy individually transcribed by individual translators was "found to be identical" in comparison to the others.[11]

From this, Augustine extrapolated that their work must be prophetic, an ongoing revelation of God's Scriptures to Greek speakers, rendering their translation faultless, without error, complete. Thus, disagreement and discord between translations vanished. Every scribe acted as a simple channel of the Holy Spirit, no corruption possible. In this story, I hear the doctrine of inerrancy played out in premodern times. One voice, one story, one interpretation, a text unvarnished by human hands.

How the Bible came to us and what it means to us are almost as important as what it says. Personally, I'm unconvinced by Augustine's account because I myself am a writer. And here's what I know to be true about writers: our hands get clammy, and we lose our grip on the pen. We lose our place on the page. We nod off. We mix metaphors, misspell words, and shuffle our idioms. My own rough drafts have taught me to approach the Scriptures with less assurance than I used to have. I now harbor doubts about translation, interpretation, and the origins of the manuscripts. I do not doubt God; I doubt the humans who collaborated in the Bible's creation. I also doubt myself.

Can I trust myself to read and interpret cleanly without the interference of my time, place, and body?

For example, consider how we, as readers of English, experience the Old Testament as its authors never intended: that is, we read from left to right. As English-speaking Americans in the twenty-first century, our eyes follow words from left to right across a page, sentence by sentence, one page at a time. The first page we attend is on the left, and the last is on the right before we flip and start again. Left page to right page, top left to bottom left, top right to bottom right. Then flip and begin again.

Hebrew, the original language of Genesis, is read exactly opposite: from right to left. In this practical way, we read backward—not out of irreverence or ignorance but because we are different from the original readers. We are separated by culture and language and geography. A twenty-first-century middle-class American is not the intended audience for the book of Genesis. We know this, theoretically, but the neat translation does not make remembering easy. It's likely, then, that purity of understanding may be out of reach for us.

Yet we try. I recall NASA's 1977 project, the Golden Record. On the gold disc, strapped to the side of the Voyager rovers, we recorded every greeting of our planet. Then, we shot the disc into outer space in search of someone to hear us. We also included whale song on the disc—after all, what do we know of extraterrestrial speech? What if an alien's anatomy resembles our neighbors of the deep?[12] Then we will need a whale to make the introduction.

The central pursuit of humankind is to knock at the sky. We seek to bridge the distance between ourselves and whatever else is out there. In so doing, we reach toward the Being who beckoned all into existence.

\* \* \*

I cannot stop thinking about whale song. Today I can play the deep-chested yawn anytime I want because the recordings are now ubiquitous. The album created by Frank Watlington and Dr. Roger Payne has been credited with the successful Save the Whale environmental movement of the 1970s and 1980s. Since the whales have been saved, hundreds of recordings give me the opportunity to study the strange noises: I can hear whales alone, whales in chorus, whales in harmony with the rumble of boats skimming the surface of the waves above them.

But the abundance of recordings does not mean I can define what I hear. The air rushes. And what sound comes out? Not a grunt or a mew. Not a note that fits neatly onto the black and white keys—it's too variable, too flexible, spanning multiple octaves more than a single voice could reach, symphonies that last for twenty minutes at a time. This is a sound with teeth, the sound of salt, water, air, and skin folding into a shape I do not recognize. The noise of an animal. The breath of a nearby alien species.

What we humans categorize as music is the barest sliver of sounds. We classify most noises as second class—unintentional, unrepeatable, unmelodic, perhaps even inhuman, and thereby lesser. Yet we call whale vocalizations songs.

Another surprise: we cannot say for sure *how* whales sing. The mechanics puzzle researchers.[13] Whales do not have vocal cords that open and close like lips between esophagus and airway like ours, air tuned by exhales. Whale song is not an exhale. Instead, whales vocalize inside their own guts, resembling the bellows of human body cavities, expanding, contracting, and resonating between the whale's organs. Air moves between lungs and a series of internal sacs, which allows whales to sing without leaking air as they travel underwater. But whale music is not gas or intestinal grumbles either. Unlike our own interior noises, whale song is a voluntary exercise.

Biologists used to assume that whale singing played a role in mating, like bird displays.[14] But while that may sometimes be true, whales have demonstrated unexpected creativity and collaboration in their songs. For example, researchers recently discovered that whales pass tunes from one ocean to the next. They have noticed symmetry in the songs of whales on opposite sides of the globe, as if whales everywhere were listening to the same radio station and memorizing the top ten hits.

This impulse likely explains why a group of male humpback whales meets yearly in the waters surrounding Raoul Island in the South Pacific, seven hundred miles from New Zealand, a detour from their migration routes. When they get there, they join a whale choir. The *New York Times* has dubbed this locale the "humpback karaoke lounge,"[15] but I think of it as a whale's Burning Man.

And yet miles separate analysis and experience. Knowing *how* does not explain *why* does not explain *what it means* in the ear of a hearer. The whale's voice stirs me up like a human belch never has. When the whale sings, I am reminded of the mournful whine of a clarinet from my days in the high school marching band, the scrape of reed against spit and taut lips, breath entering and exiting the instrument via the muscular punch of the diaphragm. When I find *National Geographic*'s transcription of whale song, performed by David Rothenberg on the bass clarinet, I feel gratified: yes, it's like that.[16] Kind of. But the sounds also remind me of a bagpipe releasing its stored air. And the trombone's top-to-bottom slide. And the orchestra tuning. And the trembly bass of Johnny Cash.

Can my words track such unmappable terrains? Doubtful. The whale seems determined to throw me into the arms of mystery. The mystery is the point: the point of aliens in the waves and speech that orders stars. The God behind the voice is unlike us. God's mind is higher; God's voice is beyond.

* * *

When we set ourselves the task of reading a book of Divine origins, a book whose words existed first on a plane beyond what the human mind can conceive, I believe that we may need to read the book with some imagination. With this in mind, here is the posture I suggest we hold as we read the book of Genesis: I suggest we read the sacred text upside down. As in, belly-up, underside exposed to the sky, head tilting backward until our cheeks flush red. Approach the words of God as if we're standing on our heads. A ritual like this could remind us to expect to be surprised. Expect that we will not understand the context on the first try. Expect that our discomfort is natural for a person accustomed to the laws of gravity—or the twenty-first century.

Such a posture should also remind us not to assume either the surety of the inerrantists or the uniformity of the scribes of the Septuagint. A single reading of this holy book may not exist. It may never have existed. Even so, here we are, holding the Bible in our hands anyway, eager to understand, at least to try.

And I suspect that our determination to understand may be exactly what's needed to encourage the one called Mystery to speak something new. As we read upside down, we may find a place to stand in the clouds. And what else might we find up there besides clouds? Maybe a cosmic goose. Maybe even the face of God.

# 02

# PLURAL

**"**

*"Let us make humans in our image,*
*according to our likeness."*

**—GENESIS 1:26**
*(NRSVue)*

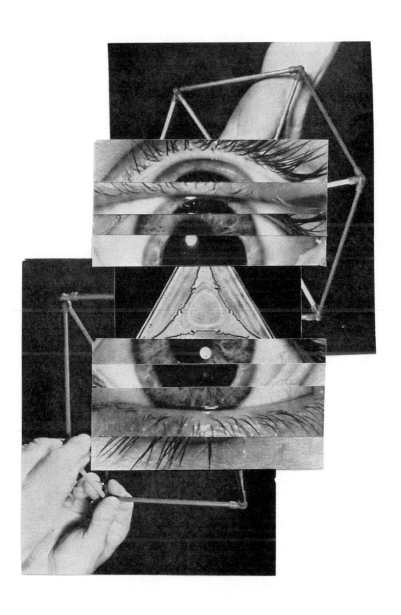

**I REMEMBER STANDING** with my toes at the concrete edge of the infinity pool. It curved behind my childhood home in the shape of a rubber duck, rather than the figure eight of California dreams. I passed many lazy August afternoons as a teenager basking in the heavy, wet East Coast heat by dunking myself in this swimming hole. The realtor had promised my parents that the diving board and slide would entertain me and my younger siblings. And the realtor got it right; I found the light on the water's surface irresistible, a shimmer almost as alluring as the television.

Sometimes, my younger siblings joined me. Then, the water became as raucous as the Atlantic, waves sloshing onto the concrete, turning to steam on contact with the pavement. We dived, kicked, raced. But when my siblings grew tired of the water, I stayed. I luxuriated in the solitude.

I had recently turned eleven. And as I squeezed into the iridescent one-piece, the fabric sparkling from black to pink to yellow, shiny like my brand-new stud earrings, I almost looked like a woman. That year, I had changed. My body had shape-shifted. My mother, watching from the kitchen window where she dutifully washed dishes, might have supposed me to be studying the bottom of the pool as I hesitated at the edge. But on so many afternoons, I caught sight of myself on the water's surface and paused, looking. Like Narcissus before me, my own reflection entranced me. I could not look away.

\* \* \*

Like a baby who recognizes her own face in the mirror for the first time, nothing fascinates a human more than *her own image*. Psychologists have discovered that mirror gazing—you, making eye contact with yourself in a mirror, "seeing yourself in the act of seeing"—calms the nervous system.[1] Mirror gazing can also teach viewers to see themselves with compassion.[2]

Our reflective obsession lies in our resemblance to the Divinity that formed us. In my glittering bathing suit, I saw the Creator's reflection: "God created humans in God's own image, in the image of God God created them" (Genesis 1:27 NIV, pronouns changed). I am made in the image of God. Therefore, in my reflection, I also see a glimmer of God. God understood that our own bodies would captivate us like an invisible deity never could, so the Divine implanted a sense of grandeur and eternality within us that mirrors God's own. But the image of God in me is hazy. How *exactly* do I resemble God? If I don't share God's eye color or height or the resonance of God's voice, what *has* God passed to me?

I am not a small woman. When I squeeze into a bathing suit and catch a glimpse in the mirror now, my image sparks feelings different from those of the eleven-year-old. My skin has curves and gullies to spare. I have borne children, have shrunk and stretched, have wrinkled. I have sometimes understood from other Christians that my body—my fat body—mars the perfection of God. Some would have me believe that only blondes under 130 pounds can enter the pearly gates, let alone reflect the heavens.

But the writer of Genesis does not see this as an issue to debate. The writer shares a bald fact: humanity bears God's image. This fact is immutable. Though my body changes, the image does not shrink or fade alongside. The *imago Dei* resides beneath our skin and not only in the division of labor appointed to us, how God has assigned us purposeful work to do. In some untouchable, immaterial part of each person, in our interiors, each of us, every shape and color and ability, reflects Divinity. All of us, a mirror.

\* \* \*

We return now to Genesis. The Spirit God was last seen hovering. Now, the Voice of God rends sky from water. And the planet teems.

Creation accomplished, God does something new. Once again, the Creator alters our understanding of Themself: God turns plural.

In Genesis 1:2, the Spirit (no *s*) hovers; in 1:7, God (no *s*) vaults the sky; in 1:9, shapes the planet's crust; in 1:20, wings the raven. "He" calls the darkness *night* (1:5), and "he" calls the gathered waters *seas* (1:10). Creation appears to be a solo act. God, the lone Spirit hanging in midair. God, singular. Then the pronouns change within the narrative. Genesis 1:26 says, "Let *us* make humankind in *our* image, in *our* likeness." The Voice has multiplied. God, plural.

A narrative inconsistency like this one could be an accident. But closer readers of the Bible have wondered if meaning can be drawn from what seems to be error. To an ancient Hebrew, this sudden plurality would have stood out because their neighbors worshiped hundreds of deities, and they would have been wondering if God resembled these other deities, if God was a multiplicity. Archaeological finds in the southwestern Levant have revealed that, in the city of Ugarit alone, the Canaanites performed cultic rituals for 234 deities.[3] Each of these deities *needed* their followers. In the second millennium BCE, Near Easterners believed worship rites performed for the right god at the right time would guarantee the fertility of crops, livestock, and households—essential survival tasks in a location that experienced dramatic climate fluctuations. Their gods also cured diseases, granted wealth, and predicted the future on demand for the price of worship.

Worship could be as simple as clothing, feeding, and bathing a representative idol daily, caring for the carved figure like an infant.[4] Worship could also require the performance of sex acts and expensive sacrificial offerings of animals or humans.[5] In return, deities offered power to agrarian and nomadic tribes. Deities also provided explanation for hosts of natural phenomena that otherwise stumped ancient man. War? Famine? Infertility? Each the result of neglected worship.[6]

Unlike these other deities, the Hebrew God does not seem to need the creatures for daily provision. Those who read these words in Genesis—"Let *us* make"—would have recognized a tone of collaboration and invitation. This is the language of the host. Later Jewish interpretation extrapolated, God is "like a king [who] has a tower full of good things, but no guests . . . [God] first created the means of man's sustenance and only then did He create [man]."[7] God prepares the feast and then creates those with whom God can share the feast.

The rabbis spent much energy puzzling over this discrepancy of pronouns.[8] They suggested that the plural may imply that God has consulted with the angels. Here God is asking the angels for their opinion about the creation of humankind: What did the heavenly host think of God's pet project? If so, the rabbis say, God must be modeling collaboration for the sake of human leaders. Or, the rabbis suggested, God is speaking to the Earth itself, from which God gathered the dust to mold man: to the pile of mud, God says, "*Let us together* shape the body of the first human."

Yet Christians took these narrative inconsistencies as a Trinitarian code. Saint Augustine says that God is *one essence* split into *three persons*: the wind of the Spirit, the voice of the Parent, the knees and palms of the Child. Christians agree on this, but even a settled argument still retains elements of mystery. For example, what *is* the Trinity?

* * *

At twenty-four, I became pregnant with my daughter, my firstborn. I remember the way she would press her hands and feet against me so that my stomach would writhe. A shadow of a handprint would emerge through the skin on my belly like a horror film, as if I had been infected by a parasitic alien. Which is to say, from pregnancy onward, I experienced my biological daughter as a stranger.

And this feeling only intensified after her birth. She arrived late and healthy. As I straddled her umbilical cord in an inflatable tub in my living room where I had birthed her, surrounded by a team of home-birth midwives, I raised her to my chest. I studied her face. Yet I did not recognize what I saw. I could not place her. I found myself asking my trio of midwives, "Whose baby is this? How did she get here? Is she mine?" The midwives roared. Of course they did; for hours, they had watched me sweat and yell to bring her into open air, expelling her from my body with punishing effort. Still, I wasn't joking. I understood the mechanics, sure, but I could not solve the puzzle of how she had arrived. How did the union of a few cells turn into a weepy infant who would eventually become a ten-year-old with ambitions to publish comic books? How had a being, whole and separate, arrived in my living room so that, where once we had been five—the three midwives, my husband, myself—now we were six? What strange magic is this life?

\* \* \*

Entire fields of scientific study have been animated by questions like these, including that of paleoanthropology. While archaeologists focus on the artifacts of culture—the remains of buildings, cooking utensils, monuments, jewelry—paleoanthropologists study the evolution of the human species on Earth through excavating the oldest human fossils they can find. Paleoanthropologists seek the origins of humanity—*paleo*, meaning *ancient*, and *anthropology*, meaning *the study of humankind*. By their relentlessness, they insist that attention to the ground can yield answers to why we're here, why we expire, and where we're going.[9]

But what I love most about these practitioners is their method. I'm not exaggerating when I say that paleoanthropologists get on their hands and knees to do their searching. They also have high-tech tools, like any scientific field does. But the final effort of identifying what's in the ground requires them to crawl on their hands and knees. With their noses an inch from the dirt, they sniff out seeds, shapely stones, any remnant of the past, beings large or small, cogent or dumb, that might protrude from the soil. All offer glimpses of humanity's past self.

To avoid damage, extraction must be patient, gentle, and relentless. The scientists do not remove the fossil alone, but samples of the "sedimentary context" with it.[10] Flora, fauna, climate, and altitude, the interdependent layers within soil narrate the past with one voice. The sedimentary context reveals a fuller picture of the artifact retrieved, and the past comes into focus.

Yet if past human life requires such attention to decipher its message, why not also the book that grounds our Christian faith in God? The Bible is by no means obvious. And a helpful starting place, when seeking to understand the Bible, is to ask, where did the words we attribute to God come from? And how do we extract meaning from the Bible, considering our great distance from its origins, a distance that ranges from geographic, cultural, and linguistic to chronological?

\* \* \*

The Old Testament was compiled and written starting within a few hundred years of Homer's *Odyssey*, which the bard composed between about 725 and 675 BCE (dates get wobbly that far back in time). We cannot say for sure who authored Genesis or when. Rabbinic tradition (and our more fundamentalist forefathers) called Moses its author, assuming that the Hebrew leader composed the book following the Hebrews' exodus from Egypt around 1400 BCE, with later additions and subtractions ongoing for most of the first millennium BCE.[11] However, the prevailing scholarly view today dates the book according to Dr. Julius Wellhausen's Documentary Hypothesis. He classified Genesis as the collaborative work of Hebrew scribes collected between 950 BCE and 500 BCE—during their Babylonian exile and after. And he suggested that the authors repurposed older non-Hebrew sources within the text, too.[12]

Yet the Bible's development depends upon its authors, these first humans who devoted themselves to scratching down the stories about God. What do we know of these first humans? What do we know of how we, as a species, developed? How did we learn language and develop the ability to write? Who were the first of us?

\* \* \*

I can imagine the jolt of surprise when Ahounta Djimdoumalbaye, an undergraduate at the University of N'Djamena, discovered the remains of our first ancestor. In 2001, he had camped with his professors in Chad's Djurab Desert for his summer break. Every working minute he spent attending to the sand, hunting prehistoric human remains of any variety, shape, or color from any era, anything at all. Crossing the desert is a laborious venture traveling upright, but these paleoanthropologists made the trek on their hands and knees. Danger marked the landscape. As they crawled, the team avoided with equal attention scorpions, vipers, heat stroke, militants of a local civil war, and undetonated land mines that other wars had left behind, hidden in the ground.

One late July afternoon, Djimdoumalbaye, his slim dark frame bent, clothes matted with sweat and dust, sees a glint in the ground.[13] Resisting the urge to reach toward the shiny object, he instead calls his advisor, "Ici! Docteur Brunet!"

Dr. Michel Brunet is over his shoulder, then on his knees beside his student. The professor uses a hand brush, then a trowel for a better look, pressing into the soil gently, giving the object a wide berth. He's bending to examine. Then, he meets the student's eyes. Yes, he says, it is bone. See the pocked center? See the hollow where the marrow once filled the crevices?

The rest of the team descends into a methodical frenzy. They don latex gloves. They shovel in wide circles around the object. They bag dirt into labeled ziplocks. And holding their breath, they brush the remains clean before lifting the fragments of bones into boxes.

Back at the university lab, the team examines a finger, an eye socket, a canine, and a jaw. Using tweezers, they puzzle together a skull the size of a coconut. It is brown and cracked, with a prominent brow ridge and sturdy features. The digital reconstruction of the skull—with skin, hair, and lips added—resembles a thoughtful chimpanzee.

But the differences between this skull and a chimp's astound the experts. For one, this fossilized skull contains teeth that resemble our canines, more worn and less sharp than a chimp's. This means the chimp chews a diet different from that of its counterparts. And the fossilized forehead is flatter. The bottom of the coconut skull, where the spinal column and head would have connected, indicates an erect posture. Meaning this creature walked on two legs: a biped. Meaning these bones, removed from the dunes of Chad, make up the oldest hominid fossil we have, dating back to 6,000,000 or 7,000,000 BCE. Hominids are the most ancient ape-like part-human species scientists know of; this is the species from whom Homo sapiens sprung.

Dr. Brunet believes no skull like this has been unearthed before. He suggests that this one fossil might be *the missing link* in the evolutionary chain from chimp to human. This skull might be the oldest fossil in the *human* line to date. The professor and Chadian officials called the skull *Sahelanthropus tchadensis*, nicknamed *Toumaï*, which means "hope of life" in the local Goran language. To them, this fragment of bone may be the beginning of humanity's story. As Dr. Brunet put it, "*Toumaï* is the oldest one."[14]

Other researchers disagree with the doctor—because nearby the skull, another team dug up a femur of a prehistoric female gorilla. So, could the skull have belonged to her as well?

Yet even if this fragment is not our ancient cousin, you can be sure we'll keep looking for the first. Our eyes will scour the ground for clues. Because our existential hunger will not rest. We need to know who we once were and who we are becoming.

\* \* \*

The Bible is a fossil, too. It is a flesh and blood memory. It is a collection of ancestral encounters with God. The Old Testament developed within a mostly illiterate ancient Near Eastern culture, its creation stretching from the Late Bronze Age and to the postexilic history of Israel. Some scholars think the scribes who constructed the biblical scrolls may have been the few Hebrews who could read and write because, in other Bronze Age cultures, literacy was the provenance of elite intellectuals. "The nonliterate public regarded reading and writing almost as a feat of magic," says Karel van der Toorn.[15] The Hebrew scribes guarded and transmitted communal experiences with God for the sake of collective worship. The Hebrew people retained their history primarily through cultic practice, a project often initiated by the monarch. The monarch alone could afford the great effort and cost of setting a story down.

This effort included funding institutions like palaces and temples where scribes trained. Training included learning multiple languages, writing, politics and religious practice, and the craft of creating the materials upon which to write.

From this side of the invention of the printing press, the craft involved in scribal activity sounds the most foreign of the processes of ancient literature. For example, making a scroll required months of labor. First, an author collected reeds, which they split, peeled into strips, dried in the sun, wove and glued together, and then laid out as a sheet to bleach in the sun before repeating the tedious process enough times to collect a substantial length of papyrus, which they then rolled up as a scroll. Alternatively, a writer could raise, slaughter, skin, and tan the hide of an animal to create parchment.

That's step one. Materials still needed: a pen (often made from hollow reeds or feathers) and ink (hand-crushed minerals). And then, after the dictation was set into the scroll, the process still did not end, but was repeated endlessly to stave off decay. Preserving any word in ancient times required near-constant restoration. A scribe would be copying and recopying, creating new paper and ink, and refurbishing the worn symbols in a loop. The writing never ceased.

So, throughout most of history, writing meant transcribing verbatim the words of the most powerful person in the room. Forget self-expression. Who cares whether the speaker conveyed the right or true or just or meaningful or beautiful to the copyist? Simply set down these words verbatim, or else you'll lose your job—or maybe your life.

And what kind of stories would rulers commission? Royals, like the pharaohs of Egypt, preferred to tell the stories that made them look divine. Yet the Bible does not shy away from the failings of its leaders, making it a unique portrait.

Knowing all of this, consider now the commitment required of a scribe to copy down a single word, let alone to compose a whole book on behalf of a patron. Consider the skill and the craft. Consider the cost. Consider what it means that the stories we possess of God and early humans do not always show humanity's best side.

As a preteen, it never occurred to me that my Adventures in Odyssey Bible might be the work of so much human innovation—from language building to paper craft to storytelling to copying. Do we mark the extremity of human work that delivered the Bible to us? Do we name the collaboration between the divine author and human hand in their joint construction? More importantly, does humanity smudging up the Scriptures shift our feeling of the book's worth?

\* \* \*

Once St. Augustine went walking. At the time, he was laboring over his tome *On the Trinity*, a work that eventually took the African early church father another decade or two to complete. I can see the man puzzling over the question as his feet followed the Mediterranean coast near his home in Algeria, taking him to the nearest beach. He is muttering to himself: how best to describe the three-in-one, the incomparable union and separation, that misty relationship of parity and distinction within the immutable uncreated that is the God of the Bible? How to box a mystery? How to wrap a human mind around an infinite communal being? Augustine cannot. It's impossible. Who would try?

Suddenly he is interrupted from his reverie. He spots a five-year-old boy on the sand in front of him. He pauses to watch the boy who has occupied himself in an urgent childhood pursuit: the boy runs between the ocean and a pit in the sand, back and forth. In his hand, he holds a shell that he fills with water and then dumps into the pit before heading back to the water's edge to refill.

The bishop draws closer and asks the boy, "Son, what are you doing?"

"I'm emptying the ocean into this pool," the boy says, as he tips the seawater in his shell into the divot in the sand before returning to the waves.

"But, son, you can't do that," Augustine replies. Because it's impossible. Because no one could do such a thing. Because to set yourself such a task is absurdity itself.

The boy, smirking and wet, responds, "I will sooner empty the ocean into this pool than you will manage to get the mystery of the Most Holy Trinity into your head!" And the boy disappears from sight that very second, leaving Augustine alone with the tide.

This legend recalls a translation of 1 Corinthians 13:12 ("For now we see in a mirror dimly . . . ," ESV). The Latin Vulgate, the translation familiar to Augustine, reads, "Idemus nunc per speculum in enigmate," which English translators have deciphered as, "For now we see as in a mirror, darkly," or more evocatively, "Now we see a reflection, as in a riddle, a mystery, or an enigma." "Enigma" seems the right word for such a legend and for the greater mystery behind it. We understand darkly God as the Three-In-One, God in happy self-communion, God in three ways of being.[16] But do we understand why God invited another into the picture? Namely, why did God make Adam?

God is a collaborator and desires to collaborate with us. From the beginning, as Abraham Joshua Heschel wrote, "God's dream was not to be alone, but to have humankind as a partner in the drama of continuous creation."[17] We bear resemblance to our Creator in our collaboration. We are relational, in constant conversation with each other and our Deity, as God intended it to be.

Just as writing is symbolic, a metaphor that represents the being behind the writing, so we are metaphors of God, reflections of the Divine on this earth. We are walking symbols. Language reflects the speaker in part as we reflect God in part.

Likewise, the Bible is only a reflection—a reflection of the collaborative nature of God, a reflection of God's very self. The Bible is a fossil made of and by the humans who came before. Does this in any way diminish the Bible's worth? Or, put another way, does God view humanity as less worthy for being a reflection and not Godself? Let us pause to marvel at what can be seen in the dark. Here we stand, toes at the edge of the infinity pool, squinting.

# 03
# THE LOADED GUN

**"**

And the LORD regretted that They had made
human beings on the earth and Their heart was
deeply troubled.

**—GENESIS 6:6**
*(NIV, male pronouns replaced with "They")*

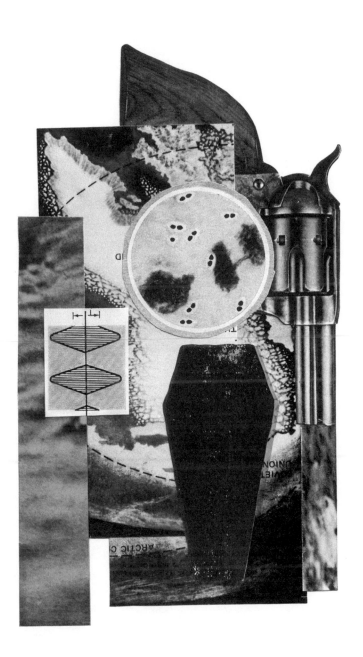

**IN DECEMBER 1994,** three cave explorers hiked along a limestone gorge in the south of France. This region, they knew, contained the remnants of prehistoric humankind, and if they could get underground, then the odds of finding the past increased. So, every weekend, every free lunch hour, the three French speleologists Eliette Brunel Deschamps, Jean-Marie Chauvet, and Christian Hillaire roamed these hillsides together, hunting for undisturbed cave systems. On this day around Christmas, they paused in front of a particular pile of rocks, stacked so that it reminded the scientists of the shape of a cave-in. Rock fall was a good sign. Then, feeling with their hands, they discerned a draft.[1] A draft could mean an opening. A draft was a good sign.

The cavers tunneled into the pile. They removed rubble with chisels and hammers, passed obstructions from hand to hand, squeezed into an aperture in the rock. They crawled, shimmed, crab-walked between two limestone walls, sucking in their bellies as they went. Inch by inch, they descended, then turned, then ascended. Then the passage widened. They discerned a roof and an edge. Then the path plunged into emptiness. They could not see to the bottom, so they hollered to measure by echo. No dice. Their voices were merely swallowed by air. But they could tell that this was a big space, and they could also tell that the only way forward was down. After discussing, Jean-Marie Chauvet, who was leading the expedition, secured a spelunking ladder over the side of the rock, swung his legs onto the ropes, and dropped into the void.

I imagine that such descents must feel interminable to cavers. With no sense of the ground, the climber loses his tether to space and time. How long did they hang on that rope ladder, grasping, seeking new footholds with a toe, core burning, steadying their hands and breath? After five stories, these speleologists touched down onto sand. A lead of rope connected them to each other and their exit as they looked around. Their three headlamps emitted faint beams of shaky yellow light onto their shoes, the walls, their helmets, and the smudged faces of their companions. The smell of clay, water, and iron filled their mouths. Everywhere they swung their lights, flecks of iridescent minerals sparkled. From the ceiling, rock hung, dripping like dried candle wax, casting shadows reminiscent of nightmare creatures. Piles of bones littered the floor. Swinging their lights to examine the dead, the cavers spotted the fossilized paw prints of wolves, hoofprints of ibexes (wild horned goats), and the claw marks and nests of bears. So far, they could count up abundant evidence of the dead and hibernating, but no signs of life, paleolithic or otherwise.

So, the spelunkers continued deeper into a stone chamber, padding single file, literally stepping into the footprints of the one ahead to minimize accidental destruction by invading Nikes. Chauvet, Deschamps, and Hillaire describe what happened next in their memoir, *The Dawn of Art*: at the front of the line, Deschamps entered a narrow stone gallery and gasped.[2] The others were already moving toward her as she said, "*They* have been here!"[3] On the stone wall before them, they saw "two lines of red ochre, a few centimetres long. On turning round, we immediately spotted the drawing of a little red mammoth on a rocky spur hanging down from the ceiling."[4] For the next ten, twenty, thirty minutes, Deschamps and her partners stood or rested on their haunches, frozen, unable to tear themselves from the drawings, stunned by their discovery. They knew what they'd found: the markings of prehistoric humanity.

The spelunkers recruited others to confirm their find, including Dr. Jean Clottes, an archaeology official in the French Ministry of Culture and historian of rock art. Clottes recalled the first time he witnessed the drawings in person just after Christmas 1994, telling *Smithsonian Magazine* journalist Joshua Hammer, "These were hidden masterpieces that nobody had laid eyes on for thousands and thousands of years, and I was the first specialist to see them. I had tears in my eyes."[5]

The cave would be named after one of its discoverers, Chauvet, and he and his crewmates' find developed an immediate reputation for its sophistication and scale. In total, the Chauvet drawings spanned thirteen hundred feet of wall over six chambers on which had been composed over one thousand naturalistic limestone etchings and drawings in charcoal and hematite (a red iron oxide). Cataloging the drawings took years: figurative sketches of wooly rhinoceroses, lions, wild horses, owls, and the predecessors of cows; narrative drawings of hunting excursions by human tribes; stencils of human hands; a mythic part-human, part-bison figure; a pictorial account of a volcanic eruption; and a half dozen doodles of female genitalia. Paint application varied, based on how the artist desired to create texture, color, or detail in the work. Chauvet artists sometimes utilized the divots and cracks in the rock to add dimension to the drawings. These early artists also seemed to have understood perspective, such as the drawing of seven rhinoceros horns side by side composed at an angle, the longest horn in the foreground and the smallest horn in the background, the size of the horns shrinking along the line so as to make the last appear further away.

But these paleolithic artists did not attempt portraiture as we postmoderns might think of it. No photorealistic ice age painting exists in any cave across the globe. But the ghosts of humans *do* appear on these walls: a hand, feet, legs, reproductive organs. Staring at the ancient pictograms can evoke the uncanny experience of recognition. In these marks, I see a family resemblance.

These paleolithic artists shared with us the instinct to record history for later generations. Humanity was not a quick study of language. Language itself—especially written language—had a moment of invention, and Chauvet is one step in this journey. The first Homo sapiens started with speech, joining sounds in our mouths, copying and synchronizing pronunciation and meaning.

Then, by their point in history, still lacking a language to wield, the Chauvet artists used their fingers to illustrate memory. In a smokey, dark chamber, they rubbed their fingers into ash and crushed mineral. They pressed their fingertips into the topography of stone, color blooming on the longest-lasting material they could find.

To remember and to be remembered: this is why all humans everywhere force our three-dimensional lives into a single plane. We flatten and distill ourselves. Line-making creates a correspondence with the future. Line-making is perhaps the fundamental Homo sapiens instinct because line-making is meaning-making. Whether we use pictures or marks or letterforms to capture memory, the receipt of knowledge happens the same way: one mind meets another by the medium of air and lips and sounds and symbols and rock and ink and charcoal. We stretch our arms in wide circles across time and space, we press coal against the wall to leave marks, we will others to read the past. And these early artists still speak to us in stone, thirty-seven thousand years in the future. We are the same.

* * *

Origin stories are a complicated genre. In the American West, being an originator is important to us. Americans are competitive, former pioneers even more so. Tellers and hearers of origin stories find themselves hungering to have gotten there *first*. We want a clear starting point, the Silicon Valley eureka moment in the garage where the code was born. But few lives feature a clear boundary between before and after. Life is not so easily delineated.

The origin story of humanity in the Bible raises as many questions as the cave drawings of Chauvet. I believe this is intentional; its authors intend the story of humankind's awakening to evoke curiosity and surprise.

At center stage, we see God kneeling. Then God shapes the first man from dust as a potter shapes a mug.[6] The form of Adam lies on the ground. God breathes into his mouth, delivering a sort of CPR, and, animated by the exhale, the first man shakes himself awake.

Humanity is created last in the cosmos. We are climax and after-thought. On the one hand, we are the centerpiece, the cosmos's raison d'être, the masterwork. The rabbis put words in God's mouth, writing, "All this world I have created, I created for your sake."[7] We bear the weight of the Creator's generosity because we are the ones who can understand what it costs.

On the other hand, the rabbis remind those of us who believe we sit at the top of the food chain that God did not create us first, but last: "The fly preceded you, the gnat preceded you, this earthworm preceded you in the work of creation."[8] We are dust: *human*, rooted in the Latin *humus*, meaning dirt.[9] Father Richard Rohr says, "We are earth that has come to consciousness."[10] Both are true: we are of heaven, and we are of earth.

Yet receiving God's generosity requires something of us. Gifts often deepen interdependence. Within minutes of Adam opening his eyes, God sets him a task: he is to name the species that appear before his eyes, an act of collaborative creation. Christening the animals marks Adam's first chance to stretch out as a being distinct from the Creator. And as Adam runs down the line of creatures over those long hours and weeks that must have made up that sixth day of creation, he begins to notice a pattern: all species are paired, but his. Each creature has a match, except for him. Suddenly, he awakens to his need. He, too, wants a partner.

Until this revelation of Adam's loneliness, God's words about the creation have been blessing: "Good, good, very good." But in Genesis 2:18, God speaks the negative: "It is *not good* for man to be alone" (NIV). Recognizing Adam's status—alone—God retracts the blessing.[11] God names Adam's lack "not good." Until now, each word God has spoken has spun out matter, but this time, God's "not good" is more judgment than effectual.[12]

Why does the quality of God's speech change? God does not speak this "not good" until Adam realizes his lack—his lack in paradise. In paradise, something is missing. Note that the man has not yet sinned in dramatic fashion, so lack cannot be wrong. What *is* wrong is Adam's lack of communion with another (which also foreshadows the potential of relational rupture, that such a thing could be possible).

God has been waiting for Adam to discover this lack. Perhaps God even provoked him (Genesis 2:19–20). It's as if God set Adam on the task to seek a match in vain. The animal-naming may have been less about the creative act—after all, how many names are recorded in the text?—and more about awakening Adam's need. Avivah Gottleib Zornberg writes, "The powerful implication here is that God's original intention [to create Eve] can be consummated *only by Adam's free perception*."[13] To get a partner, Adam must desire a partner. To get a partner, Adam must feel his lack of her and must understand he cannot meet this need independently. To get a partner, Adam must turn toward God in his lack. Adam's loneliness provides God with the first opportunity to meet a human need, to demonstrate God's ability to understand and provide for humanity. Adam's lack is God's invitation. Ask, seek, knock.

This story comforts me, but also disturbs. Because here lies the dilemma that will plague humanity forevermore: the Scriptures suggest that humans were created incomplete on purpose. God made us needy, intending us to turn to heaven whenever our bellies grumbled. Yet indulging outsize desire for anything but God—or filling our need *away from* or *apart from* God—therein lies the whole of human history, cracked open like a walnut with a sledgehammer.

\* \* \*

I once heard a piece of creative writing advice that has never left me, a word from the nineteenth-century Russian playwright Anton Chekhov: "If in the first act you have hung a pistol on the wall, then in the following one it should be fired. Otherwise, don't put it there."[14]

The prospect of this narrative commitment makes the early performances of Marina Abramović—the grandmother of performance art—frightening. She seemed to take the words of Chekhov as a challenge, making her own body the canvas, inviting her audience to abuse it. Then she called this art.

For example, take *Rhythm 0*, 1974. Abramović walks into a white-walled gallery room and places a bag of props on a folding table: pliers, a tube of lipstick, a marker, a razor, a bullet and pistol.[15] Then, the artist endeavors to become inanimate, standing impassive and silent, staring at a blank wall, barely blinking. Meanwhile, her audience is invited to pick an object and apply it to her body at their whim. Six hours pass. Visitors walk into the room. Visitiors examine the objects at the table and then stare at the artist. Then, visitors apply their own creativity to her body. At first, the responses are tame. But by the end of the artist's vigil in the museum, the audience has stripped off the artist's clothes, scratched her neck with a razor blade, slathered lipstick on her skin, and penned lewd messages on her face. In fact, the exhibition ends abruptly because one audience member loaded a bullet into the gun, placed the loaded pistol in the artist's left hand, and pointed the nozzle at her chest. So, the gallerist called a halt.

Abramović did not repeat that performance. But she did not shy away from danger either, as in the collaboration with Frank Uwe Laysiepen, known as Ulay, a fellow performance artist and the man who would become first lover and then ex. In *Rest Energy* (1980), she and Ulay hold opposite ends of a bow. He stands on the side of the hunter, and she on the side of the hunted. Between them, an arrow is taut on the strings. The shot is frozen in time, balanced by the weight of both partners as they lean away from the other, the arrow's tip aiming at Abramović's chest.

Reflecting on these exhibitions later in her career, Abramović told a Museum of Modern Art curator, "*Rhythm 0* and *Rest Energy* are two pieces, which for me, was the most difficult in my entire life of a performance artist, because in both pieces I was not in charge. In *Rest Energy*, we actually hold one arrow on the weight of our body and the arrow is pointing in my heart. We have two small, little microphones on our hearts where we can hear the sounds of the heart beating. As our performance is progressing, heart beats become more and more intense and it's just four minutes and ten seconds, but for me, it was, I tell you, it was forever. So, it was really a performance about complete and total trust."[16]

I wonder about that trust offered to strangers, to the boyfriend who will eventually leave her, to the audience across the world who encounters her work after the fact. What makes you or I worthy of that trust? And which object would you have chosen from the table, if you had seen the show in person? How would you have made your mark on the artist?

\* \* \*

The danger had always been there: Marina placed both the gun and bullet on the table. And no one could have razed Abramović's neck as effortlessly if she'd been wearing a wetsuit.

Likewise, God gave humanity a gift and weapon to use against Godself: free will. When God gave humans willpower distinct from God's own, God became vulnerable to us. Not by accident either. We can witness the reality of God's exposure for ourselves in Genesis 6:6, which reads, "The LORD *regretted* that they had made man on the earth and it grieved God to their heart" (NIV, pronouns neutral).

What has occurred between the first chapters of Genesis and this sentence in Genesis 6? Eve, the first mother and partner to Adam, has come into being (2:21–22).[17] She and Adam have failed to resist the serpent's temptations, and they have disobeyed God by indulging the illicit bite of apple (or pomegranate). Their disobedience results in the death of an animal, whose skin clothes them. And then they are expelled from Eden (chapter 3). Eve then births the first children, two brothers, but the older murders the younger (4:1–15). The first family on Earth experiences grief and estrangement.

No wonder the Deity is left mourning and regretful. The Hebrew word for regret—*nakham*—evokes a range of psychological pain: to be sorry, console oneself, change one's mind, suffer due to one's own actions.[18] Other translations render the second half of the verse as "[God's] heart was filled with pain."

Regret is desire disappointed. The Creator *desired* that the beings would welcome the abundance offered by a Creator who needed nothing yet gave everything. God's desire is exposure. Because God desired us, we discovered that we can bruise our Creator. We can disappoint and reject. Our puny actions, both done and undone, rend the heart of the Creator and sever our relationship with Divinity. Because while God longs for companionship with us we long for separation, not intimacy. To lay God aside. We pluck the fruit from the forbidden branch, and the red juice stains as it runs down our faces.

Yet the choice is still ours. I wonder, would we be having this conversation if God had remained at Adam's elbow, or had camped in Cain's field, or had refused to plant the seed of individuation within humankind in the first place? God understands better than we do that God and humanity exist distinctly from each other, that our independence is the vital tool of selfhood. That we cannot grow up without distance.

Consider how an infant's retreat from the mother does not begin at birth but conception, when the fetal cells split from hers in utero. Pregnancy is an act of creation by separation. For mother and child to survive past the pregnancy, an infant must be expelled, and the umbilical cord must be severed. The cord supplies oxygen during fetal development, but as the fetus matures, the cord impedes further growth. The mother cannot breathe for her newborn forever. The newborn must test her own lungs. God understands that untethered love is the only love worth having.

* * *

Judaism has a unique take on the push and pull of the human-Divine relationship. They recognize that the book they call Torah represents a complex collaboration between God and humanity. And they understand that the collaboration does not cease at the written expression of Torah, the scrolls they have set as their canon. Torah also includes the ongoing communal interpretation, the Jewish customs, traditions, and retellings throughout their history. This, too, is torah; specifically, Jews call this *oral torah*. Both the past written word that has been canonized *and* its interpretation, past and present, are jointly acknowledged as revelation. Some Jews even say that the book *Torah* and the practice of *oral torah* weigh the same (a shocking admission to Christian adherents of biblical inerrancy).[19]

For the Jews, Scripture "grew by accretion," as biblical scholar Samuel Sandmel wrote. "This seems to me exactly the way in which literary reflection of a live religious tradition would grow. From the oral to the written, and from the book to canonicity, and from canon to midrash, represents a continuous process."[20]

One well-known midrash summarizes the attitude toward oral torah: one rabbi, Rabbi Eliezer, speaks to a group of teachers. Eliezer insists his interpretation of Torah is correct, but the group disagrees. In frustration and conviction, Rabbi Eliezer calls on heaven to prove he's right, and God speaks aloud on Eliezer's behalf to the group, saying, "The Halakhah [law] is according to [Eliezer] in every place." He's right, says the Voice, because I say so.

But the Voice from heaven does not sway the other rabbis, and one of the group retorts, "Since the Torah has been given already on Mount Sinai, we do not pay attention to a heavenly voice, for You have written in Your Torah, 'Decide according to the majority (Exodus 23:2).'" The rabbis protest. They will not heed the Voice from the clouds because ever since God recited the law to Moses on Mount Sinai, a precedent was established: Israel's teachers had used majority opinion to decide interpretation of Torah. They trust an interpretation as true only if it has been decided democratically among the rabbis. Therefore, You, God, have been outvoted.

As modern readers, we might expect God to be angry at this strange turn, but when the prophet Elijah is asked in the account whether the rabbis overruling God has offended the Deity, Elijah says no. In fact, "[God] was laughing and saying, 'My children have defeated me, my children have defeated me.'" The story ends in God's laughter. Hyam Maccoby explains: "God is a good father who wants His children to grow up and achieve independence. He has given them His Torah, but now wants them to develop it."[21]

How does this square with biblical literalism? Isn't it true that Jewish tradition considers parts of the Torah to be verbatim dictums of God, like the Ten Commandments inscribed in stone? Yes. Could it also be true that God wants humankind to run with the story from here? Yes. God is not an authoritarian ruler threatening death to those who play loose with the story of Scripture. Instead, God invites humanity into collaboration, relishes our independent voices, and stimulates our creativity. Doubt is just another word for imagination.

\* \* \*

God places a high value on the free will of God's followers. But fundamentalist traditions do not. One of the hallmarks of these groups is a restriction of free thinking. Congregants become insulated from outside sources of information, and groupthink is encouraged. No back talk allowed. As Marlene Winell has documented thoroughly in her book *Leaving the Fold*, "In the fundamentalist system, the idea of being a 'child of God' has a charm that many relate to. You remain a child, dependent on and cared for by your heavenly father. You never have to learn self-reliance or turn to yourself for strength and wisdom. The self must be rejected. . . . Churches [may then] exploit this belief and extend their own control using the verse 'Obey your leaders and submit to them.'"[22]

In other words, Winell has recognized a sort of codependency that can occur within highly controlled religious groups between the devout and their leaders. The follower transfers the authority of God to their leader, seeing the leader and God as essentially synonymous. A leader may possess good character or none at all, the outcome is the same: the follower is disempowered. If a leader has discouraged their follower's autonomy, then they have desecrated the follower's faith. A faith like this is a case of Stockholm syndrome, rather than genuine belief.

But there is another way to practice religion. James Fowler, a psychologist and theologian, documented the opposite of indoctrination in his 1981 book *Stages of Faith*. Borrowing from child developmental psychology, he documented six phases of faith experience that occur over a lifetime, starting with stage zero (basic trust, similar to the infant) to stage six (idealistic and saintly, similar to the mature adult). He found that progression from one stage to the next *required* a devotee to move into and through doubt. The most mature believers had, in fact, reckoned painfully with every belief they held. They took none for granted, and had substantiated each belief and practice anew.

He also found that these doubting seasons tended to coincide with the times when humans naturally individuate from authorities and caregivers, as in the teen and young adult years. So, he drew a clear line between the parent-child relationship and the believer-Divine relationship.[23] The maturity of the child and the believer depends upon their ability to walk away. Can the believer adapt to change? It depends on whether they accept change as normal. A relationship between a parent and child changes, but does not need to end; if both parties engage the change, no matter how much conflict arises, the relationship can continue to mature and deepen.

This is to say, spiritual change is *normal*. Doubt is not wrong but essential. There is no authentic faith without it. Over the course of a lifetime, a religious person will undergo *many* transitions that demolish, reassemble, and reframe their spirituality. Doubt is the way we add rings to the trunk. When we doubt, we are, in fact, behaving as living beings always do: we are growing.

# 04

# DOOMSDAY

**"**

*"I am going to bring floodwaters on the earth to destroy all life under the heavens, every creature that has the breath of life in it. . . . But you will enter the ark."*

**—GENESIS 6:17-18**
*(NIV)*

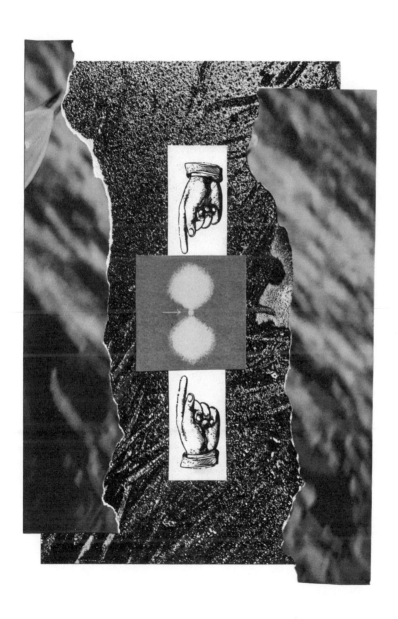

**WHEN I FIRST SAW** a medieval doom painting in person, I was eighteen, depressed, and on a supposedly celebratory high school graduation trip to Italy with my family. If it had been up to me, I would have skipped a walk around a ruined city in triple-digit heat. I would have preferred to flip channels in the air-conditioned hotel room while sampling as many plates of gnocchi as my parents could afford. Never mind that most Americans can never afford to stand beneath a European skyline; I was a bratty teenager and would have opted to stay home rather than submit to a rigorous schedule of touring. Thank God, my parents ignored my wishes. Instead, they dragged me, my siblings, and my more exuberant extended family around the ruins of an ancient empire. We wore bright white tennis shoes on our feet and dangled digital cameras from our necks. Like many American tourists, we aimed for quantity over quality: prioritize the number of sights seen above the time spent seeing. Personal comfort—or, say, the enjoyment of fellow party members—mattered less than traversing every main and side street in the city of Rome in seven days. We could rest on the flight home. Meanwhile, our itinerary would be packed to bursting with stone monuments, museums, and tours, whether we liked it or not.

One morning, we braved a wild taxi ride—a rare break for our feet— and arrived at the Vatican before lunch. We lined up among a crowd of thousands to behold Michelangelo's brushstrokes in the cathedral's Sistine Chapel. As we shuffled forward, a guard chided us—"whisper, please"—and advised against photography if we would rather not donate our cameras to the Vatican's security team. Sixteenth-century plaster does not take kindly to outside voices and flashing lights.

The chapel was smaller than I had expected. On the ceiling, Adam and God lounged, stretching a pointer finger toward the other. On one wall, the painter had created a scene of clouds and angels and harps, a depiction of heaven. On another wall, a serpent hung from a tree branch, addressing Eve as she eyes a dangling pomegranate. The line moved steadily between red velvet ropes and stanchions to the center of the chapel, which is when I began to trip over tennis shoes. There, behind the altar, was the masterwork, the fresco that arrests my memory to this day: *The Last Judgment.*[1]

I stopped, transfixed, to study the haunting image. I wanted to plant myself, to stay here a while. But the volume in the room seemed to rise, perhaps partly because I recognized one voice: a relative calling my name and whistling for me from the exit at the far end of the room, their voice echoing on the bare walls. So embarrassing.

Meanwhile, other tourists reached around me to point their digital cameras at the relic, blocking my view, and the crowd pushed from behind. Amid the heat and noise of bodies, I continued shuffling forward, and I found my contemplation thwarted, to my great irritation. Yet as I recall the scene now, I realize that my own viewing experience aptly reflected the chaos of the painting itself: a simulacrum. Maybe my viewing fit the fresco's themes more than I understood.

\* \* \*

All doom paintings, including Michelangelo's *The Last Judgment*, follow a pattern. Within wet plaster walls or onto wooden polyptychs, painters imagined scenes of Christ's second coming, the day of judgment, heaven, and hell, often employing gruesome imagery to evoke fear and introspection in viewers. The point was to remind viewers of the soul's fragility. The Catholic Church commissioned the majority of doom paintings across Europe, which were painted into enormous stretches of wall. They decorated altars and archways and cathedral ceilings. Worshipers would encounter these images walking into or out of the building, while daydreaming in the pews, and while exiting and entering the confessional. In other words, every direction you looked, you'd see theology represented visually within the structure of the church building itself, communicating the story of Jesus and the Scriptures to an illiterate congregation. Yet their most immediate purpose was to evoke repentance in the laity: doom paintings offered "a constant spectacle of the ordeal through which they would have to pass in order to reach the presence of God," according to art historian Jane Ashby.[2]

The Protestant Reformers were appalled at these scenes, in part because they decided that Catholic reverence for iconography equated to idolatry.[3] So, from the time of the Reformation onward, these frescoes were literally washed away using "a veil of wholesome Protestant lime-and-water." So began a tradition of iconoclasm that persists to this day.

*The Last Judgment* may be the most famous example of medieval doom painting. At the top of the knave, between ceiling and wall, a viewer can see the Father God's sandaled feet. Christ floats in the center, a dispassionate Italian male who presides over a chaotic end-time sorting on the ground below. Near the bottom of the wall, humans rise out of graves to be sent to heaven (into the sky) or hell (the bottom right).

Even if they rise, however, nothing guarantees that the barrel-chested Savior will notice them. In fact, the serene Christ does not seem capable of relating to the plebians at his feet, let alone counting the hairs on the heads of each follower. This Christ seems indifferent to the followers and the doomed alike. Even those who hover within reach seem to balk at the figure of their Lord. And no one hovers close enough to test the resurrection miracle, as Thomas once did by prodding Christ's scars with his fingers. Instead, access to the divine Son is limited. Christ's mother Mary claims a spot on the same cloud, while the martyred claim the next closest clouds, such as Bartholomew, who lounges in heaven with a restored body even as he holds in his hands the suit of skin that his torturers flayed from his body, according to legend. (Supposedly, this suit bears the face of Michelangelo.) Next in the hierarchy are the major Old Testament prophets, the apostles, and the Greek female oracles (sibyls). Viewing this scene, you would not be amiss in wondering whether there is room enough for the rest of us within proximity of our Savior.

Meanwhile, damnation sits at eye level. Though the left bottom corner of the fresco features the ascent of the holy to heaven, the right bottom corner depicts the opposite. Demonic figures drag the unlucky toward flames, pythons, and torment at the edge of the wall, with Charon, from Greek mythology, ferrying the damned to hell. Whether Michelangelo's viewers pictured themselves as headed up or down, no one can view the painting without reckoning with their own feelings of dread and disgust about not getting into heaven. This is horror Christianity. Humanity finds itself trapped in a two-dimensional frame, bound to the failure of the first humans, a target on our backs. We cannot escape; we are dogged until our dying days.

And who chases us down? According to the mythology of the doom painting, our antagonist is not demonic, but the abusive Father of Wrath, the one seated on a throne that barely skims our realm. In *The Last Judgment*, viewers can behold only the Father's sandaled feet at the top of the wall, while the artist has painted the rest of God's body and seat into the ceiling. We cannot approach this Deity who rules at unreachable altitudes. Nor can we understand the logic of God's anger, anger that has climaxed in brimstone and eternal torment. Meanwhile, our stoic big Brother Jesus appears at the center of the painting, unmoved by our fate and untouchable even by those who followed in his footsteps during his lifetime.

\* \* \*

When we refer to the Old Testament God, this is the popular image we conjure. The abusive Father of Wrath is *the worst possible version of divinity that humankind could think up.* When barely religious Americans open the pages of the First Testament, they interpret the most foreign, confusing, appalling, and embarrassing stories in our Scriptures through this frame: God as vindictive, all-powerful, and disdainful of creation. Especially disdainful of humanity with our tears, blood, sweat, and dramas. This is the God who obliterates Sodom and

Gomorrah in ash and flame, the God who slaughters the firstborn Egyptians in Exodus, and the God of Noah, who dooms humans, animals, and plants to extinction by drowning. This is the God who executes God's own son at Calvary.

It may surprise you to hear that though I was an exceptionally devout evangelical teenager, I rarely considered hell to be a real place. The most extreme members of my sect droned on about hell, usually at protests of one kind or another. But I believed hell was irrelevant to me. *Someone else* was going to hell; hell did not apply to believers, so, why should *I* dwell on it? Sure, I sometimes worried about friends who might not make it to heaven, but while living in the suburbs in twenty-first-century America, I found I could easily ignore the justice and judgment of God. Call it a delusion of the young, privileged, and healthy: I never had to consider hell because I was going to live forever.

I recognize now that I overlooked the parts of the Bible or God that made me uncomfortable. I did not want to remember my body's frailty. However, becoming a mother—witnessing the frailty of my children's bodies—cured me of these delusions. And I can no longer ignore those at the bottom of the frame, the objects of God's wrath. For example, how can I make sense of God's command to commit genocide or to colonize the lands of the Canaanites?

I understand why God has been painted as the abusive parent who—never having set the rules to begin with—barks up the stairs, "How many times have I told you to put the bowls on the top rack of the dishwasher?" before retaliating by setting the teenager's car on fire. Yet reading further in Genesis means we must face the horror of God. Telling the truth about God—and the book and people that represent God—means that we must come face to face with the aspect of God that makes no sense to most of us, the aspects of God that may in fact be cruel. Genesis is full of these stories. Rather than skim over the top, I suggest that thoughtful literary engagement may provide understanding.

Likewise, I believe we must face the horror done by the Christian church across its history. We must unwind lies from truth, repenting of the harms of the past and present. Only then can we understand

and embody the truth of God as expressed within the Bible. To do that, however, means returning to the site of past war crimes to identify the bones of the dead. I mean this literally and figuratively. Only a thorough reexamination of our history can initiate repair.

* * *

One such horror is the fateful 1493 papal declaration called the Doctrine of Discovery. I had never heard such a doctrine mentioned in any history class—not even in my private Christian school education—and yet, this theological conviction profoundly shaped the Christian church and the wider world from the moment the pope ratified it. Here's how it came to be: Christopher Columbus sailed the ocean blue in 1492. Then he returned to his senders, King Ferdinand and Queen Isabella of Spain. He had good news for the court: the planet had no edge; the planet resembled a globe, not a pancake; and Columbus's boats had made it there and back again. Even better, his crew had landed in unknown territory, land that, as yet, remained unclaimed by the rest of Europe. And, the explorers believed, the indigenous peoples there could be effortlessly exploited by Spain. In other words, across the sea lay land and people for the taking.

Columbus's news spread across the continent, creating competition amongst the Europeans to claim the country across the ocean before the others could. So, to protect its rights abroad, the monarchs of Spain requested that the state-funded leader of the Catholic Church weigh in. After all, the Spanish government had only sent explorers evangelistically, to "spread the faith,"[4] meaning the church only benefited from blessing Spanish efforts now, right?

As requested, Pope Alexander VI blessed the Spanish colonizers in a verdict that came to be known as the Doctrine of Discovery. In this one document, Spain claimed a monopoly over the New World in the name of God, over lands "found and to be found, discovered and to be discovered," and Spain also received a charge to overthrow non-Christian "barbarous nations" in a bid to conquer every square foot of dirt on the planet for Christ. (Spain failed at securing a monopoly but did succeed in subverting indigenous land rights.) The only exception put on this land grab: if a Christian leader or country currently claimed title to land, only then would conquest of that land be called theft. Unbelievers' property could be confiscated with impunity, as their unbelief disqualified them from full citizenship within a religious state, as Spain claimed to be.

Not once did the absurdity occur to these leaders, who claimed original ownership of the Americas while ignoring the land rights of peoples who had inhabited these continents for centuries before the Europeans ever knew these lands existed. To the European Christians, native peoples simply did not count. These beliefs were adopted widely by European settlers in the Americas, resulting in practices that further dehumanized the first Americans on the continent. Widescale abuse and eventual genocide of these communities followed.[5]

Notably, prophetic voices *did* spring up to oppose the Doctrine of Discovery during its time, especially regarding European disregard of indigenous land claims in North America. For example, Spanish Dominican theologian Francisco de Vitoria (1483–1546) admonished both the state and the pope to discontinue the policy of discounting the unbelievers' right to ownership and forcing conversion—which never works anyway, he argued, since belief is an act of personal will, not law.[6]

Another notable dissenter was Roger Williams (1608–1683), a Puritan English colonist to North America who defended indigenous ownership. He implored his fellow colonists to purchase land in the New World directly from the tribes who owned the land. He argued against incorporating with England, as such action assumed that the natives had no claim to the land.[7] Ultimately, both dissenters proved unsuccessful in their time, though their efforts would influence international law in the following centuries.

Greed is a powerful temptation, it seems, a temptation too enticing for the European Christian church to resist. So, when transplanted abroad, Christians undermined indigenous governance, property, and personhood so that European wealth could grow unhindered. Worse, this doctrine held sway even recently: the doctrine informed the writing of the American Constitution, the policies of Manifest Destiny, and even appeared in a 2005 US Supreme Court brief in reference to the legal history of indigenous Americans' land rights.[8] Pope Francis only repealed the Doctrine of Discovery decree in March 2023, 530 years after the Spanish pope formally called indigenous Americans less than people.[9]

* * *

Considering only this portion of humanity's history, is it any wonder that the next chapters of Genesis include God intervening in creation, so as to restrain human evil? Humanity needs redirection. And God's regret leads to action. In Genesis 3, God metes out consequences to Adam and Eve, the humans who have disobeyed God's single directive not to eat fruit from the tree in the center of the garden of Eden. As a result of this act and the humans' refusal to own up to the mistake, the three involved suffer—man, woman, serpent—and the couple is booted from the garden of Eden. Paradise ended. Christians extrapolate a concept of universal, inherited sin into God's consequences for Adam and Eve (Genesis 3:16–19). Jews do not. Judaism interprets these as distinct and unique judgments for individuals. However you decide the story applies, the fact that humanity has rejected God once does not bode well for the relationship between us and God. And soon enough, Abel is bleeding out in a field.

So while the curse of Genesis 3 is God's first intervention to correct a souring creation, it is not the last. Early humanity seems unremarkable for generations, though it seems to lean in the wrong direction, with corruption growing at the edges. So, God expresses regret in 6:6 and introduces another intervention, this time shortening humankind's life span: "My Spirit shall not abide in man forever, for they are flesh," an ominous sentiment (6:3a NRSVue). (The Christian Standard Bible translates "flesh" as "corrupt.") Now, God says, God the human life will end at 120 years.

When I first examined these words, I pictured a woman, midstride, who, upon reaching precisely 119 years, 364 days, 23 hours, 59 minutes, and 61 seconds, falls down dead. Her heart skids in an instant and she is no more. But I was being tripped up by my own literalism. I used to complete expository Bible studies with floral cover art, and back then, I also wanted to measure the Bible with precision, to line up what I read into neat equations that could prove the word true or false (mostly true).

But facts and truth are not the same thing, and this story does not follow its own rules. After this pronouncement, the genealogists record Noah's six-hundredth birthday (7:6), and then he lives for a further 350 years (9:29), dying at 950 years of age. Noah's descendants also live for centuries: Noah's son Shem makes it to 600 (11:11), Shem's son Arpachshad to 438 (11:12–13), and Shem's grandson Shelah to 433 (11:14–15). Eventually, the human life span does appear to retract within the Genesis narrative, but gradually, more gradually than you'd expect after a grand announcement like in 6:3.

The Scriptures register a contradiction: God pronounces that humanity's life will shrink, but the characters live into further centuries. What accounts for the discrepancy? Why does God not snap God's fingers and slay the human race instantly?

Mercy. Mercy does not make mathematical sense. God is patient with us, and God's judgment is unhurried. This is no damning lightning bolt. Instead, it's the drip, drip of water that carved out the Grand Canyon over centuries, one groove at a time.

\* \* \*

Given enough time, the force of water can reduce any boulder to dust. This is the story of the Grand Canyon: over six million years, a relentless dripping tunneled a mile deep into shale, lime, and sandstone. Probably you know that. But did you know that the canyon was once the floor of a shallow ocean?[10]

Geologists have mapped the remains of marine creatures in the rock formations. They have traced the scuttling and swimming and shedding of exoskeletons, the creases of shells pressed into mud and then fossilized. These evidences of past lives mark the walls that rim the canyon's basin.

But as the centuries passed, the land rose and the water receded. Rock pushed upward in volcanic expulsions, creating the same Rocky Mountain range that caused Spanish explorers of the 1500s to gawk, while indigenous Americans worshiped and sheltered in the shade of crevices and valleys. Where waters had once lapped, now they rushed downward to lower altitudes. As the land rose, the water picked up speed, becoming a river, the Colorado. The river carried sediment, and the sediment acted like sandpaper, flattening and smoothing the surfaces along which it ran. Deeper and faster, the waters rushed, exposing layers of striated rock, each older than the last. Erosion strips a stone of its individual parts. By means of water and wind, freezing and splitting, near-invisible divisions can eventually wrench apart the immovable. And if a glacier happens to slide past, the process of decomposition speeds up exponentially. So the canyon called Grand stopped resembling an ocean, emptying and opening until it became the natural monument we know today.

The work of erosion has not ended either. If you walk along the canyon floor now, dwarfed by red cliffs, you will witness the river as it continues to carve arteries into stone. Each year, the canyon loses one sixteenth of an inch; in two hundred years, the canyon will deepen by one foot.[11] So, when I visited the canyon over a weekend as a teenager, posing at an outlook for a photo, a thousandth of an inch of canyon floor was washed away. Infinitesimally, the altitude drops. Nothing is firm. The ground itself shifts, and human life follows.

\* \* \*

The point is this: the judgment of God is not immediate, is not inevitable, but it *is* coming. Genesis 6—the shortening of human lives—reveals that humanity has wearied God. Because as humankind multiplies in numbers, it also multiplies in wickedness. God says that God will not abide our corruption forever. So, to curb this cancerous growth, God draws a line. God will cut life short to 120 years.

But we do not heed the warning. Enter Noah.

Noah's flood looms over Jewish tradition. Christians tend to focus on the curses God places on Adam and Eve in Eden that doomed humanity to death and distance from God. Yet the rabbis considered the flood to be God's siren song. To them, the flood represented the annihilation that the Holy One might enact at any moment, if God desired. And the midrash adds the missing detail to the story of the flood: "After God had resolved upon the destruction of the sinners, He still permitted His mercy to prevail, in that He sent Noah unto them, who exhorted [the wayward] for one hundred and twenty years to amend their ways."[12] God commissioned Noah, the first street preacher, to urge repentance of those due for judgment. Perhaps every day of their lifetimes, Noah hammered out the mercy of God in full view, one plank on top of the other, a hand-hewn prayer for their about-face.[13] Even those damned creatures who coal-walk at the bottom of the doom painting get the chance to change.

In case this legend sounds far-fetched, Peter, the disciple of Jesus, alludes to it when he writes, "The patience of God kept waiting in the days of Noah, during the construction of the ark, in which a few, that is, eight persons, were brought safely through water" (1 Peter 3:20 NASB). Peter goes further, claiming that Christ descended into hell (or purgatory?) after defeating death to preach to the "imprisoned spirits, to those who were disobedient long ago when God waited patiently in the days of Noah while the ark was being built" (1 Peter 3:19–20 NIV). Noah is not the only prophet God sends to the would-be victims of the flood; Christ also preaches repentance to these ancient ones. The persistence of God exhibits on a national scale.

Yet God's patience includes the individual, too. Consider God's approach to Adam, Eve, and Cain after their sin: God arrives not with judgment but questions. God asks Adam and Eve, "Where are you?" (Genesis 3:9), and "Who told you that you were naked?" (3:11). God asks Cain, "Why are you so angry and why has your face fallen?" (4:6), and "Where is your brother?" (4:9). To all, God asks, "What have you done?" (3:13; 4:10).[14] God's questions invite a response. Explain yourself, and repent. God respects each person's choice: to obey, or not to obey? Even when we reject God, God gives us time to change our minds. Adam, Eve, and Cain are the earliest prodigal children of

God, leaving the family farm with half of God's bank account and returning to the pantry when the funds run out.

But God's radical commitment to independence goes both ways. God *wants* relationship with us, God does not depend upon or require it. And God makes demands of God's creation and the creatures within it.

\* \* \*

Yet even as I consider this question of God's judgment and mercy, I remember a midrash that astounded me when I first read it, a midrash that asks, What if this world was not the first created by God? One Jewish myth considers this question:

> Before the world was created, [and] . . . the thought arose in Him to bring the world into being, . . . He began to trace the foundations of a world before Himself, and in this way, God brought a heaven and earth into being. But when God looked at them, they were not pleasing in His sight, so He changed them back into the emptiness and void. He split and rent and tore them apart with his two arms, and ruined whole worlds in one moment. One after another, God created a thousand worlds, which preceded this one. And all of them were spent away in the wink of an eye. God went on creating worlds and destroying worlds until He created this one and declared, "This one pleases me, those did not."[15]

Reflecting on this midrashic myth, Howard Schwartz hypothesizes that the reason God would have created and then destroyed so many worlds before our own was a means of modeling. God sought to model repentance to God's creatures. Starting over (and over) provided a methodology by which humanity could live, too. Schwartz writes that the world "would not stand until God created repentance. Thus repentance is the key element that made our world possible."[16] God changes God's mind about the other worlds; God repents of the earlier designs; and so God established repentance (*nakham* again, as in Genesis 6:6), the changing of the mind, as the singular means by which our reality came to exist. Nuances within *nakham* suggest error, as in "regret," but also "change." God *turned around, changed Their mind, tried something new.* This is God, the Potter, returning the misshapen bowl to a lump of clay.

I find this instructive as regards the way we view the Scriptures themselves. Can we change our minds? To interpret a passage one way and then, later, to reverse course? To decide we're undecided? We are free like God. And apparently, changing our minds is one more way in which we mirror the Creator. Because, like you and me, They are independent. God is not limited by anything, including God's previous intentions and actions. God can change God's mind.

So, in an act of characteristic mind-changing, the Deity can enact judgment and consequences at this point in Genesis, a novel mode of interacting with God's human creatures. Or God can reverse course. God is free to choose.

Two things appear to be true: God is mercy; God is also justice. God is not evil, yet determinedly overlooks the evil of God's creatures, demonstrating God's own patience, which in no way compromises the purity of God's justice. Are you confused yet? We, the beings so easily crushed beneath the Divine's sole like ants beneath the sandal of a cartoon Zeus, cannot always make God's actions square. However, the prerogative belongs to the Creator. The Creator alone can mash the clay to nothing and then set the wheel spinning again. Judgment is not immediate, or inevitable. But we can expect that it is coming, eventually.

\* \* \*

The end of the story of Noah is predictable: Noah's neighbors do not heed the warning of the prophet. The biblical text is spare, so the midrash fills in the imagined details: after the 120-year waiting period—and then an extra week of mourning for the holy man Methuselah, who dies on the eve of the flood and is spared the judgment—the midrash states that the sky turns black. Water drips, then rushes.

Noah, his family, and a zoo settle inside the ark. Then, they hear a banging on the door. A crowd of seven hundred thousand rush at the boat. The waters rise, and the crowd outside becomes desperate. They wail and curse, demanding admittance. Is this repentance? Noah doesn't think so. Noah speaks to the doomed through a crack in the hull: "Have I not been prophesying this unto you these hundred and twenty years, and you would not give heed to the voice of God?"[17] The crowd gives no response except to push down their own children into the water, hoping to dam the rising waters with the corpses of their drowned (drowning?) children.[18] So much for the next generation. The adults care only to save themselves. (Is it any wonder that evil has been passed along family lines, hand to hand, over centuries?)

But the legend leaves no character unscathed, not even the prophet of God. The rabbinic texts call Noah undeserving of God's grace because "he had so little faith that he did not enter the ark until the waters had risen to his knees."[19] Noah does not seek shelter within the structure he's spent a century of his life constructing until he can no longer stand in the tide. I want to hold the man by the shoulders and shake. Did Noah *need* to soak his calves in order to trust the Voice who had foretold the flood? But I do understand. I would do the same. Any of us would. We would only enter the ship's hull if we had first swum for our lives. Since before time was counted, every human alive and dead would resist God's crazy command until the last second, only yielding when we finally lost our footing. Of course, we would. We always have.

Lord, have mercy.

# 05

# TONGUE IN KNOTS

**❝**

*All the earth was one lip, and there was one*
*language to all.*

**—GENESIS 11:1**
*(Brenton's Septuagint translation 1851)*[1]

Fig. 1

**THE STORY OF GENESIS** continues like this: the ark docks. Noah, his family, and a menagerie swarm onto a remade landscape, a moment of déjà vu, as when God first filled the world to teeming. Second creation. God also repeats the original command: procreate and spread out. And Noah's family complies enthusiastically. According to Genesis 10, the Table of Nations, Noah fathers the kingdoms of Babylon, Assyria, Chaldea, Egypt, Philistia, and Canaan. These nations may share a common heritage, but Noah's offspring have dispersed themselves widely across Asia and Africa by the time these Scriptures were compiled, resulting in distinctive cultures that bicker and trade and intermarry for centuries to come.

At this inflection point, it's worth asking, has the purpose of the flood been accomplished? Has the rebellion against God, initiated in Genesis 3, been quelled?

For the answer, we turn to Nimrod, Ham's grandson and the great-grandson of Noah (10). Nimrod is first mentioned in a genealogy. Unlike Noah's other descendants, the author gives Nimrod a special honorific, a title plus his familial identifiers (son of, father of, etc.): Nimrod is a "mighty hunter before the LORD" (10:9). The text calls him "mighty" three times, the equivalent of an ALL CAPS, bolded and exclamation-pointed social media caption. This language harkens back to the mysterious angel-human-giants, the Nephilim of Genesis 6:4 (or, in Darren Aronofsky's reimagining, the rock giants).[2] The author has planted a flag: expect great things of this man.

Then Genesis 11 directs our attention to a movement of people to the east, and though the text does not specify the instigator of this movement, I imagine it to be Nimrod. I imagine Nimrod instigating this migration to a new land, away from the western ancestral lands allotted to Ham's relatives[3] and toward Shinar in the east—Shinar, also known as Babylon, also known as Mesopotamia. I can imagine Nimrod walking with a blend of extended family, livestock, mercenaries, and a mass of slaves. A company like this was meant to intimidate the locals, a tactic of egomaniacal ancient Near Eastern kings. An entire city block on the move.

In fact, Nimrod is the kind of strong man leader who invokes kingdoms to rise in his wake. All the nations mentioned in Genesis 10 seem to come from a single outpost that Nimrod erects in the desert. And then he conscripts his followers to build a tower whose top reaches the stratosphere, a tower that will earn Babylon's ruler the same respect above as he demands on the earth below. They will raise the Tower of Babel high enough that even God will take notice.

*  *  *

Few of us can spare the time or funds to reconstruct the Babylonian tower like the multimillionaire Ken Ham. He intends to build a replica within his Creation Museum, located seven miles west of the Cincinnati airport so that devout tourists can stop and stare, dwarfed by the past. (I suppose he hopes for a different outcome for his construction project than the Bible describes.)[4] Others with more limited ambitions have re-created the sky scraper in two dimensions. Pieter Bruegel the Elder's oil painting depicts a leaning stone structure rising as a serene Romanesque ruin in Italian farm country, a cousin perhaps to Pisa's tower.[5]

Yet my imagination is caught by neither Ham nor Bruegel. Instead, M. C. Escher's 1928 woodcut seems to capture more closely the chaos of the construction site.[6] Escher is known for his psychedelic lithographs of staircases heading in all directions. These optical illusions mimicked a disorder that Escher confessed to having, "an inexplicable passion for heights, [in which he] experienced almost religious ecstasy when looking up at a tall building or hill."[7] Heights made the artist high. The closer to the clouds, the more giddy the transcendence.

Escher's *Tower of Babel* captures this sensation. At the front and center, the tower is rendered in lines of black ink, surrounded by coastline on two sides. The perspective is extreme with no horizon line to steady the vision: a viewer stares from the top of the tower downward at a sharp angle, coastline bending toward the center, and the city lies so far below that the ground turns black, bottoming out. Because the eye has nowhere to rest, I find my gaze repeatedly dropping from the top of the tower to the black city below at speed. Escher evokes the anticipation of a wooden roller coaster ride, the drop of the stomach as the lead car in the train disappears over the first peak. Construction workers hang off the structure—they stack blocks, balance on ledges, and pass stones upward by ropes and pullies. They also argue. One pair even exchanges blows.

Viewing Escher's woodcut seems to put the viewer in danger of losing their balance. To witness this scene, a viewer would have to perch on a nearby tower of their own. Which gets me wondering: whose perspective am I seeing? As these humans wrestle and sweat at the tower's top, who witnesses their work? As the figures swing on ropes and admire the view, who else could witness their activity but the Divine Observer?

The dizzying surrealism of Escher's print appeals to me because the Babel account has never seemed to be pure fact. The narrative edges blur like a Salvador Dalí dreamscape. For example, in this alternate reality, the whole world shares a single "lip." This brick structure reaches, not to the cloud line but into *heaven*. Then, in a Bugs Bunny move, God descends on a cloud, ties the opponents' tongues into knots, and, holding the entire human race in God's palm like a packet of seeds, God scatters humanity across the globe with one mighty puff of air. The narrative of the Tower of Babel reads like a cartoon, but in reality, it is another story of pain and judgment.

\* \* \*

Humanity perpetually seeks to overcome the limits of human power through innovation. This is the story of the Tower. Another parallel story has come to be called the European Enlightenment of 1685–1815 (also called the Age of Reason). The Enlightenment initiated a period of questioning and remaking. Scholars inaugurated an age of catalogs, see-it-for-yourself expeditions, democracy and sovereign governments, and theorems that flipped inside and out our ideas about the universe.

And then, after innovating in science, art, philosophy, and government, the thinkers remade Christianity, too. Consider the work of Charles Darwin, a scientist profoundly shaped by Enlightenment ideals. As historian Janet Soskice wrote, "Darwin's theories [of evolution], readily generalized, had led to the notion that everything— from the shape of barnacles to the beaks of birds—had been subject to the long processes of development, *and if barnacles and beaks, then why not human institutions and artifacts—even religions and the Bible?*"[8]

Before the Enlightenment, the testimony of Christian church leaders (no matter how corrupt) had defined past religious knowledge; now, the faith of the powerful no longer sufficed. The individualism of the Enlightenment demanded free thinking, and Christianity had not been tested in the cold light of science. The Enlightenment gave an intellectual permission to reject God without facing social consequences, as they had in the past; their god was no god. More precisely, their god was material reality itself, as discovered through repeated experiments that tested reality's veracity. A measurement that could be replicated could be trusted. No surprise, then, that atheism and agnosticism trended during and beyond this European movement, supplanting religion with materialism so thoroughly that Europe to this day remains post-Christian.

So, the post-Enlightenment church found itself in crisis. Left and right, members abandoned their former beliefs. Institutional trust evaporated. The faith seemed to be expiring. Yet devout intellectuals still had a card to play. They understood that the simplest way to dispute antireligious materialism was with *divine* materials—as many as possible, and the more ancient, the better. Soskice again: "There was thus avid popular interest in any new [biblical] manuscript finds that might push reliable testimony back to earlier dates."[9] Religious scholars understood that these artifacts would never offer skeptics the hand of Christ to prod. But it *could* validate the prooftexts. Discovering more copies of our sacred text within the Holy Lands would be evidence. So, with pickaxes and cash in hand, the Bible hunters of the nineteenth century headed east to excavate God from the sand.

In their travels, I see the capacity for both good and evil to exist within a single frame. Some Western scholars, influenced by the free travel and scholarship of the Enlightenment, inheritors of the Doctrine of Discovery, took advantage of easy travel, leaping across oceans to stick a flag into as many acres as possible, snatching up every artifact that crossed their paths. They plundered histories and landscapes. They exploited the generosity of local peoples and stole the monuments of indigenous cultures. And they enacted this evil in Christ's name, yet again. The imperialists reasoned that if they dragged Christ with them, then wasn't the eternal gain of a single soul worth the plagues that decimated Native American tribes, that enslaved Africans and Asians, or that plundered Egyptian ruins? Didn't Christ's entrance make up for any other bad result?

The harm of these Europeans is reprehensible, and reparations remain too slow in coming. However, abuse is not the whole story. The post-Enlightenment hunger did great harm *and* it also created a well from which scientists continue to draw hundreds of years later. Advances in methodology such as the development of the scientific method of inquiry, the cataloging and equitable sharing of knowledge, the discovery of the processes of evolution, and the democratic ideals that eventually dignified every member of a society as a citizen—all these arose during this Enlightenment and post-Enlightenment era of scholarship.[10]

Along with our generalized knowledge, our understanding of our holy book increased dramatically, too. Some of the Bible hunters who headed East *did* return home with proof of God. Or at least, they returned to the West with bundles of God's tattered texts, either with the original manuscripts or with photos of those manuscripts (some borrowed, some stolen). In a century and a half of traipsing through the Holy Land, Christianity gained tens of *thousands* of biblical manuscripts, libraries of preserved and handwritten texts, passed from hand to hand across centuries. At least twenty thousand New Testament texts and ten thousand Old Testament texts (some fragments) were recovered, and even more biblical quotations and references were discovered within other contemporaneous nonscriptural manuscripts.[11]

Yet not every manuscript discovery required skill. In fact, the most influential Old Testament manuscripts we possess came to us by accident and luck . . . In the spring of 1947, a young Palestinian bedouin shepherd followed a stray goat up a Jordanian hillside and noticed a cave he had never seen. Idly, he chucked a stone into its depths, and heard an unnerving cracking. He ran away as all children do when they fear they've broken something. But later, he returned with a friend. At the back of the cave, they found tall clay jars. They removed the lids and found "oblong lumps" inside, as Edmund Wilson described in the *New Yorker* magazine.[12] Bringing the lumps into the light, the boys saw that these were papers "wrapped like mummies" in linen and dipped in pitch. After they delivered the scrolls to a black market in Bethlehem, the Syrian Orthodox Archbishop Mar Athanasius Yeshue Samuel bought the scrolls for fifty pounds. Eventually, after much trial and error, Samuel discovered that these were the handprinted words of the Dead Sea Scrolls (also called the Masoretic Text). They were the oldest, most complete copies of the Old Testament we have to this day, dating from the third century BCE to the first century CE.[13]

Today, the Masoretic Text, due to its completeness and age (marking its closeness to the originals), makes up most of the Old Testament that sits on your nightstand. Other manuscripts act as comparison. Some of our Old Testament verses appeared as fragments, crumbling scraps of papyrus or parchment. Other chapters arrived within fraying scrolls and bound books called codexes. Remarkably, these texts contain more likenesses than differences, and the similarities affirm a consistent story about God and humankind, as narrated by the Hebrews.

Alongside this unrelenting hunt for manuscripts spurred by the Enlightenment, other fields related to biblical study deepened our understanding. The disciplines of archaeology, ancient language study, biblical literary theory, and anthropology grew by bounds. We created methodologies to guide even the laity in Bible study. We discovered that bending to understand the geography, cultures, peoples, and artifacts in the soil also offered hints about the holy book, helping us to decipher God's words in the present.

Then again, our hunting did not produce every desired effect. Artifacts mean something only if we approach the evidence with openness and seek to engage what we see honestly. If we approach with bias, we will find ourselves blinded and deceived. The most important lesson that we learned, then, is that the materials of God are not synonymous with God. A stack of paper cannot substitute for faith.

\* \* \*

Though the authors of Genesis do not spell out humankind's motivation for erecting the Tower of Babel, Jewish historian Flavius Josephus hypothesizes that Nimrod built the tower as an insurance policy against another flood. If God decided to wipe out the population again, the Babylonians would circumvent death by sheer altitude.[14]

Another compelling interpretation posits that the tower was meant to be a meeting place between deity and humanity, a ladder from heaven to earth, earth to heaven. Of course, a ladder allows travel in both directions. While God needed no help descending,[15] a construction foreman may desire to ascend. And what better way for a skin-and-bones king to secure his subjects' eternal loyalty than to attain the height of divinity? If Nimrod is anything, he is undoubtedly a king with ambition.

Archaeologists have also unearthed the remains of brick foundations across Iraq, wide and square, sticking out of the sand like the nubs of teeth. These foundations resemble pyramids with stairs zigzagging across the outside, leading to a platform or altar where priests may have sacrificed animals. (Though no one knows exactly how worship looked at these temples.) So, they postulate that Babel was a ziggurat, a pyramid-like Babylonian temple, seeing similarities between these foundations and the tower in Genesis.[16] In fact, the story of the Tower of Babel may be an allegory of the ziggurat Etemenanki, the Babylonian temple of the god Marduk, a name that means "temple of the foundation of heaven and earth."

But while scholars cannot say with certainty that Etemenanki and the Tower of Babel are the same, I can imagine that a tower rising from flatlands would have had another purpose: it would have acted as a warning. Other tribes would have gawked at the Babylonian innovation, the force of numbers required to construct such a monument, and the military strength suggested by its height. And the king responsible for these towers would have become known as a threat.

A Jewish midrash clarifies the fable further, setting the story as one of oppression:

Many, many years passed in building the tower. It reached so great a height that it took a year to mount to the top. A brick was, therefore, more precious in the sight of the builders than a human being. If a man fell down and met his death, none took notice of it: but if a brick dropped, they wept, because it would take a year to replace it.[17]

Here, a brick counts more than a human life. Josephus interpreted, "When God saw that they acted so madly he did not resolve to destroy them utterly, but he caused a tumult among them, by producing in them diverse languages, that they should not be able to understand one another."[18] Rather than bring about another flood—which God has promised never to do again—God twists the creatures' tongues into knots. God does not even need to topple bricks: instead, a few letters swapped here, a typo there, a fatal misspelling in the final proof.

For a God whose speech has initiated the universe, the distortion of the creatures' speech means more than confusion. Augustine argued that the tongue was "the instrument of domination," and so to strip the tongue of its power is a way to humble any of those who ignored the commands issued by the mouth of God.[19] Dr. Walter Brueggemann also surmises that the divine does not judge *all humans generally* but the *powerful ones specifically* through limiting human language. Those whose lust for power has dominated their people, they alone bear the brunt of God's judgment.[20] Words are power, authority, and dominion. Like free will, words can become instruments of harm or mercy. Words can be Chekhov's loaded gun in our palm. So, by restricting the human tongue, God restricts human power, tuning down the amplification of human will to a manageable volume.

\* \* \*

Jesus once proclaimed in Mark 11:23 that faith can remove a mountain; but so can an army of slaves. Unfortunately, this is the story of the Suez Canal, the famed Egyptian trench whose creation represents another story of historic colonial oppression. The French chief engineer of Egypt's public works, one of the men responsible for overseeing the project, declared that it would allow "communication between the two seas."[21] I consider this a poetic, yet naïve framing, in that it ignored the logistics of moving a small planet's worth of dirt out of the ground so that a ship could sheer two continents.

The European imperialists France and Great Britain adopted the canal as a pet project in 1860. Starting at the Mediterranean Sea, they aimed to send ships of cargo through Egypt, Sudan, Eritrea, Djibouti, Somalia, Saudi Arabia, and Yemen, a path straight to the Indian Ocean. This route would create a shortcut from Europe to Asia, reducing travel time by a full month. But making a canal is not so easy; in fact, the pharaohs and Alexander the Great, despite their ambition and unchecked power, both failed to do it. One hundred miles of African dirt needed to be hauled away, one hundred miles of clay, sand, limestone, gypsum, salt, and shells removed without the help of modern-day excavators.[22]

The colonizers saw this as a challenge of funding and organization. They did not consider the problem of labor, those poor souls conscripted to dig on the Europeans' behalf. They assumed that the

Egyptians, whom the colonizers had once declared "a race of slaves," would do their dirty work.[23] And the Egyptian officials complied with this demand.

In 1862, British Anglican missionary George Percy Badger visited an active digging site several years into the decade-long canal project. As he traveled, he met a group of *fellahin*, Egyptian rural peasants. While Badger played sightseer, the Egyptian government had conscripted these men to a month of canal digging. The missionary wrote in his travel diary, "[The groups of fellahin we met] were all on foot, but accompanied by a few camels carrying their scanty store of provisions for their monthly term of labour. I asked several of them, as we went along, whether they came of their own free will. The uniform answer was, 'We are taken bizzór,' i.e. by force. 'Are you to receive pay?' 'We know nothing about that, but from what we have learnt of others who have been there, we expect nothing.'"[24] The Egyptians understood plainly: they had no choice, would receive no reward, and would be punished if they refused. So, they traveled to the dig site, unable to resist the imperialists.

And the labor demanded of Egyptians was brutal. The imperial nations relied upon cheap Egyptian laborers to unearth the canal *by hand*, a gallon of mud at a time muscled into woven baskets. In fact, though the French project managers of the Suez Company had access to steam-powered earth movers, they never employed them in the decade it took to dig the trench. Dr. Abdelaziz Al Shennawi, a history professor at Cairo University and author of the book *Forced Labor in the Digging of the Suez Canal*, explained, "The Suez company did not bring any machines except for two tractors brought a month before the digging officially started. Despite the size and depth of the canal, the intention was clearly set to exploit the Egyptian people to dig it."[25]

The conditions, too, led to the deaths of thousands. Nearly 130,000 Egyptians died due to insufficient drinking water (much of which was brackish), dehydration, heat exhaustion, and cholera. Some Egyptians now consider these to be the casualties of an invisible war.[26]

There is no excuse for the evil of these European colonizing nations against the poor in Egypt. Yet, as I consider the past, I wonder, how might such a venture be completed today? On whose backs would a continent's worth of dirt be carried? The Suez Canal still funnels the planet's imports from Asian to American shores. It remains an irreplaceable artery of commerce, enriching industrialized nations at the expense of the poor. While we rightly scoff at the evil of the oppressors 150 years ago, we should admit our own sin, too. To this day, the West continues to benefit from the labor of those slaves. We are not so different from our European ancestors.

What one man calls progress, discovery, and innovation, another calls slavery. It has always been this way and will always be so. Free will works like that. A single coin flip can yield evil or beauty. We battle the two faces every week, day, minute. And the powerless feel the brunt.

* * *

Another way to understand the fable of the Tower of Babel is by means of a rare psychological condition called casadastraphobia: that is, the fear of falling upward. Not "the sky is falling," but a reversal of gravity.

Casadastraphobia looks like this: you're walking in a Kansas cornfield. Your feet crunch on stalks and the fallen bodies of grasshoppers, your nose fills with the scent of earth and sweet starch. Suddenly, gravity fails. Your body lifts and flips in the air, and you're tumbling upward into the "wide, carnivorous sky," as one sufferer of this phobia put it.[27] The open blue can terrify as much as the fall to the bottom of a crevasse.

This is like the moment in a science fiction movie when the spacewalk goes wrong. The astronaut misses a handhold and catapults beyond the human outpost and into the black. His body, encased in its plastic and metal suit, floats along the endless horizon; meanwhile, all we hear is breath, coming in short, throaty gasps. Until the oxygen runs out. Then, silence.

Sufferers of this phobia report needing to wear a hat and sunglasses just to walk outside to the grocery store. A hat can offer the sense of a false ceiling. Some sufferers even avoid rooms with double-height ceilings, which can evoke the feeling of "falling upward" indoors.

However, if I had to guess, I'd say that Nimrod suffered no such malady. No, Nimrod the Mighty could have slapped the ceiling of any room he entered, and he would have been first in line for a fight. Even so, history has forgotten the king named Nimrod. To this day, we cannot identify one particular Babylonian ruler by this name; his identity remains obscured, legendary.[28] Though historians have combed through the records of Babylon, no Nimrod has surfaced. In fact, in the original language of the text (Hebrew), Nimrod's name shares a root with the verb, "*marad*, 'rebel,' and can be translated as 'let us rebel.'"[29] What identifies the man is the fight he picks with God. And then his loss renders him anonymous (if he ever existed at all). Only the word of God against the man has survived him, five slim verses in the Bible.[30] His memory lives within the judgment imposed upon him.

Humanity both needs and fears the notice of God. God does not overlook injustice. To God, none of us are anonymous, and no actions go overlooked. No matter who you are or how high you sit, the Creator sits higher. No one knows this better than Nimrod the Fallen.

# 06

# WHITE NOISE

**❝**

*Now the* LORD *said to Abram, "Go from your country. . . ." So Abram went away.*

**—GENESIS 12:1, 4**
*(NASB)*

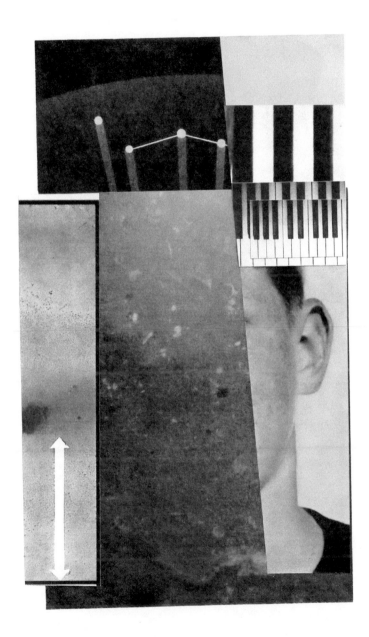

**A MAN IN A TUXEDO** walks on stage and sits on a bench before a grand piano. He opens the lid, extends his fingers toward the keys, and then . . . nothing. Nothing, except the pianist has removed a digital stopwatch from a pocket and set it counting with a loud *beep*. A long minute passes. Audience members glance around; then murmuring fills the hall. Meanwhile, the man in the tuxedo stares into the face of the timer. *What is going on?*

The composition—if you can call it that—is "4'33"." John Cage, avant-garde composer, offers this score to us as a corrective to our overfull soundscape. This performance tests a listener's ability to endure silence.

The timekeeper at the bench repeats this charade three times, three acts in all, each time starting and stopping the watch, and, with stiff attention, studies the papers on the stand as if counting out the bars of four minutes and thirty-three seconds of rests. Cage premiered his work in a venue near Woodstock, New York, on August 29, 1952. The composer sat in the audience to judge its reception. Later, he'd say this first audience had "missed the point" because some of the audience had walked out during the last movement rather than sit still for one more minute. Another audience member suggested to his friends that, instead of the audience vacating, Cage should do the leaving.[1]

This became a trend whenever Cage premiered this composition: audiences revolted. A recording of one performance is marked by the squish of tomatoes thrown onto the stage at the immobile performer. Another time when Cage himself sat on stage in the pianist's chair, performing at a Buddhist school in Colorado, the event "turned violent; people whistled and shrieked; one audience member leaped onstage and ripped off Cage's glasses."[2]

Why such extreme reactions? An audience expects a composer to provide a premade sonic experience. Yet Cage compels an audience to attend to the noises they want to paper over: the coughs, creaks, and sniffs of the fidgety human body. Also, the ambient noise of their natural and human-made environment: the blare of traffic, the whirring air conditioner, the flush of a toilet across the hall, bird song. In "4′33″," Cage insists that white noise adds up to something. Each sound wave that vibrates along the ear canal is noteworthy. He wrote, "Many people question whether my 'music' is music at all. For in this new music nothing takes place but sounds: those that are not notated appear in the written music as silences, opening the doors of the music to the sounds that happen to be in the environment."[3]

Silence, as we think of it, is an offer to pay attention to our surroundings. Silence is presence. As the novelist Paul Goodman once wrote,

> Not speaking and speaking are both human ways of being in the world, and there are kinds and grades of each. There is the dumb silence of slumber or apathy; the sober silence that goes with a solemn animal face; the fertile silence of awareness, pasturing the soul, whence emerge new thoughts; the alive silence of alert perception, ready to say, "This . . . this . . ."; the musical silence that accompanies absorbed activity; the silence of listening to another speak, catching the drift and helping him be clear; the noisy silence of resentment and self-recrimination, loud and subvocal speech but sullen to say it; baffled silence; the silence of peaceful accord with other persons or communion with the cosmos.[4]

Each silence is its own language, filling in space with meaning. And the strange silence of John Cage asks only one impossible thing of his audiences: to listen.

By listening, we meet the universe beyond ourselves. We also meet the universe within, who we *actually* are. And that quiet place of truth is also where we encounter God. This is how the story of Abram, the originator of Israel, begins.

\* \* \*

The canonical text offers no indication that God and Abram had met before, yet in Genesis 12, God demands a total upheaval of the man's life. The Voice of God comes out of nowhere, and the Voice is commanding. The King James Version of 12:1 is forceful: God tells Abram, "Get thee out," exclamation points implied. "Go from your country, your people and your father's household to the land I will show you," says the NIV. Leave all you know, and everywhere and everyone to whom you belong *now*. Why? God offers exchanges for prompt obedience. Abram, at age seventy-five, will become the unique recipient of God's care. Land, children, legacy, you name it, Abram can have it all, if only Abram will *get out*.

God's speech to Abram reminds me of Christ's call to fishermen centuries later. Christ beckons with the seemingly innocuous words, "Come, follow me." Yet to follow requires total abandonment of the rest. "First let me go bury my father," says one hesitant disciple, to whom Christ responds, "Let the dead bury their own dead" (Luke 9:59–60 NIV). "For whoever wants to save their life will lose it, but whoever loses their life for me will find it. What good will it be for someone to gain the whole world, yet forfeit their soul?" (Matthew 16:25–26 NIV). Christ seems to be saying, do you want to see God? Then, leave your life behind. This is the example of Abram: "So Abram went, as the LORD had told him" (Genesis 12:4 NIV). And, having proved he can listen, he and God keep talking.

\* \* \*

Language travels indiscriminately, democratically, and I am obsessed with its travel, so much that I have made my occupation the conveyance and reception of language. Language is spoken, implied, scratched down. Language is the work of mouths and minds. And rarely, language is even passed between heaven and earth.

Despite my obsession, I only recently learned that humans develop language so early in our existence. We used to think babies began their language learning at six months of age, about when a baby starts to sit up without support. But we were wrong. Researchers now know that *newborns* can recognize the vowel sounds of their mother's native language. In one study, researchers asked expecting parents to play a recording several times a week for their baby, including the sound "tatata" (they called this a "pseudoword"). By birth, the newborn had heard the word more than twenty-five thousand times, and when researchers played the recording again for those "tatata" hearers, the infants reacted, demonstrating recognition. (The control group did not respond to the same sound.)[5] So, if a newborn, freshly vernixed, can distinguish her mother's native tongue, then language learning begins in utero.[6]

The inner ear matures in a fetus at sixteen weeks gestation. From that point, babies respond to their own personal soundscapes. They leap and pummel their mothers' insides at surprise noises, ordinary speech, bumps, and burps. Even with organs and amniotic fluid insulating external sound waves, a fetus can perceive low frequencies. Her mother's muffled speech makes up the background of her days. The mother is already preparing her offspring to communicate with her, and the baby, too, is already in training, noticing the inflections of her mother's pronunciation by osmosis.

So, I feel justified in saying that our human preoccupation with communication is an essential characteristic, seeing as it begins before consciousness does. And this first step toward communication is facilitated *not* by our mouths but our ears. Before we ever learn to speak, we listen.

I first understood this mystery of early recognition at my daughter's birth. When she fell into my husband's open palms, she spluttered, coughed, and then wailed, furious at the light, the cold, the open air. "It's okay, it's okay," my husband and I cooed, "Baby, my baby, you're okay," and like a light switching on, the child went still. She opened her eyes and searched. She found my eyes and stared, then turned and looked into her father's eyes. Back and forth, her eyes traveled between our faces. Time slowed, then stopped as we stared into the eyes of this foreigner, this child who recognized us by our voices. Our presence meant safety to her because she already knew us. We had met before.

\* \* \*

While I marvel at Abram, the man so quick to listen, doubts nag. How did Abram decide that the invisible voice from the clouds was God's? What convinced him? How did he justify his actions? If you or I heard such a voice, ordering a move with no reason or destination, would we be persuaded to roll up our rugs and head into the unknown? Whether from desperation or mistrust, I need more than the spare biblical account offers me; I need to know *why* Abram listened.

The theory of Yale psychologist Julian Jaynes takes my doubts into account. In his 1976 book *The Origins of Consciousness in the Breakdown of the Bicameral Mind*, he postulated that humans of earlier centuries, like the patriarch Abram, did not mentally process their experiences as we do in the post-enlightened West. He wrote that ancient people would have "experienced thought as a series of auditory hallucinations, commands that they ascribed to their leaders or gods. These voices . . . may have been similar to those heard by people with schizophrenia."[7] According to the bicameral (two-sided) mind theory, a simple tweak in prehistoric neurology meant that Abram and his contemporaries would have interpreted *their own thoughts* as external commands. Their brain, split in half, would separate out verbal processing and automated action, with their actions appearing less like decisions and more like compulsions. By this definition, Father Abraham would barely be considered conscious.[8] Rabbi James Cohn, agreeing with Jaynes, determines that if this theory is to be believed, these voice-hearers would have understood God's speech as a product of their individual minds, even as they "perceived the voice as externally produced."[9]

While his theory interests me, I suspect an element of chronological snobbery lies behind Jaynes's supposition. For one, it relies heavily on particular prooftexts while ignoring contradictory evidence within the same literature—such as the fact that the majority of Abram's contemporaries *within* the biblical narrative *disagree* with Divine directives. In fact, that's the notable point of the narrative of Abram—no other character in the story would have left home, as he did. Abram's quick response is unique, even compared to lauded scriptural protagonists, many of whom famously waffle in their allegiance to God (look at Moses, Jonah, Jeremiah).

Jaynes also operates from the assumption that God's speech was common in Abram's era.[10] However, God's speech appears to have been as rare then as now. For example, though the genealogical dating of Adam to Abraham is hazy, a conservative scholarly reading would set two thousand years between the creation of the first human and the call of the patriarch.[11] The majority of recorded conversations between God and humanity either occur within the garden of Eden or offer direction to Noah. So, measuring by one of Jaynes's primary sources, only a few people *ever* carried on a conversation with God in the Bible. And those conversations were so infrequent that, in two millennia, discussions between Deity and humanity could be counted on two hands.[12] In fact, this trend of God's infrequent speech continues in the time of the Hebrew patriarchs Abraham, Isaac, and Jacob. As one rabbi writes, "For 502 years, the Holy One communicated with the patriarchs, and in all those years, He voiced to the three of them no more than 15 utterances."[13] That's one word every thirty-three years, assuming God's words were split equitably over time between the three fathers—which they were not.

And Jaynes's theory contends that prehistoric humans had no interior life and no decision-making capacity *except* by way of divine speech; yet the narrative shows even the loyal protagonists to whom God speaks making plenty of unauthorized decisions. Abram moves the family to Egypt and back to Canaan, takes a second wife, and fights a war or two, all without express permission or direction from God.

That said, I resonate with what lies behind Jaynes's objections. Historically, Christians have assumed that God speaks and that we can perceive God's speech. Jaynes considers this assumption too outlandish to take seriously—it *can't* be true—revealing his own bias. I understand this bias. I sympathize with Dr. Jaynes, Thomas Jefferson, and the crowd of academic German commentators who enthusiastically excised miracles from the biblical text with a scalpel and a red pen. Even for devout Christians, we should be unnerved by a Divinity who can appear at whim, either externally or internally, and demand urgent compliance from us. As followers of the Bible's Deity, we should ask hard questions about why biblical characters obeyed God.

As writer and psychologist Dr. Charles Fernyhough has written, "We're so rooted in the idea that there is some unitary self, that we are alone in our bodies [that] any kind of intrusion on that [idea] is deeply existentially troubling."[14] Auditory hallucinations—whether spiritual or physiological in origin—disrupt our sense of self. Whether Abram heard a "word from heaven" as a vibration in the eardrum, within a dream, or during a psychedelic high, any such hearing contradicts a human's sense of autonomy. We are not alone on our planet. In fact, the Bible suggests we may not even be alone inside of our own bodies.

\* \* \*

One way Jaynes's theory stands up: God's voice does seem to have quieted since the days of the patriarchs. The canon of God's revelatory speech has been gathered and refined, and the story seems to be approaching its conclusion. Even so, humanity continues to seek out the voice of God. And while direct conversation may seem unlikely, the laity has more of God's speech in writing than believers have possessed at any other time in history.

Before the post-Enlightenment Bible hunters searched the Holy Land for manuscripts, Christian texts were few and rare. Withheld from the public, monasteries and libraries hoarded the words of God, protecting and maintaining them as relics. Primarily, our Old Testament comes from the Masoretic Text and from the Septuagint, early Greek translations of the Hebrew text.[15] Yet these remained inaccessible to the unordained and to those outside of contemplative communities or institutions like the Vatican. Until after the Enlightenment. Then, the manuscript hunters began the search abroad. My favorite among these scholars are the Scottish twins Agnes and Margaret Smith.

Their lifelong pursuit of manuscripts began after hearing about the work of explorer Constantin von Tischendorf. Von Tischendorf turned up manuscript gold in 1844. After visiting the library of Saint Catherine's, an Eastern Orthodox monastery in Egypt's Sinai Peninsula, he returned to England with a biblical manuscript so complete and so ancient that no other available New Testament text compared. The find would be called the Codex Sinaiticus. Janet Soskice described the shock that accompanied publication of von Tischendorf's translation of the manuscript, writing in her book *The Sisters of Sinai*, "One reviewer [at the time] wrote . . . that 'the appearance of a new island would scarcely have been regarded with more interest.'"[16] Von Tischendorf became the Darwin of biblical manuscripts.

His discovery and the stories of another scholar, Dr. J. Rendel Harris, who had visited the same Egyptian monastery, had roused the curiosity of Agnes and Margaret Smith (a custom of the era). They had already visited the East once and had experience traveling without male chaperones. They had inherited a large fortune from their father which they intended to spend on the Lord's work, true to their Presbyterian heritage. And though their hometown university—Cambridge—did not admit women until 1869, they began to take language lessons on their own, developing reading fluency in Aramaic, Syriac, and Hebrew, the languages they would need to do the work of studying biblical manuscripts. They already spoke fluent Arabic and Greek, allowing them to converse both with the monks at Saint Catherine's and with their Egyptian guides. So, in 1893, the sisters set off on an Eastern treasure hunt.

After a two-week camel-back journey through the Sinai desert led by Bedouin guides, an orthodox monk at Saint Catherine's monastery showed them into the closet beneath the archbishop's room. By candlelight, the trio removed two chests of moldy documents. One, in particular, caught Agnes's eye. In her travelogue, she later wrote, "It had a forbidding look, for it was very dirty, and its leaves were nearly all stuck together through their having remained unturned probably since the last Syrian monk had died, centuries ago, in the Convent." The top layer of text told seamy stories of female saints. But as Agnes turned over the bound parchment book (the codex), she noticed underwriting in Syriac. Syriac, she knew, was the particular Aramaic dialect spoken by Jesus and his disciples.

She reckoned that she had found a palimpsest, that is, an erased manuscript. Most palimpsests existed as imprints in the fibers of the papyrus or parchment. In the past, monks had erased the oldest words in order to reuse parchment for another literary end. But as the sisters discovered, even after the ink had gone, the shape of the original letters remained as divots and dips pressed into the paper by an earlier hand, as if embossed. The parchment contained a topography of memory, the ghost of past writings.

Imagine, then, the heart-stopping moment in the monastery library as the Scotswoman bent toward the page, squinting to see the words underneath the overwriting, the moment she discovered something else had been written there. Her hands must have shaken as she steamed apart the fragile leaves with an iron to confirm her suspicions, unpeeling stuck pages before brushing astringent chemicals across the surface to reveal the lost text. The work of rebuilding lost manuscripts is like trying to complete a ten-thousand-piece jigsaw puzzle made out of tissue paper while a crowd of politicians and protestors stares over your shoulder, ready to contest the picture as it emerges. Yet slowly, with the patience of a preschool teacher, words of God from the deep past appeared before Agnes Smith's wide eyes.

The page headings read, "Of Matthew" and "Of Luke." Sentences emerged, and she noted a date in one corner of the codex: a scribe had scribbled "697" to mark the year when he'd completed the overwriting. That made the undertext even older, perhaps by two hundred years or more. With the revelation of each new word, the Smiths understood that theirs was an unprecedented find. Both the oldest and most complete translation of any gospel discovered before, Agnes Smith's codex came to be known as the Syriac Sinaiticus.

Throughout the sisters' stays in Egypt, the originals never left the monastery. Instead, Smith and a handful of scholars spent time with the pages, photographing for later study or embarking on crude translation. They dated the inks and discovered the Syriac Sinaiticus had been penned in the third century within this very monastery. The dialect of the writing—Syriac, a local form of Aramaic that Jesus and his disciples likely spoke conversationally—also verified its age. Amid a climate of religious doubt, the Smiths' manuscript added credibility to the faith. An American journalist wrote of their find, "Two English women, twin sisters, . . . have just brought to light a document that antedates all other scriptural records by two and a half centuries. . . . Now the gap between the Crucifixion and the record has been reduced to 150 years at most."[17]

Yet the discovery of any manuscript that purports to contain the words of God begs for criticism. First, other jealous scholars wondered, were the finders worthy of the discovery? Could the discovery of two widows in their fifties, unknown to the academy and new to the world of translation, be trusted? Also, how did these gospels compare to other Syriac texts discovered? What should be made of any variations in turns of phrase or structure compared to other gospel copies?

In response to the first criticism, the sisters worked to qualify themselves as worthy scholars, mastering the languages of these manuscripts and checking and cross-referencing their work with the most respected scholars in their field. Eventually, they would even found a Cambridge college, and they were two of the first women to receive degrees from the university.

As to the second, the sisters remained unshaken. The most notable variation between their codex and other copies of the Gospels appeared within the genealogy at the beginning of Matthew. Agnes Smith translated the passages: "Joseph, to whom was betrothed Mary the Virgin, begat Jesus, who is called the Christ" (1:16).[18] In contrast, most contemporary translations of Matthew 1:16 read, "Joseph, the husband of Mary, and Mary was the mother of Jesus who is called the Messiah" (NIV). Did Joseph "beget" Jesus or not? Was Mary impregnated by the Holy Spirit or by her fiancé? According to this manuscript, the answer is yes: both-and, either-or, we're not sure, and all of the above. While many biblical critics of her day took the textual ambivalence as evidence that disproved the supernatural claims of the Bible, its Protagonist, and perhaps even the codex, Agnes did not balk at the variant.[19] To Agnes and her sister, the surprise of these words did not offer a threat but an invitation to learn. Surprise invited curiosity.

In the publication of the translated manuscripts, Agnes wrote,

Why, we may ask, has God allowed these variants [in the Scriptures] to exist? Why has He not made the very copyists of His Word infallible? . . . God, having provided us with the Revelation of His truth . . . left to His human prophets perfect freedom to use their own words in delivering His message, and to human scribes to embody their own ideas of accuracy in copying it. [As they were,] we are called to be fellow-workers with Him also in the transmission of His Word . . . for the very variants which frighten the weak-minded amongst us act as a stimulant to others, inciting them to search the Scriptures more diligently, to eliminate the mistakes of mere copyists, and to ascertain what it was that the Evangelists actually wrote. Thus it was that the seed of the Word sprouted anew.[20]

Like a seed whose roots descend toward deep pools, so too, the word of God lives, breathes, seeks. The Word did not cease to live after the first writing ended. In the recopying, translating, and studying, as relentless as the Mind that conceived it, God's words do not end. And God will continue the work of revelation among any willing to listen. Let us, like the Smiths, remain open to surprise.

\* \* \*

Ultimately, what intrigues me most about the story of Abram's call is that the man is unperturbed by a voice from heaven. Though we see none of Abram's interior battle, we witness the man leaving "as the LORD had told him" (4:12 NIV). (Abram *does* dissent, but that comes later.)

Fortunately, legendary writings offer the backstory. Within Jewish and Muslim traditions—both religions that count Abram as founder—storytellers assert that Abram listened to God in Genesis 12 because *Abram had been communing with God already.* Abram and God had met before.

One story suggests that as a newborn, Abram's mother left him in a cave in the desert to die in order to protect him from the evil king Nimrod of Babylon. Yet God preserved Abram's life by sending the angel Gabriel to nurse him to maturity (milk flowed from the child's pinky, which he sucked until he'd reached ten days old; then, he stood up and walked out of the cave. Within ten days, Abram was talking and walking for miles, so that, when his mother returned to the wilderness and found her son alive, she remarked, "My son, how thou art grown! But twenty days old, and thou canst already walk and talk with thy mouth!")[21]

Yet another legend envisions Abram at home with his family in the city of Ur, a city ruled by King Nimrod. His father, an artisan entrepreneur who crafts idols from wood, conscripts his son to help in the shop. Yet the teenage Abram is disgusted by the foolishness of his father's customers. Instead of selling the figurines, he belittles them, saying, "Thou art thirty years of age and yet thou wouldst worship this idol which I made but today?" Then, he walks through the market square, dragging behind him two idols face down in the dirt, proclaiming, "Who will buy an idol? It has a mouth, but speaketh not; eyes, but it seeth not; feet, but it walketh not; ears, but it heareth not."[22] His anti-idol campaign—which evokes later prophetic shows of disgust—escalates when Abram is asked to babysit the king's idol stash, at which point the teenager takes a hatchet to the lot. Then he blames the vandalism on one of the idols, in whose hands he has placed an axe.[23]

Abram's puckishness does not make him popular, and he is eventually run out of town. (One version of the story has Nimrod burning him at a stake, from which God rescues the patriarch-to-be in the style of Shadrach, Meshach, and Abednego.) According to this telling,

Abram's leaving has less to do with the divine command. Instead, Abram is retreating from his angry kinspeople. No one likes rocks flung in their direction.[24]

But to assume that Abram was *already leaving* at the same moment God's voice told him to *get thee out* misses the point. Hebrews 11:8 summarizes: "By faith Abraham went forth, not knowing to where he goes" (Literal Standard Version). He leaves his ancestral tribe and caravans into the desert, following the voice to nowhere. At the whim of a word from heaven, no proof of destination required, no other reason for leaving proffered, Abram goes. As Charles Spurgeon wrote in his sermon on Hebrews 11:8, "Towards God a blind obedience is the truest wisdom."[25] This is belief with the lights out. The thrust of this story is devotion. Stupid devotion.

Every legend of the young Abram reveals a man who has determined to unearth the truth of the universe and the Being at its bleeding heart. Even if the search alienates him from his family and culture. "Leave your father," says God, and the man leaves. Why? Because of God. For Abram, the call of God was enough. To grow, Abram and Sarai must abandon the land on which they are planted. To find home, they must wander. Or at least they cannot stay. "Come and see," says Jesus to Peter and James, and they leave their father in the boat, following after a mystery.

# 07

# **EMPTY**

**❝**

*"I will make your offspring like the dust of the earth, so that if anyone could count the dust, then your offspring could be counted."*

**—GENESIS 13:16**
*(NIV)*

SEA BOTTOM
TRENCH →

OCEANIC
RIDGE

**WE USED TO BELIEVE** that the deep ocean was empty. No life whatsoever. Not a whisp of seaweed or neon coral, not a glow of jellyfish, not a single flutter of fins in the deep blue, nada. The idea of ocean emptiness originated with Edward Forbes in 1841. The Irish surgeon-turned-naturalist dipped a net into the Aegean Sea to measure what creatures lived there. The lower Forbes's net descended into the Aegean, the fewer creatures he captured.[1] At three hundred fathoms (eighteen hundred feet or one-third of a mile down), the living disappeared altogether.

So, Forbes and the scientific community inferred from this single survey of this single section of ocean that life and light were inseparable. For us who depended on solar energy for our sustenance—either by photosynthesis or by consuming those photosynthesizers for energy—we could not imagine an environment without light. What creature could survive perpetual freezing temperatures? Could withstand water pressure that would compress an adult human's lungs to the size of a pea? Could endure a dark so final that no ray had ever penetrated? Surely none. Forbes called his theory the Azoic hypothesis (azoic, meaning "no trace of life"[2]). Life stopped at an invisible line in the waves, and this idea ruled the burgeoning field of oceanography for twenty-five years.

Of course, Forbes got this wrong.[3] For those who grew up with *National Geographic* photography on our bedside tables, such a conclusion is laughable. How many strange jelly-like deep sea aliens have I beheld on my television screen courtesy of diving documentarians? Yet these mysteries—considered science fiction only—remained unreachable and unimaginable to humanity for most of our history.

Only later, after we had invented the means to travel to the ocean floor safely, could we amend our imaginations.

Another survey of the ocean floor debunked the Azoic hypothesis. In 1885, the *H. M. S. Challenger* crisscrossed the globe over a thousand days, collecting and studying the flora and fauna caught in its trawling nets. At the end of three years of travel, the team led by scientist Sir C. Wyville Thomson counted five thousand new species, including one worm that sheltered in a patch of mud in the Caribbean Sea three and a half miles below sea level.[4] A new species and a new ecological environment had been discovered simultaneously, obliterating the Azoic hypothesis.[5] No longer was the deep ocean barren, but alive. Actually, the ocean had never been empty, but we humans could not conceive of its fullness.

*  *  *

The call of Abram is the high point of the patriarch's story. He hears and obeys without delay, and the rewards seem to be arriving imminently. The family will receive land (Genesis 12:7), legacy (12:2), and a lineage of children as numerous as "the dust of the earth, so that if anyone could count the dust, then your offspring could be counted," God said (13:16 NIV). Yet the fulfillment is delayed, and with that delay, doubt enters. The problem: Sarai remains barren.

From my point in history, it's easy to forget that the couple does not know the end of their own story. They do not yet understand the power of God. They do not have the New Testament testimony that says God impregnated the virgin Mary. Abram and Sarai also do not know the stories of their own relatives, whose infertility was no match for God.[6] From their limited perspective, nothing would have felt certain. God had not yet proved trustworthy (at least, not to Sarai). But Abram and Sarai *could* trust biology: Abram is 75, Sarai is 65, and so far, even in their prime years, they had delivered no progeny. Unfortunately, every other divine promise depends upon knocking down the first barrier. And no postmenopausal body had ever gone backward in time. No wonder there's so much laughter whenever the topic comes up. (See 17:17; 18:12–15; 21:6.)

Still, God seems to be goading the patriarch, asking, "Do I measure up? Try me." As readers, we share the couple's suspense. *Can* God cure Sarai's emptiness? *Will* God? We don't know yet. For a long time, for decades, it looks as if the answer is no.

\* \* \*

Sarai is not the only barren matriarch of Israel; three out of four were infertile, and Sarai is the first in line. So then, why does God build a lineage out of women whose wombs resist filling? Unlike many questions I ask the Genesis scroll, this one yields a straightforward answer. The rabbis speak in unison: "Why are the matriarchs barren?" they ask. "Because the Holy One . . . yearns for their prayers and supplications."[7] The Deity of Abram does not seek only men as followers and witnesses. God also seeks the allegiance of the mothers of faith. The rabbis understand the matriarch's barrenness as God's pursuit of Sarai as an individual. Sarai does not matter to God only because of her tie to Abraham, the chosen patriarch; God has also chosen *her* to be Israel's matriarch. God is catching her attention. God is calling Sarai, too.

\* \* \*

Every text of antiquity has a complex origin story, and the story of the Christian Scriptures—and particularly the Genesis scroll—is no different. As we've discussed, artisan scribes set down the words on homemade papers and inks at the request of their governments. Then, scribes continued the process of maintaining the stories, adding and editing as they went. Then, explorers like the Smith sisters rediscovered the discarded relics of God, beginning the cyclical process anew. In a few chapters, we have covered centuries of determination and creativity.

Yet, the last few chapters of the story of the Christian Bible's origin require even greater human participation than American evangelicals may be comfortable admitting. Much of our Bible reading today is a matter of judgment. Scholars must judge between the thousands of manuscripts—for example, the historicity of individual papers or the trustworthiness of particular scribes—in order to create a translation. Preachers then select among the abundance of translations in order to do the work of interpretation. And readers decide how to apply the words to their own circumstances. This entire process requires nuance, specificity, and humility to get right. And even when we try to find the one right reading, we often discover that a single way does not exist.

For example, consider the question of the "original" Bible: is there an original manuscript, the first ever story of God written down? And how would we tell if there were? Can we judge the trustworthiness of a manuscript by its age alone? And among manuscripts of equal trustworthiness, how do we parse the variations between trustworthy manuscripts to determine the most authentic word or phrase? What level of consensus between scholars and readers decides the truest (to the original) version of the Bible?

And then there's the issue of translated manuscripts. Translators and scholars seek to set down literally the words from Hebrew, Aramaic, and Greek into American English, yet to make these words legible to the average reader, they must also bridge time and culture. So, scholars must consider, how can a dead language be rendered into a living tongue? Literalism goes only so far. What to do about idioms? Metaphors? Humor? How much interpretation has entered the translation to begin with? And what do we make of the vast disagreements of interpretation between even serious *contemporary* scholars engaged in parsing the nuances of these texts? Do you see how reading the text "plainly" will not suffice to answer the complex questions of translation and interpretation?

In fact, we have proof that the collaboration between God and humanity does not always occur faultlessly. Notable errors in Bible translation have accrued over time, errors that sometimes have been reinterpreted in their error form. One example is the question of women's roles in the Bible, a question that represents a tower of errors built up over time within religious tradition. Katharine Bushnell, American medical missionary to China, herself fluent in all the biblical languages, took on these translation errors directly in her 1921 commentary, *God's Word to Women*. She painstakingly retranslated and corrected one hundred Bible passages that referred to women and women's prescribed roles within the home and church.

And she starts at the very beginning. While many (male) translators had written that Eve was formed by God from Adam's "rib," the Hebrew word used in 2:21 (once translated "rib") is translated "side" in every other of the forty-two times it recurs in the Old Testament by the same male translators.[8] She explains that the Hebrew language contains a different word that explicitly means "rib," a word that the Genesis author does *not* utilize in the account of Eve's creation. Yet even today, a corrected translation appears only as a footnote in my NIV Bible.[9] So, why has the mistranslation of Eve created from the "rib" of Adam—rather than his "side"—persisted?

Bushnell points to the bias of the translators and the rabbis before them. One proof comes in the Mishnah, the most ancient part of the midrashim, where one rabbi compares women to "meat . . . which one may eat, salt, roast partially or wholly cooked."[10] Misogyny has been a near-universal feature of human society, and the Jews were not uniquely blameworthy for their poor treatment of women. But these biased attitudes toward females *do* appear to affect the rabbis' translations of Eve's creation in Genesis. Bushnell points to one particular tale attributed to Rabbi Joshua, who in trying to understand why God has created Eve from a rib and not another part of Adam's body, ultimately concludes that God must have assumed the best way to create Eve was to construct her body from "the member which is hid, that is, the rib, which is not even seen when man is naked."[11] In other words, God is hiding the woman. Rabbi Joshua's logical error continues: since we can expect a contentious relationship between man and woman (3:16), then we can expect that if the woman had been made from a more visible part (not the hidden rib), then the natural contention between men and women would worsen. The two would vie for dominance. Instead, God makes the hierarchy clear from the beginning, hiding Eve behind Adam at her creation.

Another assumption underlies the former one: the rabbis lay particular guilt on Eve—and through her, womankind—for yielding to the serpent's temptation. In Rabbi Joshua's telling, God sees Eve as marked by evil even before her creation. Because God has anticipated womankind's rebellion, God prepares to check her bent nature. So, Eve is prematurely hidden away and demoted. She will not be made from Adam's heart because if she is, she will be envious (rather than, say, compassionate). Such clear bias against women of course raises eyebrows about the rabbis' objectivity to the "women question," as Bushnell termed it.

While the rabbinic writings do get this translation wrong nearly universally, they also contain other contrary opinions about the making of the first woman. One midrash asserts that God made Adam with "two fronts" so that Eve was created when God "sawed [Adam] in half," as if the man was created as a double, conjoined with an unawakened Eve.[12] Another suggested that "when the Holy One created Adam, He created him hermaphrodite [bisexual], as is said, 'Male and female He created *them* . . . and called *their* name Adam' (Gen. 5:2)." A footnote clarifies, "Normally *androgynos* [translated as hermaphrodite (bisexual)] means one who has both male and female genitals [intersex]; but here it means two bodies, male and female, joined together."[13]

In her commentary, Bushnell herself draws on this tradition of halving Adam in Eve's creation, rather than limiting the creation of Eve to a single rib. She speculates that another method for Eve's creation could have resembled "fissiparous" reproduction, in which an organism divides into a near copy, like mitochondria reproducing itself under the lens of a microscope. Picture Adam's organs splitting into two like the colored liquid inside a lava lamp. Here is parity. Unlike the first translation, Eve made from Adam's *side* communicates equality. The two humans are seen as a true match, literally made of the same quantity of the same material; they would weigh the same in every respect.

Because of the range of interpretations of this single passage (not to mention others), I no longer buy the "plain reading" approach to scriptural interpretation. And I cannot assume that my preferred English translation is divinely inspired. To this end, Bushnell offers a corrective: "When we speak of the Bible as inspired, infallible and inviolable, we do not refer to *our English version*, or any mere version, but to the original text."[14] The holy part of the holy Scriptures is not the commentary or the translation, but that the story somehow evokes the presence of God, God transcribed on a page.[15]

Reading the Scriptures requires attention and spaciousness. Reading the words of God responsibly requires a willingness to learn we were wrong. Scripture has the effect of widening our insides. It requires both the humility to learn, interpret, and explore, and the conviction to settle lightly. And Bushnell's one-hundred-year-old commentary demonstrates how what is false can be continually rediscovered and reinterpreted. The fact that our fingerprints have muddied the text has not extinguished the presence of God on the page. God still hovers between the words: a wind, a breath, an unrelenting and stubborn guide. But to receive, we must clear space. We must become an empty cup ready for the faucet's stream.

\* \* \*

Though I now see Sarai's infertility as God's pursuit, I admit that I struggle to relate to Sarai. Like so many other female characters in the Bible, she feels flat. These women seem not to count, not even in their own households, not even to their own husbands. In comparison to the male biblical characters, women are hardly mentioned outside of the "who begat whom" formula. Their worthiness is most often defined by whether they birthed a prominent male child, or if they had the misfortune to be raped by a male closer to the center of the story (take Dinah and Bathsheba as examples).[16] I do not mean to diminish the wonder of childbirth. In fact, I trained as a birth doula years ago, and I have endless fascination with the intricacies of childbearing. Yet I take offense at the biblical authors reducing these women to their fertility status.

Still, I understand that I am a product of my time, a time in which womanhood looks dramatically different than it did in Sarai's. For example, scholar Stephanie Lynn Budin describes sex in antiquity: "For males, reproduction [was] simple, almost effortless. There [was] no downside to a plethora of offspring, merely the pride of proven fertility and potency. For females, reproduction was dangerous, stressful, and exhausting . . . [, and] women bore the full drudgery of childbirth and rearing."[17] For all ancient Near Eastern women, reproduction was their life and their livelihood. Yet women who failed at this particular female task seem to have been treated as disabled, according to disability biblical scholar Jeremy Schipper.[18]

Sarai, being Babylonian, would have been accustomed to a patriarchal culture that still allowed female priestesses to lead the cults of the maternal deities Ninhursaga (also called Nintur) and Inanna (later called Ishtar). Further, Babylonians assumed these female gods were responsible for the fertility or infertility of their subjects. Yet despite the couple's extended time in Ur, they had not conceived. In contrast, Abram's Deity, Elohim, seemed to have male tendencies.[19] If Sarai had already failed to produce an heir under the influence of Babylonian fertility goddesses, then how could Abram's male God manage it?

Jewish scholar Anna Goldman-Amirav hypothesizes that this impossibility is why God picks Sarai to fulfill God's promise of children. God intends to perform a miracle. Goldman-Amirav writes, "Yahweh has to demonstrate his power precisely in the areas where the hegemony of the [Mesopotamian] Goddess has been total. She who made the womb contract, she who started the birth process, she who was the mother and midwife of the nation, must be defeated and crushed. Yahweh [must] prove that the power of fertility now is in his hands. He turns nature up-side-down, emptying young women, filling the old."[20] So, God's pursuit of Abram's mate does not mean God has fuzzy feelings for the woman, or that God is a feminist, per se. Rather, the call of Genesis 12 belongs not only to Abram but also to Sarai because leaving Ur meant abandoning land, family, heritage, and *the ancestral fertility goddesses.* As they traveled away from the deities who could have cured her sterility, Sarai must have given up hopes of motherhood.

So then, I believe that Sarai's twenty-five years of barrenness can best be understood in the form of a question. God asks the matriarch the same question that God once asked Adam in the garden of Eden when Adam fervently sought a partner. Sarai, will you trust me to fill your lack?

\* \* \*

Once, Saint Teresa of Ávila grew frustrated with God. The sixty-six-year-old abbess had embarked upon a thousand-mile journey by carriage in midwinter to visit the Carmelite convents she had founded across Spain. Before she'd left, she had asked God about this journey, about the cold and the wet and the potential for illness. And she had heard God speak back to her directly, saying, "I will be your heat." Do not fear the cold, I will keep you warm.

Yet despite this promise of God, nothing had gone to plan for the traveling party.[21] Teresa had been ill for weeks—feverish, a hacking cough and unyielding pain in her throat, plus insomnia. The party had already faced snow and ice on the roads between convents. Then, she and her traveling companions found their carriage stuck in the mud at the center of a flooded river. To reach their destination, the whole party needed to descend and ford on foot before walking to the next abbey. The abbess, already grumbling, nearly slipped into the freezing water as she stepped across the slick stones lining the river bottom. Sopping and furious, she prayed to God, "When will you stop throwing obstacles into our path?" Did you not say that you would warm and sustain us? The legend goes that God answered the abbess's complaint directly, saying, "Teresa, this is how I treat my friends." And with the type of honesty that comes only when hypothermia is imminent, Teresa sniped back, "No wonder you have so few."

\* \* \*

When God delays, most of us retreat. Confusion is our cue to give up. Doubt is another name for disappointment—and Sarai is the case study. When God's word to Abram first arrives promising a child, perhaps she dares to hope. Then a year passes, then another, and then five and five more.²² After ten years of silence, Abram is eighty-five, and Sarai is seventy-five. Is it so surprising that the woman jumps ship? Her previous gods had not fixed her problem, and now God, too, appears impotent.

Sarai will no longer wait. Here, she tells Abram, take my slave and bear our children through her (Genesis 16:2).²³ We must fix our lack. God must never have meant it, anyway. Sarai suggests surrogacy through the enslaved girl in their household, a common practice in the ancient Near East. The children of the enslaved will belong to Sarai because Hagar the slave, their mother, belongs to Sarai. And the enslaved Hagar has no say in the surrogacy because she is a slave. Goldman-Amirav explains, "Hagar is totally at Sarah's mercy."²⁴

Abram accepts Sarai's offer. Abram's attitudes toward God have also shifted between Genesis 12, the moment of God's original call, and Genesis 15:2. This time, when God appears again to the patriarch with another round of promises, Abram interrupts to ask God, "What can you give me since I remain childless?" It seems that Abram, too, has given up. What can God give him? *Nothing* is the implied answer. God, your promises are barren.

So, unlike the Hebrews who follow Abram—Abram's son and grandson, who both pray to God on behalf of their infertile wives— the first in the line does not pray for a child. (Eventually, Sarai notices Abram has not prayed for her, but too late.)²⁵ Abram accepts the enslaved woman into his sheets, and Hagar becomes pregnant.

\* \* \*

Considering the slowness of God, as slow as the deepening of the Grand Canyon, I understand why the patriarch and matriarch gave up. Yet I take heart in Katharine Bushnell's example. When she discovered holes in biblical translation, she did not despair but set to work. In the introduction to her commentary, she wrote, "Supposing *women only* had translated the Bible, from age to age, is there a likelihood that men would have rested content with the outcome?"²⁶ She makes the case for why it matters that she and other women turn their attention to the biblical text. But who is she speaking to? She is not speaking to women, but to her male critics. To them, she makes the case that we can only understand the words of the Bible truly when the outsider revisits the words translated by insiders, each perspective adding interpretative depth. She anticipates the objections to her commentary and seeks to persuade her detractors to her side. She is educating women and men alike. Bushnell is generous, even to her opponents.

Her willingness to explain, to seek to convince rather than dismiss, reminds me of the generosity of Abba Moses, the third-century Egyptian slave turned thief turned monk. Abba Moses was once asked by a community of priests to act as judge between themselves and another priest who had wronged them. Abba Moses refused to mediate at first. But the brothers pressed him. The erring brother *must* be corrected, and preferably by a more respected outsider, just to prove their point more emphatically. Relenting, Moses left his cave, heading to their monastery where the offender and a council of priests would be gathered. On his way, Moses carried a clay jug full of water on his shoulder. But the jar was cracked, and as he walked, the water leaked out, leaving a trail in the sand to mark his journey. By the time he arrived, the jug was empty. The brothers noticed first the jar and then the trail of water. They asked Abba Moses about it before the trial began, and Abba Moses explained, "My sins run out behind me, and I do not see them, and today I am coming to judge the errors of another?" My sons, he said, the empty jar is a symbol. And the jar says, he and I and you are no different. We are all children, empty, only filled and sustained by grace. The monks, humbled, "said no more to [their] brother but forgave him."[27]

The story of Abba Moses still speaks to me. I see myself clearly, so desirous of another's judgment. I also see Abram, Sarai, and the enslaved pregnant woman, Hagar. When I witness the failures of the matriarch and patriarch, using the enslaved Egyptian woman as their pawn, I want God to disappear, to withhold Godself from the chosen family as a reproach. Abram and Sarai, I believe, do not deserve God's blessing.

I feel the same anger when I view the words of the Bible sharpened to a point and wielded as a spear to impale the so-called heretic. I want to turn the spear around, to instead take a run at the accusers. But this is not the way of Abba Moses, nor of God.

In the end, I see the greatest mystery of the patriarch, matriarch, and enslaved woman's story is not God's absence, but God's presence. God remains. God keeps speaking to Abram. God keeps blessing the couple. God's stick-to-itiveness offends my sense of fairness—because God does fulfill every promise God has made. God gives Sarai a new body, a body that conceives a child. God gives the parents a miracle son.[28] God expands the influence of the man and woman, and they become an innumerable nation. And by my reckoning, the two do not deserve it, because of Hagar.

But God has not forgotten the enslaved woman. To the lowest and least of the three in the love triangle, to the abused woman, God speaks face-to-face. And Hagar listens.

# 08

# WASTELAND

**"**

*"Hagar, slave of Sarai, where have you come from,*
*and where are you going?"*

**—GENESIS 16:8**
*(NRSVue)*

**"**

*"What troubles you, Hagar?"*

**—GENESIS 21:17**
*(NRSVue)*

**IMAGINE THIRST** that does not end. Thirst that pins your tongue to the roof of your mouth like a spoonful of peanut butter. Thirst that cracks your lips, empties you of sweat, dries your tears before they well, sets your vision spinning. Dehydration is as personal as spit evaporating off the tongue and as public as the scorched lawns of Los Angeles. A lack of water can wipe life off a landscape. Thirst can topple empires.

When the American archaeologist Dr. James H. Breasted visited the storied lands of the Bible on an expeditionary trip in 1905, he bestowed a misnomer on the region. He called Israel and the lands nearby the "fertile crescent." He also called out the land's contradictory features: the land is mountainous. It is shoreline, plateau, and limestone canyons. It is also "sandy waste."[1] The assessment of naturalist Dr. Albert T. Clay, a contemporary who visited the same spot twenty year safter Breasted's trip, strikes me as more accurate: "The land even in the spring looks like a desert."[2] An engineer involved in the building of the Suez Canal likewise remarked on the scarcity of drinkable water in the region, describing springs that gushed from Egypt to the Mediterranean as so murky with sulfur and salt that men who drank from them became ill. (During construction, the canal laborers needed to dig ten or more feet into the ground to ensure they were drinking clean water.)

So, the lands of the Testaments have experienced more than their share of drying up. The rarity of water even becomes an organizing feature of the biblical stories. Egyptians, Midianites, Babylonians, Persians, Hittites, and Sumerians—each empire extinguished by drought and correlating famines. Cultivated rows turned to sand, olive and citrus trees to cacti.

From this extreme landscape came the tribe known as the Israelites, the descendants of Abram. The children of the patriarch grew up as agrarian herders in the lands southeast of the Mediterranean Sea, those lands of uncertain rainfall and fallen kingdoms, within borders established by the promises of God to their founder. Their territory resembled the mountain plains of the American West. Theirs, like that of my home state of Colorado, was a landscape marked by wind and sun and mudslides and thirst. When drought inevitably ravaged their lands,[3] they migrated south into the Negev desert and east toward Egypt, seeking shelter in that subtropical zone insulated from their region's swings of climate by the Mediterranean Sea above and the Nile below. The Israelites' time in Egypt was long and hard: first, they were farmers and herders. Then, they were slaves. Eventually, they wandered back to their ancestral place, circling through the high desert plateau and red rocks of the Sinai Peninsula for forty years before reclaiming Abram's lost homeland in Canaan.

The Hebrews' slow road to rootedness meant that they understood the drama of climate from the level of hands in the soil. In each generation, the Hebrews had to reckon with inhospitable weather that did not care about keeping them or their children alive.[4] So, they would have understood better than we do the danger that Hagar, the woman enslaved by Sarai, faces when she flees pregnant into the desert to escape the wife of her baby's father. Reading this story, the Hebrews would have understood that heat stroke can end pregnancies. That isolation in the sand leads a human to the brink, not just physically but psychologically. That Abram and Sarai would have assumed that the carrions and heat would take her.

Yet the story does not end with vultures. Instead, God arrives.

\* \* \*

But first, how did Hagar come to live with the couple? Jewish tradition supposes that because Hagar is Egyptian, she likely joined the family unit during Abram and Sarai's sojourn in Egypt (Genesis 12:10–20). To avoid famine, the patriarch headed south and west, and upon arrival, Pharaoh took an interest in Sarai. Abram feared the ruler. So, when Pharaoh requested Abram's wife for his harem, Abram gave her up, lying about their relationship (*we're siblings, nothing more*). However, God is displeased with this deception and inflicts plagues on the Egyptians until the matriarch is returned to her husband's bed. The Egyptian monarch, hoping to make amends to Abram's Deity, sends the family away with gifts. And the rabbis assume that one of these gifts is the slave girl Hagar, a maid for Sarai.

Another theory says that Pharaoh offered one of his daughters to Sarai—a child of one of his concubines, an act of worship to the God who cured his court of illness. In Bereshit Rabbah, the ancient rabbinic commentary on Genesis, a legend describes Pharaoh saying, "It would be better for my daughter to be a handmaiden in this house than a noblewoman in another," an attitude that marks a dramatic contrast with the Pharaoh the Hebrews meet in the book of Exodus.[5]

Then again, Hagar might not have been royalty. Sarai's parents might have gifted Hagar to their daughter as part of her dowry, which would make her Sarai's legal property alone and not Abram's. (That would explain why Sarai seemed to have more control over the girl's fate than her husband.)[6]

However she arrived, by Genesis 16, Hagar has resided in the household for at least ten years, their entire time in Canaan. Abram and Sarai have tried and failed to produce an heir. Hagar is volunteered to play the surrogate mother by Near Eastern custom. Sarai and Abram believe that a child will fix the family's problems; instead, problems compound. First, on discovering Hagar's pregnancy by Abram, Sarai's shame increases—because any confusion about the cause of the couple's former childlessness evaporates. If Abram could get Hagar pregnant, then Sarai is guilty of their past sterility.

Also problematic, whose son is the child inside of Hagar? Though Hagar provided half of the baby's genes and birthed him, by cultural custom *Sarai* held the maternity rights to the son because the mother was enslaved to her. But the issue seems unsettled in the patriarch's household. Though Hagar does not officially become the patriarch's second wife, according to some midrashic accounts, Abram begins to treat her that way, perhaps out of gratitude for his son, Ishmael.

Because of this confusion, the women feud. Hagar has accomplished what her mistress cannot, and the Scriptures say, she "look[s] with contempt" (16:4 ESV) on Sarai. But "contempt" does not capture it, according to disability biblical scholar Sarah J. Melcher: "A closer translation from the Hebrew emphasizes the change in status [between Hagar and Sarai] that occurs as a result of Hagar's pregnancy: 'When she saw that she had conceived, I became slight in her eyes,' [said Sarai]" (16:5).[7] Hagar's side-eye lessens Sarai further, making her feel emptier than she had before. Or at least, Sarai *perceives* this slight from the enslaved woman. Notably, we lack Hagar's defense of herself. But whether the slight is real or imagined, the feud between the women is very real.

Of course, Hagar and Sarai are not equal sparring partners. The power imbalance becomes plain when Sarai complains about Hagar to Abram. Abram tells her that Hagar is Sarai's problem, not his: "Your slave is in your power," says Abram in Genesis 16:6 (ESV).

So, Sarai "deal[s] harshly" with Hagar. To understand this harshness, we must recall the fact that Abram and Sarai never refer to Hagar by name within the text that tells this story. Abram and Sarai identify her only as the "slave" or "servant" (16:2, 5, 6). No doubt, this habitual dehumanization is one of many repeated afflictions Hagar experienced within the household. To them, Hagar is a tool to produce the child they need. Her body is not hers, nor is her place in the household secure. Hagar is, in every respect, enslaved.

Now, Sarai adds a new level of cruelty to this perpetual unnaming, a cruelty exacerbated by Sarai's own envy and self-hatred. Feminist interpreter Phyllis Trible points out that the verb to describe Hagar's suffering under Sarai's hand—"afflict" (*'anah*), translated "mistreated" in the NIV—is the same verb that describes the oppression of the Hebrew slaves in Egypt (Exodus 1:11–12).[8] The Genesis authors are drawing readers' attention to the parallel enslavement narratives. Hagar, the Egyptian, is afflicted in her enslavement, just as the Hebrews will be afflicted by the Egyptians in their enslavement. (And just as God responds later to the afflicted Hebrews in Exodus 2:24 NIV—"God heard their groaning"—God will also respond to Hagar.)

But no one in the household seems to care what happens to Hagar. Abram, no doubt a witness to the mistreatment, remains silent. He does not intervene. He refuses to pass judgment on his wife's treatment of the slave, and he refuses to nurture any relationship with the slave beyond her utility.

Hagar is on her own. So, when Hagar's suffering becomes unbearable, she runs.[9] She heads south toward Egypt, a place she may have once called home. She carries no food or water. If she's early in pregnancy, she may be fighting nausea with each step. And as she grows dehydrated, her stomach cramps and tightens with Braxton Hicks contractions. Upon setting out, she must have understood that her odds of successfully crossing hundreds of miles of desert while pregnant and without supplies were poor. Yet she does not hesitate. She preferred the wilderness to the tent of Abram. She preferred death. And Hagar does not look back, only forward across the empty sands and vast sky where, at the horizon line, she seeks relief.

* * *

In the same desert where Hagar once wandered, St. Anthony wandered centuries later. By his time in the fourth century CE, the church and state had moved in together.[10] The Roman emperor Constantine (306–337 CE) had converted to the faith, which meant, for the first time, Christians were no longer being slaughtered for sport. And the church gained a state budget. In Constantine's empire, claiming Christianity no longer required an appetite for controversy, unlike in the previous two centuries when martyrdom at the hands of the state had become a popular and revered cause of death. Now, to be Christian was to have power. Hypothetically, someone could wield the name of Christ for political gain. Someone like, say, the emperor, could poison his son, hang a rival, and still receive the Eucharist each Sunday if only he screwed up his face into a penitent frown.

Whenever the church has gained power and wealth throughout history, corruption and exploitation follow.[11] The age of Constantine resembles our own with uncomfortable clarity. Then and now, church leaders sidle up to candidates with whom they share nothing in common except the hunger for power. Yet this is not the way modeled by St. Anthony, the founder of monastic life.

Anthony's conversion was dramatic: according to legend, at age twenty, the young Egyptian had inherited considerable wealth at his parents' death, which he set about squandering. Then, one day, he stepped into the doors of a local cathedral and heard a priest read Christ's call to the rich young man (Matthew 19:21). Anthony felt overwhelming conviction, and he reversed course, embracing the poverty that the rich young ruler had rejected. He relinquished his land and assets to his neighbors, enrolled his younger sister in a convent, and moved into the North African desert. And for the next sixty years, that's where he stayed—holed up in caves among the remains of mummies, determined to know God without distraction.

He committed himself to a life of total asceticism. To follow God was to embrace pain. So, Anthony starved himself. Only a few times a week, he consumed bread, salt, and water, forgoing stronger flavors. He lived in silence, alone, only encountering other people when his neighbors delivered his rations. He battled thirst, starvation, heatstroke, wild animals, insects, and vivid hallucinations that he attributed to demons. (Often, these dark angels haunted him in the form of busty women). He aimed to extinguish all desire except the desire for God.

Anthony's extreme devotion did not go unnoticed. Following a move of conscience, Anthony had exiled himself, renounced his former identity, and sought God in pain, and this way of life turned out to be a contagion. Suddenly, nearby caves filled with pilgrims. This annoyed the originator, who retreated further; after all, he'd adopted this lifestyle to *avoid* society, *all* society. But pilgrims kept arriving.

When he confined himself to an abandoned fort, pilgrims spent the night on his doorstep, calling through the gaps of his walls for Anthony's spiritual counsel and prayers. When he retreated to a southern mountain range—putting a harsh desert landscape between himself and civilization as he knew it—novice monks would trek in the direction of his hermitage, sometimes dying of heatstroke or dehydration on the way, risking death for the slim chance of speaking with him. What could the monk do? Anthony touched them, prayed for their healing, and consoled them. As a result, "His words persuad[ed] many of those who heard him to reject human things: this marked the beginning of the desert's colonization," writes his biographer Athanasius. Anthony became the unwilling leader of a crowd who was determined to follow his example.

Though Anthony reluctantly made peace with his fame, he never stopped fearing the temptation of authority. So, when he received a letter from the emperor one day, he refused to respond. Athanasius writes, "[Anthony] called the monks together and said, 'The rulers of this world have sent us letters—why should Christians be impressed by this? For although we are different in rank, yet our mortal condition is the same. What business do monks have with the letters of emperors?'" But the brothers urged him to respond. So, Anthony took the opportunity to topple the Roman Empire, gently. He told the leader of the free world not to be fooled into thinking that "imperial power was anything wonderful" and "not to forget that they, [the rulers, are] human and they would be judged by Christ." He urged Constantine to do justice, to love mercy, and to give what he had to the poor. Because, Anthony reminded him, "Jesus Christ is the one everlasting king of all ages."[12] In other words, Caesar is not Christ. Christ is the eternal ruler, not the emperor. Like all those in authority, Constantine needed reminding that he, too, was mortal. Anthony says, remember that power today is weakness eternally.

Yet while Anthony did experience popularity, as is so common for marginal religious movements, the religious establishment viewed the monk with suspicion. They feared Anthony would split the church by his teaching. Or they feared that the movement "could be regarded as a tacit criticism of the 'secular' Church for having become too involved in the things of this world."[13] They were right to be affronted. The self-consciousness of the detractors could also be read as the pangs of conscience. But they misunderstood the protest of Anthony—he did not speak division, but purity. So, while the man never purposefully backtalked the institutional Christian church (or the empire), his example unveiled their hypocrisy.

The saint echoes the same message to our time. The United States is a country where politics and religion intertwine dysfunctionally. Pastors reach beyond the pulpit and into the White House—not for the sake of the vulnerable, but for their own dominance, for the sake of authority. Likewise, politicians claim religious allegiance for a competitive edge. The rich fill our closets with clothing constructed by impoverished hands. And marginal populations starve as food pantries lose funding while billionaires blast rockets into the stars for four-minute joy rides. In other words, every human society, including our own, including Anthony's, has the potential to use God as a tool to uplift strength and denigrate weakness. We prefer comfort to the poverty and homeless wanderings of Jesus and his prophets.

But Anthony's example condemns these power grabs. The monk in the desert believed that pain and humility were the means to revelation, which is to say, the only valuable thing was the chance to meet God in the desert. All else must be excised, discarded, composted, or firebombed. Even when power came knocking, Anthony refused it. Instead, he wandered, and, in his wandering, he was found.

* * *

Initially, Hagar's story does not have much in common with Anthony's. The Genesis narrative in which Hagar appears centers the feelings and words of *other* characters, not Hagar's unique experience. She is not a main character in her own story.

Others, the powerful characters, overshadow her. Abram becomes the father of three faiths. Sarai, the envious and infertile wife, becomes the vehicle for God's miracle, despite her cruelty to Hagar. Ishmael, the son taken and restored to Hagar, becomes the father of Islam. Isaac, the child of God's promise, becomes the progenitor of Israel, and he is also the reason Hagar must eventually leave the patriarch's compound for good. Hagar's story has been hijacked.

Later Jewish and Christian commentators also misuse Hagar further, turning her story into a foil for the patriarch and matriarch. Again, Hagar's story is about Abram, and not her. Is he righteous or unrighteous? Look at how he treats Hagar. Unfortunately, when Hagar is mentioned, these comments tend to sound defensive. Many of the early church fathers bend over backward to excuse Abram and Sarai from their abuse, pride, and cowardice toward the enslaved woman in their household. They perform a spectacle of creative reinterpretation.

For example, Augustine decides that the whole debacle of the female feud and double sons is *Sarai's* fault due to the "defect in her nature," that is, her infertility, thereby neatly excusing Abram of the sin of bigamy. (He also claimed that Abram experienced *no* feelings of lust toward Hagar.)[14] Ambrose, bishop of Milan and teacher of Augustine, says, "After the flood, the human race was still numerically sparse. Hence, [impregnating his wife's slave] was a matter of moral obligation. . . . And it is not without significance that the wife is presented as the instigator of the deed."[15] Again, Ambrose is saying, Abram *had* to do it, moral obligation, no other way, and *Sarai* is at fault again as the "instigator" (in that word, I hear echoes of blaming Eve for the sin in the garden of Eden). Didymus the Blind, a fourth-century Eastern Orthodox theologian, decides Abraham must have felt nothing toward the woman, and Abram performed the sexual act without passion, "passionless [*apatheia*]," without a hint of lust and for the sake of progeny alone, a move never before achieved by a male in all of reproductive history.[16]

These interpretative cartwheels miss the point of the story. They ignore the central character: Hagar. This is her tragedy. And Abram and Sarai are her abusers, end of story. We cannot draw further interpretative conclusions until we acknowledge her suffering. How can these commentators be so deluded and hard-hearted?

They did have a reason. These early commentators so fervently defended the patriarch because they assumed that Abraham prefigured Christ. Meaning readers should engage the patriarch as symbolic rather than actual. Abram becomes an archetype. And because Christ endured a life among women without lust; ergo, a stand-in for Christ must do the same, or else Christ's own integrity comes under fire. (I doubt the patristic fathers would have gone as far as saying the patriarch was *sinless*, but they do their best to absolve his actions toward Hagar.) Their inflexible reading of the story of Abram, Sarai, and Hagar is a means of justifying the divinity of Jesus.

Their defensiveness, however, reminds me of the American Christian church's scandal management communications. *No, the holy man with the microphone did not sin, could not have sinned, not possible.* But if all the evidence, carefully measured and examined, adds up to the opposite, how can such a stance be anything but gaslighting?

Of course, the patristic fathers are not unique in having poor interpretative technique. They, like we often do ourselves, had picked a hermeneutical stance and would not move from it. Reading the Bible objectively may be impossible for any of us. We come to the words with our own vocabularies, preferences, histories. And if these fathers could read the holy text with bias, commentating only a century or two from Jesus's own lifetime, then how much more do our biases affect our reading of the Bible today?

Theologians call the reading and application of texts *hermeneutics*, which means interpretation. Hermeneutics can be understood as the set of glasses through which we read the Bible, the particular prescription. But the word has broader implications, according to philosopher John E. Murray: "The purpose of hermeneutics is to make meaning intelligible [through] expression (utterance, speaking), explication (interpretation, explanation), and translation (acting as an interpreter)."[17] Interpretation happens internally and individually, and then these learnings are conveyed externally to others. Hermeneutics includes teaching. Reading a book is independent; interpretation is independent *and* communal.

The dilemma of the interpreter is balance. The hermeneutic we use will necessarily deem some questions unimportant and others salvific; some experiences superfluous and some essential; some interpretations worthy and others illegitimate. Interpreters apply value to words and sentences and paragraphs so that the text can be understood by a nonexpert audience, and how they determine value is personal. How can it not be?

However, I believe most Bible translators and teachers take on the task of transmuting God's words with gravity and humility.[18] Yet the job is not easy. Consider the interpretation of a text message. A sender (the writer) may find its meaning plain, but does the recipient (the reader)? How many ways can the skull emoji be read? Does it portend literal death—the perishing of a pet or grandparent—or laughter so extreme as to render the sender incapacitated, as in the expression, "I'm dying"?

Interpreting a text message is one thing. Now try interpreting a text dubbed *divinely authoritative*. In the case of Bible translation and interpretation, the interpreter becomes an intermediary of divine speech. The stakes could not be higher.

This is where those who have chucked wholesale inerrancy, like myself, become twitchy. We understand that reading any Bible story—like Hagar's—happens from a particular seat. And this seat determines how we translate the language, interpret the culture and characters, and make sense of inconsistencies. Certainly, there are objective truths; but the context can require nuance to understand the objective (is the narrator reliable or unreliable?). This is especially the case within a text from which we are so distant contextually.

Yet populist American Evangelicalism has often resorted to a lazy cut-and-paste exegesis, transcribing the Bible literally into our culture today without exception or appropriate application. We apply the rules of antiquity to today, writ large. Such thoughtlessness harms people and misrepresents God.

For my peers who have rejected the Bible altogether, it's not the Bible as a work of literature to which they object necessarily, but how people *apply* the Bible *today* that spooks them. The object of interpretation is the problem, not the words themselves. And no wonder.

\* \* \*

Last we saw her, Hagar was staggering through the sand. She's been on the run for hours, maybe days, and she is thirsty. Perhaps her body is nearing heat stroke. Perhaps she is wavering in her decision to run away. She sits, resting near a spring. Since the Genesis narrative clarifies that this spring was well known in the region, we can assume that someone had claimed it. Because in the desert, water means power. So, the fact that Hagar has stopped here signals her desperation: as desperate as Hagar is to escape, she's now equally desperate for a drink, whatever the consequences.

Here, an angel appears to the runaway woman. By angel, I mean God, as the authors and Hagar assume that God and the angel are interchangeable. The text tells us that the angel "found Hagar," implying God was looking for her. Genesis 16:6–7 reads, "Then Sarai mistreated Hagar; so she fled from her. Then the angel of the LORD found Hagar near a spring in the desert" (NIV). In fact, God had been paying attention to the slave all along.

So, the angel speaks to Hagar, calling her by name, "Hagar." No other character has dignified the enslaved woman like this. The Visitor says, "Hagar, slave of Sarai, where have you come from, and where you going?" And Hagar responds with surprising honesty: "I'm running away from my mistress Sarai" (16:8 NIV). The woman may have a destination in mind, but the most relevant thing is leaving, not arriving.

Then God shocks me with an incomprehensible demand: return. Go back to your slavery. Submit to Sarai, says God. This breaks from the mold of the slavery narrative of the Hebrews rescued from Egypt. Does God only deign to rescue Hebrews from slavery? What about Hagar?

But the angel has not finished. God gives Hagar promises reminiscent of Abram's call in Genesis 12—except this time, an enslaved woman is the beneficiary. God says, you're pregnant with a son, and he is not the only child in your womb. "I will increase your descendants so much that they will be too numerous to count" (16:10 NIV). See that sand at your feet? Try to count a teaspoon full and then consider the legacy that will come from your diminished, dehumanized frame. Right now, you're growing the future. While your maternity rights seem to be at stake, no one can take away the matriarchy I have planned for you. You will be the mother of a nation, too, just like Sarai. Though you and your son have been disinherited from the family of Abram, God has seen and heard her affliction. And for whatever reason, God does not offer deliverance, but presence. You, too, Hagar, are a child of God.

Yet how can a return to slavery be mercy to Hagar? The most tender commentators remind me that the desert is no place for a pregnant body. The survival of mother and baby requires that they return to the household. Hagar and Ishmael may not be *safe* in returning, but they will be *alive*. And Ishmael, born into the family of Abram, will join the line of God, even if theirs remains a side story in the Bible. The protection that God offers the enslaved woman in this moment *is* the household of Abram.

Still, is that good enough?

* * *

Here is an uncomfortable truth: every interpreter of the Bible is in danger of fundamentalism. On one side, fundamentalism looks like thoughtless, cut-and-paste application. These are the "plain readers" who assume the application of the ancient words is obvious and accessible without effort. Genesis spins the heads of these readers one hundred and eighty degrees, causing fantastic leaps in logic and judgment that result in laughable interpretation. As a person who appreciates direct speech, I understand the desire these readers possess that the Scriptures be plain, clear, and obvious; I, too, have flipped open the Bible at random, pointed at the page, and found a word that spoke specifically to me in my specific daily circumstance. This is not wrong. Some of the Scriptures can and do comply with the demand for simplicity. Yet this hermeneutic is woefully inadequate at providing a holistic scriptural understanding.

However, the opposite pole also exists within American biblical hermeneutics: let's call these readers the hyper-scrupulous. These interpreters attempt to approach the Scriptures as an academic discipline, preferring the scientific hermeneutic known as the historical-critical. Historical criticism applies the tools of the European Enlightenment to the ancient story to clarify the "objective" meaning of the holy text.

I certainly lean this direction. Yet feminist theologian Kwok Pui-Lan points out the inherent bias with asserting claims of objectivity about this complex work of literature. She argues that historical criticism preferences "white, male and middle-class academics, because they alone can afford to be 'impartial,' mean[ing] 'non-committed.'"[19] In this case, "objectivity," "impartial," and "non-committed" act as coded language, the wealthy Western academy's way of whitewashing biblical studies.

Our biases are often subtle. Those of us of a dominant heritage struggle to see the ways that our majority culture inflects our translation and interpretation of our holy book. Academic examination of the Bible is certainly valuable. However, this Western reading method should not be the *sole* mode of biblical interpretation, and it should also not be elevated as the *best* interpretative mode either. For example, the fact that total objectivity has not been rigorously maintained does not mean an interpreter got the interpretation wrong.[20]

Scholar Renita J. Weems agrees that historical criticism has often "undermine[d] marginalized reading communities," who have tended to approach the Scriptures less objectively and more personally. These readers seem to find a way to combine the academic and the personal immediacy of a plain reading. In other words, an academic approach to the Bible is to read at a distance, while marginal communities without access to more academic commentary can still find answers to the questions of their daily sufferings in the text. These readers are the survivors, and to them, the Bible's message is urgent and immediate. They do not have the luxury of reading the Bible at a distance.

When we interpret the Bible, study and story must balance each other. We need biblical fan fiction and we need Sunday school sword drills. God isn't picky, so long as our engagement with God's Word is authentic and embodied. And if our Bible study does not include times when we engage personally, immediately, and emotively, then our hermeneutic has missed the mark.

\* \* \*

An example of this latter biblical hermeneutic—that of the survivor—came to me by way of Howard Thurman's grandmother. Dr. Thurman was a theologian whose work inspired the founders of the American Civil Rights Movement, and his grandmother, Nancy Ambrose, had been an enslaved sharecropper from Daytona Beach, Florida, before her emancipation after the Civil War. Throughout her life, she cultivated a devoted trust in God, yet her "master" limited her worship to his own all-white church. At these services, he could maintain control even over his slaves' religious yearnings by asking the minister to tailor his teachings to the topic of "submission to authority."[21]

Yet Ambrose did not allow her master to hijack her spirituality. In secret, she joined meetings held by an enslaved minister who preached the same message to his congregants each week: "You—you are not slaves," he would say. "No, you—you are *God's children.*"[22] All week long, these enslaved men and women heard dehumanizing lies about themselves from their oppressors. Yet when Sunday came, their pastor offered them words of blessing. These words were the truth according to God, the God who saw, knew, and valued each one. No, they were not slaves; they were children of God. From these words, Thurman's grandmother developed an interior strength that could endure even abuse and disdain.

This simple message also guided her reading of the Scriptures after the Civil War when she obtained her freedom. Though she never learned to read or write, her grandson, Howard, often read aloud to her from the Bible, as she requested. Reflecting later, her grandson wrote in *Jesus and the Disinherited* that she "never ever" chose to read the Pauline Epistles. One day, he asked her why, and she explained that her "master's" minister had exclusively preached Paul's writings during her enslavement:

> "At least three or four times a year he used as a text: 'Slaves, be
> obedient to them that are your masters . . . , as unto Christ.' Then
> he would go on to show how it was God's will that we were slaves
> and how, if we were good and happy slaves, God would bless us.
> I promised my Maker that if I ever learned to read and if freedom
> came, I would not read that part of the Bible."[23]

She abstained from these passages for the rest of her free life. She did so because she understood the plain message of God to her: she was loved, safe, and whole because she was a child of God. And any traumatic memory of her life before, when she daily heard the opposite message, she could forgo in freedom. She recognized that she could not receive the words of Paul as anything but the tools of hatred, manipulation, and abuse. So, she soaked in the Psalms, the Gospels, and the book of Isaiah instead—passages that reaffirmed the identity bestowed upon her by God from birth in a way she could receive it. Her interpretative matrix allowed her to read the Scriptures with creativity and personality. She read plainly, without any academic instruction or perspective, and she read for the sake of survival. We need her mode of Bible study as much as we need any other—maybe more. A wider variety of reading modes displays the variety of God-self. While Thurman's grandmother's method may not be the Western norm, it is contemplative and wise, and her freedom with the Scriptures is my inspiration.

\* \* \*

Another metaphor for the freedom of God can be discovered in the story of Judith Scott, a renowned fiber artist. But no one would have called Judith Scott an artist until the last two decades of her life. That's when she became one of the most revered outsider artists in the United States.

Born to a middle-class family in Cincinnati, Ohio, in 1943, Scott was the fraternal twin with Down syndrome. As an infant, she also contracted scarlet fever, which impaired her hearing. Because of her deafness from infancy, she never learned to speak. Yet her doctors did not understand that she'd gone deaf, so they misdiagnosed her as "severely retarded." Because she was deaf, mute, and developmentally disabled, doctors pressured her parents to institutionalize the little girl at age seven. So, Judith became a ward of the state. Not much is known about Judith's institutionalization except that, once, when she showed interest in drawing with other children her age, her institutional caregivers took the crayons out of her hands and told her she was "too retarded to draw."[24]

Thirty-six years passed before her twin sister, Joyce, became Judith's legal guardian. Judith left the institution and moved to San Diego to live with her sister, and her sister enrolled her in a local art studio for people with disabilities. For two years, Judith observed artists working in the studio without revealing any propensity or interest in making art herself. Then, after a fiber artist offered a workshop to the students, Judith snapped to. She had found her medium: Judith was a fiber artist. From that day in 1988, she began to express herself through fabric.

Judith's sculptures developed layer by layer. Her sculpture would begin with an object collected from the studio—an umbrella, skateboard, tree branches, chairs, magazines, a bicycle wheel, her own jewelry (or another's appropriated jewelry). She hid that object in the center of her sculptures, and each became a "talisman of a significance known to Judith alone," wrote a curator for the American Visionary Art Museum.[25] She often built spines into her sculptures, combining soft curves with sharp angles, blending loud and soft colors into sophisticated palettes. Then, over days, weeks, and sometimes months, Judith hid the object. She wrapped, wove, and knotted together yarn, thread, fabric, and any other fiber strips around the center armature.

Some of her sculptures remained small. Others expanded to nine feet, dwarfing even the tallest NBA stars. All contained secrets within.

Over eighteen years, Judith produced two hundred sculptures. She worked five days a week without interruption. Sometimes, her hands bled with the effort of winding fabric. And no one could tell her when the work was finished. She alone identified a work's completion. And when she reached the finish, she would dust off her hands, push the bundle away from her, and start immediately on the next.

Her creations evoked cocoons, nests, and wombs, an association curators often emphasized by hanging her sculptures from the ceiling at exhibition. Her sculptures appear to be places of safety for vulnerable beings, a representation of safety she had not known in her early life. The director of Judith's art studio, Tom di Maria, hypothesized that these artworks helped Judith to develop a sort of language. Through fiber, Judith learned to speak.

Work like Judith's has been named "folk" or "self-taught" art, which means art made without institutional support or direction. But I prefer the term "outsider art." This art bucks trends. It exists unselfconscious of viewers. It is created apart from the gnawing desire for fame, wealth, or significance, earning it a sort of expressive purity. Outsider art is made only for the joy of making. Judith's art is a story of art created apart from the ordinary containers, expectations, categories, and ambitions. She's free of the burden of canon; she can innovate without fear of criticism. She and outsiders like her can wander, and their wandering teaches the normative what we lack.

* * *

Do you see how the story of Hagar is a form of outsider art? How interpretative modes like that of Howard Thurman's grandmother become a healthy corrective for those of us who read the Bible as science? How reading the story of Hagar from this lens decenters the main characters in favor of the secondary character? And how a side-reading reveals a new side of the patriarch, too? Do you see how God's love resists boundary lines? And do you sense how desperately we—the majority, the normative, the neurotypical—need the outsider to see God clearly?

Hagar's son, Ishmael, is the means of her salvation. "Ishmael" means "God hears." It can also be translated "God will listen," future tense.[26] And God has listened in the present tense, too: "The LORD has heard of your misery," says the angel to the woman in the desert. As in, the justice of God *will* come in the future for Hagar and her son. As in, God will make all things right because God sees beyond the handpicked family of Abram. Hagar, the undervalued and afflicted enslaved woman with no name, is proof that God hears and God responds with particular attention to those at the bottom. Liberation may delay, but it will not be thwarted.

Case in point: Sarai, matriarch of Israel, never meets God face-to-face. She hears secondhand about Abram's encounters, and once, she overhears God's messengers through the tent walls. Yet God speaks with Hagar without any mediators in between. And according to the midrash, the rabbis presume that even if Sarai *had* been standing right beside the enslaved woman at the well, God would have remained opaque to Sarai. Even then, God would have refused revelation to the matriarch. Because God intended to speak to Hagar alone.[27]

I read this as condemnation of the wife of Abram. Ramban agrees: "Our mother [Sarah] did transgress by this affliction [of Hagar], and Abraham also by his permitting her to do so. And so, G-d heard her [Hagar's] affliction and gave her a son who would be *a wild-ass of a man* ['a wild man'], to *afflict* the seed of Abraham and Sarah with all kinds of *affliction*."[28] Ramban sees Hagar's son, Ishmael, and the line that will come from him as God's justice on his mother's behalf—because from Ishmael come the Ishmaelites. And the Ishmaelites, in turn, become the enemy of Israel throughout the rest of the Old Testament, "afflicting" the Israelites as Sarah once afflicted Hagar. Which is to say, God sees and knows each one of us—every deed done and undone. Justice comes like a spring in the desert.

# 09

# PROTEST ART

**“**

*"Shall not the Judge of all the earth do justice?"*

**–GENESIS 18:25**
*(NASB)*

**THE MONK WALKS** into a busy street. Pedestrians, motorbikes, and cars vie for space on the sidewalk. Apartment buildings tower above. In his hand, he holds a can of gasoline. He drenches his orange robes so that the liquid runs down his bald head, drips off his back and shoulders, and puddles on the pavement. Then, he strikes a match. The flames spread like water. At first, no one notices, and then, someone is screaming. The monk falls to his knees. Pedestrians stare, yell, weep, but they do not interfere. The police will arrive soon to arrest what's left of this protestor, and if the observers save him now, the police will torture him, too. Better to die than be taken into custody. Better to respect the ultimatum. The monk clutches to his chest a photo of the Dalai Lama, the most holy of Buddhist Tibetans. He is burning in remembrance and in protest. He is mourning the land his people once possessed before China removed them in 1950. And he is dying to bring them home.

Nearly two hundred have performed this act of self-immolation, a dramatic final moment of pain and outrage against China's occupation of Tibet.[1] Sometimes, protestors drink kerosene to ensure a quicker death. Witnesses often play citizen journalists, recording the deaths on smartphones to be smuggled to Western media outlets who may take up the cause of their tribe. And Tibetans need the support. As one of the most oppressed people groups in the world, they have little power. Only Nagorno-Karabakh experiences less national autonomy than Tibet, whose experience ranks worse than South Sudan, Syria, and Crimea (according to a 2024 Freedom House evaluation).[2]

In the West, we may be tempted to judge these deaths as pointless. Nothing has changed for Tibet, not for decades. Yet Tibetans call these deaths holy. An immolator's body, alight, glows as an altar, like the fires that burn in homes and temples. Anthropologist Dr. Carole McGranahan explained to a journalist, "The flame is an eternal form of prayer to the gods and has been a part of the Tibetan Buddhist tradition for as long as we know."[3] They stand as breathing monuments, martyrs who spend their bodies in prayer and protest. They reject the power determined to extinguish their religion, culture, and language in the pitch dark. And they object in the strongest possible terms.

\* \* \*

Protest exists in Genesis, too, in the textual detour that arrives in Genesis 17–19, the story of Sodom and Gomorrah. Since the events of Genesis 16, a decade has passed: Ishmael has nearly grown to adulthood (he's thirteen). God has demanded that the men undergo circumcision, which Abram compels his household to do. And a trio of supernatural beings has arrived at the tent of ninety-nine-year-old Abram to announce the coming birth of Isaac. Ninety-year-old Sarai will become pregnant, and one year from the angels' arrival, Isaac's arrival will make them a family. This event also occasions the renaming of both matriarch and patriarch (Sarai to Sarah, Abram to Abraham).

Then, as the supernatural visitors turn to leave, God confides in Abraham: God has not only descended to deliver good news, but also to pass judgment on two nearby cities (17:20–21 NIV). God explains that the "outcry" from Sodom and Gomorrah has been so insistent—"so great," "so grievous"—that the Creator cannot ignore it. The Hebrew word for "outcry" is gendered feminine, as Rashi points out, and the city seems to stand in for the voices of oppressed women in that city.[4] The same word also appears in Job 16:18 when the tormented man begs, "O Earth, do not conceal my blood. Let it protest [cry out] on my behalf" (Living Bible). This cry of physical suffering also reminds me of Genesis 4:10, when, after the first murder, Abel's blood "cries out from the ground" (NIV), pleading for justice on the dead man's behalf. Suffering this severe requires the Earth itself to moan with the weight of death. All these sufferers—Abel, Job, and the women of Sodom and Gomorrah—are reduced to blood and bone, their fundamental parts flayed, souls desecrated, voices anguished. And the dirt weeps with them.

A legend in the Talmud describes an emblematic Sodomite victim: a young woman has compassion on starving beggars who sit outside the city's gates, despite the citizens of Sodom outlawing aiding the hungry. So to hide her kind act from her fellow citizens, the young woman conceals provisions for the beggars in a clay pitcher. But she is found out. Her punishment? "The people of Sodom smeared her with honey and positioned her on the wall of the city, and the hornets came and consumed her."[5] A brutal death for an act of kindness.

In the biblical account, we need to skim ahead only a few verses for evidence of evil from the citizens of these cities. In Genesis 19:4–5, "All the men from every part of the city—both young and old" (19:4 NIV) demand that Lot, the nephew of Abraham, refuse shelter to a group of strangers that has appeared on his stoop; the men want to gang-rape Lot's guests instead. Unfortunately, the strangers turn out to be the angels tasked with measuring the city's morality, a test these men fail fantastically.

The rest of the Scriptures also reinforce the evil of these cities. Uttering the name of either Sodom or Gomorrah invokes images of an empire bent on total abuse and complete rebellion from God, one that urgently needs heaven to set it right.[6] Sodom and Gomorrah represent hell on earth where the abuser is not an angry God or Satan, but the bent desires of humanity violently enacted against itself.

Even so, the evocation of brimstone on these cities still makes me and Rabbi Nachmanides squirm. The rabbi writes in the midrash, "Surely there are many nations whose citizens are evil, wicked, etc., and nothing even remotely as drastic seems to happen to them."[7] Because their destruction is imminent and yes, drastic.

Even so, remember that when God pauses to confide his plans to Abraham, God has *not yet decided* the fate of these cities. The indecision of God is striking. God has arrived to investigate, which means the conclusion is not predetermined. God's messengers plan to examine the city and report back before taking action against the citizens. And God confides this to Abraham as if asking for Abraham's opinion.

Thus begins an astonishing dialogue: Abraham talks back to God. God asks, and Abraham objects. And remarkably, God, the Creator of black holes and brain stems, hears him out.

\* \* \*

Not every protest takes on the urgency of the Tibetan martyrs. As you'd expect, the most memorable acts of resistance do put a protestor's life in immediate danger. But protestors can also pace themselves, making protest a lifelong endeavor. Chinese artist and activist Ai Weiwei has modeled this slow-burn resistance.

After the 2008 Sichuan earthquake that decimated the rural province, the Chinese government refused to release an accurate death count. Many children had died, crushed under the rubble of poorly constructed public elementary schools. When their parents begged for answers, Ai noticed the government's reticence to provide accessible information. He found this unacceptable. So, for the sake of the grieving, the artist gathered a team of one hundred volunteer investigators.[8] They examined the ruins closely, interviewed the bereaved about their lost children, and repetitively called government hotlines for information until the operators refused to take their calls anymore. Their pressure campaign gained attention and results. In all, Ai's team documented the deaths of 5,219 local children, offering closure to their families and accountability to a government unused to such protest.

And then Ai went further: the sculptor memorialized the dead. One by one, he lined up nine thousand primary-colored backpacks on the facade of a Munich art museum. Together, the backpacks spelled out a sentence in Mandarin, the words of one mother's grief for her daughter recorded during an interview with Ai's team: "She lived happily for seven years in this world."[9]

When Ai's government noticed the artist's dissent, they retaliated.[10] Officials excised his work from China's national museums, scrubbed his name from the state-monitored internet, tapped his phone, surveilled his house and studio, bulldozed his properties, and eventually arrested him. Once released, Ai began to understand that if he stayed in his country, he could anticipate lifelong imprisonment. So, he fled. Now he lives abroad, exiled.

Protest leaves the dissenters vulnerable because protest discards the narrative or identity that the powerful project upon the weaker. Conscience wins out. The lives of the group trump the safety of the protestor's single, fragile body. Fear is useful in keeping our species alive, but it cannot overturn corrupt governments. Only justice can do that.

\* \* \*

In this light, how should we measure Abraham's protest against God? Does Abraham's objection strike us as dangerous?

God says to the patriarch, I am here to investigate Sodom and Gomorrah. Abraham, disturbed by God's intention toward the cities, blocks the path of the divine Presence. Abraham demands God's attention; since God asked, Abraham will test the boundaries of his welcome. Genesis 18:22 says, "So the men [angels] . . . went toward Sodom, but Abraham remained standing before the LORD" (NIV). This standard translation puts Abraham before God in a posture of subordination, as if Abraham has not yet been dismissed from the monarch's presence. Yet theologian Dr. Walter Brueggemann writes, "A very early text note (not to be doubted in its authority and authenticity) shows that the text before any translation originally said, '*Yahweh* stood before *Abraham.*'"[11] The subject and object reverse. This reversal implies that Abraham is the host, Abraham has called the meeting, Abraham holds God accountable and not the opposite. But this grammatical construction disturbed the scribes. And they changed the scroll with a *tiqqun sopherim*, literally a "correction of the scribes."[12] The scribes reversed the order of the sentence—Abraham before Yahweh, not Yahweh before Abraham.

Whoever has brought the court to order, it's noteworthy that God, undoubtedly the most powerful one in the room, does not strike Abraham dead for insubordination. Abraham's disagreement with

God does *not* mean annihilation. So then, what meaning can we draw from this reversal? Perhaps God welcomes Abraham's examination. Perhaps God wants to teach us about relationships. Here, God submits to questioning, heeds argumentation, and *desires* to hear our human thoughts, even when they differ from God's own. The Divine Conversationalist does not quash the freewill and freethinking of the patriarch, but encourages it.

So Abraham interjects himself into the conflict between God and the peoples of Sodom and Gomorrah. "Will you indeed sweep away the righteous with the wicked? Shall not the Judge of all the earth do what is just?" (18:23b NIV; 18:25c ESV). Can God's anger be quenched for the sake of the innocent? For the sake of God's own integrity? What if God finds fifty innocents within the city? What if forty-five? Forty, thirty, ten? Then what?

Abraham seems to be playing a philosophical game, a sort of "would you rather" in which God can pick the side of either the oppressed or the guilty, and God does not blink. God listens. God agrees, saying, you know me rightly. I am justice, and I will do justice. I will *never* destroy the righteous. The Holy One promises, "For the sake of ten, I will not destroy [the city]" (18:32b NIV). Then God and Abraham part ways, crisis averted.

. . . Except that the following morning, the city goes up in smoke, despite the dialogue of the day before. The text reads, "As the sun rose upon the earth, . . . God rained upon Sodom and Gomorrah sulfurous fire out of heaven'" (Genesis 19:23–24 Contemporary Torah JPS). Which raises the question: if the patriarch's protest did not save the cities, did God listen to Abraham? Or was Abraham's questioning irrelevant?

Perhaps there were no righteous people left in the city, or at least less than ten. Even Lot, Abraham's nephew, supposedly righteous by association, proves evil. He rejects the violent demands of his neighbors to gang-rape his guests, but he offers his daughters in trade. He says, if you leave my guests alone, you can have my daughters. His actions are despicable and cowardly, meant to spare himself at the expense of the children under his protection.

So, the city burns. "God annihilat[ed] those cities and the entire plain and all the inhabitants of the cities and the vegetation of the ground" (Genesis 19:25 Contemporary Torah JPS).[13] I guess that settles it. Or at least, no witness survived to appeal the verdict.

* * *

The story of the cities destroyed by fire reminds me of humanity's tendency for revision. God's version of revision is much more dramatic than ours. God can wipe a city off the planet. Yet humankind also practices the act of revising history. Humans rewrite out of habit, necessity, and sometimes, malevolence.

My vocation as a writer attunes me to this tendency to boomerang because revision is my craft: writing is revision, and revision is writing. I see no distinction between the two. The real art of words appears in the drafts that come after the first. When I sit at my desk and rest my hands on the keyboard, I work and rework the words formerly set down. The first act of creation means nothing compared to the labor of making those words clearer, truer, more vivid. I see revision as an act of generosity and respect to a reader, who must muddle through an author's sentences without context. As an author, I cannot occupy the reader's extra armchair, waiting and available to answer questions as they occur. So, I must labor to make the words stand up on their own so that the reader can decipher the meaning in their own way. I also expect each reader to extract different shades of meaning from my words, meanings I may not have anticipated. This is the mystery of the autonomous human mind.

God's version of revision might be to initiate a natural disaster, or to smash the premade world back to dust, starting creation anew. Yet what about the words of God? Do they ever undergo revision? Does God truly change God's mind? And more specifically, have the words of the Bible undergone revision, and if so, how does that shift the Bible's authority over human lives?

Applying the concept of revision *to the Bible* can stink of heresy to an evangelical (or even a former evangelical like myself). Yet scholars of the biblical manuscripts posit a believable theory of revision based on their close study of these literary texts. Manuscript critics suggest that various redactors (editors) have rearranged and shifted our beloved book over time. Sometimes these editors have added their own clarifying notes to the original words, sometimes crossing out and correcting, as in the *tiqqun sopherim* of Genesis 18:22. Scholars have identified these edits because certain edits give away scribal styles and emphases.[14] In other words, the earliest physical copies of the Bible that we have are not identical, as illustrated by the Smith sisters' palimpsest. While scribal changes and revisions make up a small percentage of our Bible, I find the fact of any revision within the Bible significant.

Especially because my fundamentalist forebears would have assumed that acknowledging revisions would devalue the holy book, disrespecting the God at its center. Yet these complexities of authorship remind me that reading the Bible is, and always was, an exercise in discernment. Acknowledging revision is not the same as doubting God. God is not God's words; God is more.

While we might wish the Bible would conform to our black-and-white thinking, it resists us, as works of art always do. We must be patient with the text. We must sift through the revisions, engage the discrepancies in manuscripts and translations, examine the text for the influences of scribes and outside sources, meet the tiqqun sopherim with creativity and curiosity. We must admit that meaningful disagreements arise as we interpret the Bible, even between people who take these words equally seriously. We are foreigners to the Bible. A chasm yawns between the Bible's readers and writers. To cross this chasm requires humility. Ask God the question and then allow God to answer.

\* \* \*

We may understand the Bible better by contrasting our Western culture of high literacy with the ancient Near Eastern culture of illiteracy. In twenty-first-century American culture, reading precedes all else. Education, work, and entertainment function due to a culture of reading and writing. The fact that the tools of literature are so accessible makes the least among us richer in written-down relics than past royals ever were. According to Westerners, literacy is intimate, individual, singular, fundamental, essential.

Yet while we may assume reading is an act of individualism, the experience of writing and publishing is not. Every book and article require collaboration. Though attributed to an individual author, a published work has absorbed the feedback of multiple sets of eyes, fingers, and minds. Editors are heroic for guarding their anonymity, and so maintaining the illusion to the reading public of *the* author, singular. Even more extravagant is the humility of copy editors, whose names rarely attach to the works they comb for errors in punctuation.[15]

Even inspiration is communal. Over a lifetime, an author absorbs the contents of hundreds of thousands of conversations in real life, virtually, and on the highways of culture—the zeitgeist. These influence and amend an author's thinking before she ever composes the brilliant, immutable, and original concoction of words. (So we suppose.) No book is *ever* an individual affair. No book rises spontaneously and without precedent from the mind of one author. Books take a crowd to produce. That crowd takes years to settle on a final written version, which, ever after, will be nominated the original. Yet individual authorship is a myth of the romantic era that will not die.

The debate surrounding the Bible's authorship suffers the same fate. We prefer the idea of the singular author in a room, urgently scratching a quill to parchment until the candle goes out, only to start again the next morning at sunrise. Probably, this biblical author is possessed, we think, haunted and animated by God's spirit to the last word.

Yet we must flip ideas of authorship by one hundred eighty degrees to approach a more historically accurate model of biblical authorship.[16] In the ancient Near East, there was no reading public, no stack of books on the bedside table, not even for the wealthy. Only scribes engaged texts. Scribes composed scripts to be performed orally to each other, to crowds, to their monarchs. No one read for fun.

And no such thing as *an* author existed. When and if a single writer did arise, he would often obscure his identity on purpose. An author did not care whether he received credit for his unique words; he preferred to put his thoughts in the mouth of an author already deemed singular, influential, and authoritative. Claim your words were written by Plato, and earn instant credibility.

But this complicates the question of biblical authors. Who wrote Genesis? The Bible's own internal evidence disputes Moses's authorship of the Pentateuch (the first five books of the Christian Bible)—for example, by narrating events that happened after Moses's time, including an account of Moses's death. Yet early commentators still named Moses as the author of Genesis.[17] Why? Perhaps attributing Genesis to Moses offered authority to a nonauthoritative group of scribes scrabbling together the threads of their culture after Israel's return from exile, as some scholars suppose happened. These scribes then constructed a cohesive national story around which the battered nation could rebuild.[18] Or perhaps these scrolls traveled with them into and out of exile, already whole, a collaborative work of Moses and a few aides. Frankly, I do not care which, though I believe the first to be the most probable, based on scholars' assessments.

What matters most to me is that the Bible is a work of collective writing, rather than a work of singular authorship. Biblical scholar Karel van der Toorn expounds: "The quest for an individual author is pointless [because] the Bible is a repository of *tradition*, accumulated over time, and the texts they produced were often coproductions. *[Therefore,] the making of the Hebrew Bible is owed to the scribal class rather than a limited number of individuals.*"[19]

Rather than obsessing over singular authorship, what if we embraced the theory of collective authorship? These preserved stories and teachings were always meant to imprint the community. The Bible is no private diary. Rather, a scribe canonized the *cultural* memory through the collected stories, songs, and liturgies by his people about God. Scribes were "the guardians of literary heritage."[20]

Better yet, what if we embraced the tension between communal and individual authorship in the Bible? For example, researchers keep trying to unmask the individuals behind the Bible; such is our post-Enlightenment obsession with singular authorship. In 2020, manuscript researchers found a way to test the DNA of the animals whose skin made up the parchment of particular manuscripts in order to isolate the age, location, species of these animals. In turn, this provides further context about the unique scribes commissioned to compose the disparate scrolls. (Which scribes lived in which regions alongside *this species*, and what does this information tell us about the scribes as individuals and also about their communities?) Contextual data like this could teach us about each scroll's distinct origin story.[21]

More importantly, studies like this continue to affirm that the Bible was created collaboratively. The Great Isaiah Scroll is one of the most complete discovered in the cache of Dead Sea caves. And in 2021, Israeli researchers used an algorithm to determine that *two* distinctive styles of handwriting marked the parchment. Meaning at least two scribes contributed to the copying of the single scroll.[22]

Do we see how wide and deep the canon is, how much taller than we presumed? Only with help—the help of hands behind and ahead—can we discover the wide-ranging truth of the Scriptures. We need others to pronounce the words we cannot, to turn the pages we cannot reach, to aid our ascent. We need a leg up. While I used to see revision of the Bible as a decay or a loss, now I see it as an illumination. Revision is communal expansion. Meaning is not lost but gained. Accepting the Bible's revisers does not mean wielding a red pen, but instead, illuminating the page with gold leaf.

\* \* \*

But we must return to Sodom and Gomorrah, the burning cities, the cities God revised off the surface of the planet. On the morning after Abraham questions God, the patriarch wakes to see "the smoke of a kiln" on the horizon (Genesis 19:28 JPS). We presume that, for the sake of the victims, slaves, impoverished, houseless, addicts, and immigrants, God's anger has descended on the city as a fireball. There was not one righteous left, not even one.

One midrash hypothesizes that the fate of Sodom was less fiery than the biblical account: instead of destruction by flames, destruction is wrought when God uproots the cities like a weed.[23] Another rabbi remarks that the land of Sodom and Gomorrah used to overflow with gems and fruit; now, even birds shun the place.[24] In fact, "When a person takes soil from a piece of land that once was Sodom and he transplants it, it will never grow anything again." The desolation is ongoing.[25]

The Enlightenment practitioners, too, have tried to answer the question of how and why the two cities disappeared. Archaeologists hypothesize a meteorite touched down,[26] while geologists see tectonic shifts in the East Africa Rift system during the Middle Bronze Age, the time of Abraham.[27] Perhaps Sodom and Gomorrah were swallowed by sink holes? One measurable effect of regional geologic activity was the marooning of the Dead Sea. This body of water that stretches from Gaza to Israel is lifeless, lying so far below sea level that any water that drains into it cannot escape except by evaporation. In its depths, minerals and salt pile up. The high salinity then kills any creature that ends up in these waters.[28]

Perhaps it's no coincidence that the rabbis assume that the Dead Sea used to be Sodom's Lake, a body of water that assured the city's prosperity—until it didn't. Imagine the Dead Sea as the spot where the judgment from God rained down. God's wrath falls on Sodom and Gomorrah, and the destruction is total: not only today but hereafter. The soil itself dies. It is still dead.

This is terrible news for the children of Lot, we who bear the genes of oppressors. A story of a prosperous and powerful city flattened reminds me to fear God. My Anglo-American ancestors have abused so many. If it is true that God is an unquenchable fire, then anger could be headed toward me, too, coming for me and mine. Do I desire the justice of God? If so, I am burnt toast.

Yet Lot escapes. Lot escapes not because he's good or worthy or sorry, but because "God remembered Abraham" (19:29 NIV). In fact, the angels drag the reluctant man and his family out of the city. On the way out, Lot's unnamed wife glances backward—in longing? In curiosity or vengeance?—and her body is transfigured into a column of salt, salt that then empties into the Dead Sea, its final resting place.

The autonomy of God means that God can mete out judgment and extend mercy, just because. Judgment is confusing and makes God appear monstrous. But if the story of Lot is anything to judge by, you'll always have the chance to duck and run for cover, an angel tugging at your sleeve. God jealously guards human freedom, so why would I assume that God is not also free? Free to judge and free to pardon. How should we make sense of these dueling powers, ours and God's?

\* \* \*

However, there's another reason I find myself bothered by the story of Sodom and Gomorrah (other than the obvious): the story is in the wrong place. The Genesis narrative has focused on the love triangle for chapters and chapters, centerstage. We've witnessed the infertility of Sarai, God's promise of lineage, and then the family breakup. This story of brimstone interrupts the family story. Genesis is a book that rarely requires events to line up chronologically, so the authors of Genesis did not put the story here for the sake of precision. Rather, I suggest that the story is placed *here* to draw eyes to Abraham, the only character that stretches across the chapters. The authors intend to reveal the guts of the man.

Consider how Abraham, the chosen of God, advocates for the not-chosen Sodomites in this passage. These Sodomites are strangers and Abraham names no names when he brings up the hypothetical righteous citizens of the cities. After hearing that God may act dramatically, Abraham, despite God's prior warning, does *not* warn his nephew. He simply returns home and goes to bed. Abraham protests the loudest when he has nothing personal to lose. Yet when the patriarch has an opportunity to advocate for those he knows and loves—even those within his own household—he falls quiet.

The conclusion of the story of the two sons, Ishmael and Isaac, clarifies the character of Abraham further. Sarah receives her promised son, the son who restores her laughter, Isaac—if only Ishmael will not interfere. So, taking up the mantle of God, Sarah suggests judgment for Hagar and Ishmael in 21:11. They no longer fit well within the family structure now that she's had a son. Sarah's solution? Throw them out. Dump the enslaved woman and the illegitimate son into the desert to die.

Abraham finds this suggestion "very displeasing" (21:11 ESV) and "distressing because it concerned his son" (21:11 NIV) (and no mention of Hagar). But Abraham does not argue with Sarah.[29] And when God affirms Sarah's actions, to my consternation, Abraham does not argue with God either.

Abraham has a streak of passivity: he does not pray to relieve Sarah's infertility, does not protest Sarah's ill-treatment of Hagar and his oldest son, twice does not protect Sarah from marauding kings (12:10–20; 20), and twice does not object to the slow death of Hagar and Ishmael in the desert. Abraham may have been called righteous for his faith, but the narrative shows off his faithlessness. So, the judgment and negotiation on behalf of Sodom and Gomorrah may be meant as a foil. Pay attention to the inconsistency of the patriarch. God *wants* the man to speak up, invites him to speak for Sodom and Gomorrah, in fact. Wouldn't it follow that God desires Abraham to advocate for others' well-being, too, even at the risk of God's anger? But the narrative has not concluded, and God intends to give Abraham one last chance to practice advocacy. This time, God tells him to climb a nearby mountain—just father, son, and a knife.

# 10

# HOLY TERROR

**❝❞**

*"The fire and the wood are here," Isaac said, "but where is the lamb?"*

**—GENESIS 22:7**
*(NRSVue)*

**THE DAY THE WORD OF GOD** arrives, the old man rises early with his son. The birth of this son made God's word true—after decades, Abraham finally has a child on whom to pass the extravagances of God. This miracle renovated the mother's body so utterly that the rabbis named it a double miracle: first was the pregnancy. The second, Sarah's age rewound. The wrinkles disappeared, and her organs returned to working order, a regeneration. Some rabbis even hypothesized that before the annunciation, in all those previous decades, the mother never had a womb. Her organs had been incomplete for ninety years. Then, at the birth announcement (Genesis 18:10), God created a womb within her from scratch like a starfish regrowing a limb. The son's arrival meant that, as Sarah's body was re-created, so too, a people was born.

But the word still arrives to take the miracle away. In a dream, Abraham receives the final demand of God: "Some time later, God tested Abraham" (22:1 NIV). The Hebrew verb for "test" is sometimes translated as "prove" or, rarely, "tempt." I prefer "assay," as in determining a metal's purity, achieved by burning or drowning the minerals in acid. As in, God assays Abraham to remove the impurities in his faith. The rabbis imagine a scene similar to Job, with Satan demanding God offer proof of loyalty. Pain is the proof.

So, God says, rise, go to the mountain with your son and a bundle of fire and a knife, and slaughter him for my sake. Then the narrative cuts to Abraham rising early in the morning. He wipes his eyes, splits wood, loads up the donkey, two servants, and his son. Together, they set out for the place where Abraham will end Isaac's life according to God's impossible demand.

\* \* \*

When lightning strikes, each person experiences the flash differently. The US National Weather Service collects self-reported stories like Rachel's. She was struck while bathing in California's Donner Lake. "I was swimming, and I was treading water when all of a sudden BAM! And it felt like all my bones broke. A bolt had hit a boulder on the other side of the lake and the current went through the water. My sister was with me and she described it as having all of her joints dislocated. I was shaking afterword [*sic*]. The people on shore felt the shock too . . . but they didn't seem to understand the terror and pain."[1]

Glenn felt surprised when a bolt ripped through him on a Long Island beach. He and his wife had huddled beneath an umbrella as a storm front approached. Then, suddenly, "NO warning, NO thunder, a bolt of lightning blinded us like a flashbulb, hitting the umbrella I was holding. I felt the lightning travel through my left arm into my chest and then out my feet in the sand."[2] After a quick escape to a nearby hotel (and a few gulps of vodka), Glenn walked away unscathed.

Anita was not so lucky. When lightning struck her outdoor porch, she heard a hum as violent as cicadas in heat. She remains permanently deaf in her right ear. She wrote, "I live with the loud locusts sound 24/7."[3] Other survivors have experienced temporary paralysis, burns, heart arrythmia, memory malfunctions, PTSD, and an array of emotional disorders due to their encounters with lightning.[4]

Johanna from Denmark, who was struck while unlocking her bike from a pylon in the center of Copenhagen at age nineteen, described "screaming very loudly." The feeling of electricity coursing through her body has stayed with her: "Indescribable, unfathomable, a power going through me and being surrounded by intense white and purple colors. And you're overwhelmed with sadness, ridiculousness, confusion, laughter and luck. The incident changed me, and it's debatable whether it was for the better or worse."[5]

Who hasn't enjoyed the sight of lightning from afar as it arcs across an ink sky? We like to be startled by a bolt now and then, to witness phenomena we cannot explain or predict. But up close, lightning leaves a mark.

\* \* \*

Here is God arriving like a bolt of lightning traversing the patriarch's nervous system: "Take your son, your only son, whom you love—Isaac—and go to the region of Moriah. Sacrifice him there as a burnt offering on a mountain I will show you" (22:2 NIV). Despite God's statement, "Your son, your only son, whom you love—Isaac," Isaac is not Abraham's only son. Isaac is the only son *left* in the patriarch's home.

The other son, Ishmael, has been chased from the father's house with his mother, Hagar (21). Mother and son barely survived this abandonment. Their story of near extinction has been carefully preserved within the pages of the Scriptures. I can imagine Abraham, standing at the tent flap as Hagar balances the supplies on one shoulder—a skin of water, a bag of barley, a leg of roasted goat, a handful of green herbs—and with her other arm, she supports her teenage son.[6] Then Abraham turns away, and Hagar and Ishmael continue into the blinding heat. Gradually, they cannot see the tent anymore. Then their skin is searing. Their provisions dry up. Still, the pair keep walking. By now, the boy may be weeping, begging for rest. Finally, Hagar sets him beneath the sparse shade of a wild bramble. Then, his mother walks in the opposite direction. She might be delirious herself, but she knows what comes next, and she refuses to witness the final blow.

We readers peer through our fingers and wait for vultures to circle. Except the two survive. God speaks again. Here is a well that Hagar has not noticed, hidden beneath overgrown brush, and God tells the mother to give the boy a drink. Here is a way the two can survive. Around this spring in the arid dunes, mother and son can build a life. Here, the disinherited mother and son find themselves shaded by the blessing of God. They become a people, and their story is picked up by the founders of Islam. God's word is proved true. Ishmael becomes a nation, and Hagar is its matriarch.

Delores S. Williams, a womanist theologian, makes sense of Hagar and Ishmael's abandonment through the lens of the Black American experience. About the well, she writes, "God provided Hagar with a resource." As God always does for those at the bottom, Williams contends, God "makes a way out of no way," a future out of exile.[7] And though God's way may not be total liberation, God's resourcing provides resiliency, the means by which the oppressed can become whole.

\* \* \*

The divine mercy shown to Hagar and Ishmael offers a clue for the story of the mountain, the father, the second-born (?) son, and the knife. Yet, while I can blame Abraham for abusing Hagar and Ishmael (one bad human actor), who can I blame for demanding Isaac's death? God utters the command to kill.

I suspect that God is muddying the waters. The total autonomy of the Being Above has been proved in Genesis—in the firebombing of Sodom, the toppling of the Tower of Babel, the dramatic drowning of Noah's flood, and Sarai's infertility. God's actions do not always appear just. Yet each preceding narrative has demonstrated God's preoccupation with justice. Does this command fit the pattern?

I am certain the same urgent questions occurred to Abraham, the man who received the impossible command. Imagine the agonized journey to Moriah. The journey takes *three days* of travel on foot. The landscape is immense, towering sandstone mountains that dwarf the travelers in the valley. What do the father and son discuss as they walk? We never learn the mind of the patriarch. All we can measure are his footfalls—his silent, plodding steps. In fact, Abraham offers no explanation to Sarah or to Isaac before or after.

Not until Abraham glimpses the peak on the horizon does he clear his throat. And he speaks to the servants, not to Isaac. Stay here, Abraham says. My son and I will climb alone. We will worship at the top. And we will return. *We, we will*, we will *return*, the both of us (22:4). So, the servants seek shade, the donkeys nose for green, and the father and son ascend.

How can Abraham bear to keep the secret he carries? Philosopher Søren Kierkegaard has made much of Abraham's silence. In fact, the philosopher understands the father holding his silence to be the trial itself. God's command makes Abraham a moral outcast. The father cannot confide in anyone because, in everyday terms, humanity's universal moral code would classify the man as a murderer. Yet now, improbably, God redefines the code: to kill the son is to love God. How can this be? The text confounds.

Later God sets similar paradoxes before other biblical characters. Take the case of Mary's pregnancy and her conception by the Holy Spirit. Mary, the mother of Jesus, who from the outside, appears as an adulterer. Kierkegaard elaborates: "No doubt Mary bore the child miraculously [and] no doubt, the angel was a ministering spirit [who announced the pregnancy], but he was not an obliging one who went round to all the other young girls in Israel and said, 'Do not despise Mary, something out of the ordinary is happening to her.' What is left out is the distress, the fear, the paradox. The angel came only to Mary, and no one could understand her."[8]

Like Abraham, God traps Mary in a moral paradox. She maintains her silence about the angel's visit—who would believe her?—and is condemned by it; yet her silence also confirms her faith, for which God rewards her. As Kierkegaard says, "Isn't it true that those whom God blesses he damns in the same breath?"[9] Who can hope to judge Mary or Abraham truly? In the sight of God, these two are known. To the rest of us, only time tells the difference between a murderer and a worshiper, an adulterer and the Mother of God.

* * *

Like most acts of God, lightning cannot be predicted. Yet we can explain the mechanics of lightning, sort of. We know that lightning is electricity. That the entire universe runs on electrical pulses of a kind, powered by the magnetism of every cell's mass. Also that electricity accumulates during storms and that lightning is a sudden release of that stored energy—like a static jolt you receive in the winter months that makes your hair stand on end, multiplied by a million. We know that lightning is fast and hot, so that if you could straddle a bolt of lightning, it would launch you to the moon in fifty-five minutes flat (rather than four days in a NASA rocket). That is, if that bolt of lightning did not incinerate you during the ride, since lightning is hotter than lava and up to five times hotter than the surface of the sun.[10]

We know that these spontaneous bolts of electricity do not confine themselves to rain clouds either. They also arrive in storms of dust, snow, hail, earthquakes (the phenomenon known as earthquake lights), and occasional volcanic eruptions.[11] Lightning appears during any atmospheric disturbances, whenever electrical currents fluctuate—such as a meteorite crashing to Earth. A space rock pelting toward the ground will likely be accompanied by lightning. Lightning can also appear as a ball of light, hovering, so that, occasionally, viewers of this phenomenon have assumed that "ball lightning" was an unidentified flying object of alien origin.[12]

There, our knowledge halts. We cannot predict it or prevent it. We cannot even say for certain which storms will generate it. Our inferences about when lightning will appear resemble a joke more than a scientific theory: Did this exact storm *already* produce lightning? If yes, then run for cover.

Electrical currents that jump at random from the sky to the ground, defying prediction, offer an example of the chaos of weather. In fact, meteorologists consider *all* weather to be part of a "chaotic system." Which is to say, we humans can barely predict the sky beyond a ten-day chart of likelihoods. Massachusetts Institute of Technology researcher Edward Lorenz first applied his theory of chaos to weather in a 1972 paper, asking, "Does the flap of a butterfly's wings in Brazil set off a tornado in Texas?"[13] Can minute disruptions of regional climate zones set off monumental disruptions in the style of a falling domino? Chaos theory suggests that anything that disrupts air and water and light, even the air disturbance caused by the flap of a butterfly's wing, could affect weather in the future. Meaning that all climate everywhere is connected. The actions we perform within our specific climate bubble can change things *anywhere on the planet*, though we cannot predict how. No neat formula can sum up the effect of a Brazilian butterfly's flight pattern on weather patterns in Texas.

But other meteorologists take issue with Lorenz's theory. They believe weather *can* be measured, or at least that trying to measure it is worthwhile, and that we *will* understand how these systems function eventually, if not today. As physicist Spencer Weart explained, "Most scientists agreed that climate has features of a chaotic system, but they did not think it was wholly unpredictable. To be sure, it was impossible to predict well in advance, with any computer that could ever be built in the actual universe, that a tornado would hit a particular town in Texas on a particular day (not because of one guilty butterfly, of course, but as the net result of countless tiny initial influences). Yet tornado seasons came on schedule."[14]

Determined scientists like Weart pass days gazing at sunspots, calculating the rotation of the stars and planets, and removing minerals and remains from thousand-year-old ice to search for clues about the climate's future. They seek any repeating patterns to make sense of how our climate functions over the long term. They have not unearthed the Rosetta Stone, not yet. The question remains unsettled. Whether the universe bends toward chaos or order remains up for debate.

\* \* \*

But what about Isaac? What did he think of the silent hike with his father? Scholars debate Isaac's age at the time of the journey to Moriah. Isaac is called a "boy,"and he has not yet married within a culture that married young. (And his parents would have certainly prioritized matchmaking as the means of securing the generations promised by God.)

Yet whether adult or child, Isaac *is* intuitive enough to guess his father is hiding something. As they ascend, Isaac says, "Father? Father?" a refrain familiar to parents, whose children say our names more often than their own. Isaac has realized that he and his father have forgotten something important. If God lives at the top of this mountain and awaits our offering, where is the animal to satisfy God's hunger? What will burn? "The fire and wood are here," Isaac says, "but where is the lamb for the burnt offering?" (22:6 NIV).

Abraham demurs: "God himself will provide" (22:8 NIV). I hope the father means what he says, that he does not intend to carry out the terrible act. Or that he's decided that God cannot be serious. Can the love of God mean hatred of the son? How could such an act be forgivable? What can explain Abraham's idiocy? What can justify God's decree? Is it any wonder that Abraham's family must unwind generations of dysfunction after the first son is nearly set alight on top of a mountain, in supposed worship of God?

A rabbinic tale sets my doubts in the voice of Samael, an accusatory angel who functions as Satan throughout the midrash:

> Samael went to our father Abraham and said: "Old man, old man! Have you lost your mind [lit. have you lost your heart]? You are going to slay a son given to you at the age of a hundred!" "Even this I do," replied [Abraham]. "And if He sets you an even greater test, can you stand it?!" "Even more than this," Abraham replied. "Tomorrow He will say to you, 'You are guilty of murder, you murdered your son!' Abraham replied: "Still I go."
>
> [Samael then] approached Isaac and said: "Son of an unhappy mother! He is going to slay you!" Isaac replied: "Still I go." . . . So [Abraham and Isaac] went both of them together—one to slaughter and the other to be slaughtered.[15]

This legend suggests that our main characters do not flinch. Another retelling sees Abraham so determined to obey God that when the moment comes for Abraham to sink the knife into his son, the angel must intervene by literally dissolving the knife in Abraham's hand. At which point Abraham begins to strangle Isaac instead.[16] (In the legend, the angel ultimately stops Abraham.)

Isaac is also set on obedience.[17] To emphasize this point, some rabbis assume Isaac is a thirty-seven-year-old man and not a boy at the time of this event, and they wonder, could Abraham, at age one hundred, "really tie up a man of thirty-seven?" Not by force alone. "Rather, it was with [Isaac's] agreement" that the father tied the son tightly to a stone and lifted the knife to make the incision that would kill the promise.[18] At least, that's the theory.

* * *

Only one aspect of weather can be reproduced at will: sometimes, we can make clouds drop what they are carrying. "Seeding clouds" means a plane flies over a range of threatening cumulonimbus, dropping dry ice or silver iodide crystals into the vapor. The clouds release, and water in the air clings to the crystals so that they grow heavier and heavier until they succumb to gravity. In other words, we can make it rain. Through cloud-seeding, governments combat drought. But if there are no clouds, then there is no way to wring out the sky.

No wonder humanity has so often equated God with the weather. The Presence is like a cloud. Barely visible yet powerful, consuming, uncontrollable, transforming. Sometimes, God even confounds the moral senses. Sometimes, God is known only by absence.

The Dutch artist Berndnaut Smilde has made clouds his art form, playing on these resonances. He fills a warehouse, auditorium, cathedral, or white-walled gallery to humid. With a spray bottle, he coats the floors and walls with mist until the air becomes thick and heavy. Then, with precision, he turns on a fog machine and a fan, and a cloud appears. The vapor morphs into a shape we recognize from a blue May morning, hovering above the concrete floor for a few breathless seconds. And Smilde snaps a photograph. He has only seconds before the cloud has dispersed, the air invisible once more. In fact, if you stood in the spot where the cloud had once been, you'd never recognize that the visitor had drifted by—except for the documentary record. Smilde warns, "If you're seeing a photo, you've already missed it."[19] Yet an image can be doctored. Perhaps the potential for deceptive editing is exactly the reason Smilde's work is worth viewing: was it there, in situ, or not? The question, the doubt, the mystery makes the work stranger, makes a viewer look harder. The presence of doubt awakens hope.

* * *

In the case of Abraham and Isaac on Mount Moriah, we know that the tragedy does not occur. God's demand evaporates. After Abraham binds his son and raises the knife, an angel restrains him (Genesis 22:12). God does not make the father kill the only son. It seems that God demanded only the intent to kill the son. I wonder, which counts most: the demand or the retraction? I measure God by these pages, applying a lighter to the edges to assay the Deity for purity. Why does God ask the unaskable of Abraham? And why does God change God's mind a few days later? (How dare God?)

Is the moral of the story that God is capricious? Or that Abraham, as Hebrews 11:17–19 describes, believed God could resurrect the dead (and is that solution to the riddle tolerable)?[20] Or might it have to do with the chapters that arrived before, in which God obliterated Sodom and Gomorrah for their cruelty to the vulnerable? If Sodom, then why not Abraham and Sarah, too? Have they not tormented the enslaved woman and her son so that Hagar and Ishmael have cried to God for rescue in the same pitch as those victims of Sodom? God's silence about Hagar and Ishmael has me wondering whether the sacrifice of Isaac is God's own judgment against the evil of the patriarch and matriarch toward the pair in the desert.

Yet this too evokes grief. Why must the following generation bear the weight of punishment? I keep returning to Caravaggio's painting *The Sacrifice of Isaac*. A balding and gray-bearded Abraham forcibly holds down a boy that looks about ten years old, palming his neck, a knife in the opposite hand. The boy screams, his eyes fixed on the blade that glints a few inches from his face, and he desperately tries to escape his father's grip. The canvas is primarily deep blacks, a technique of Dutch masters like Rembrandt that spotlights faces and hands while obscuring the rest of the frame—I cannot see the subjects' immediate surroundings, nor can I see their legs or the whites of their eyes. Meanwhile, an angelic figure who resembles Isaac, perhaps barely older than twelve, appears to the left of the father. And though Isaac cannot break free, the angel secures Abraham's wrist with one hand, immobilizing the knife. With his free hand, the angel points to the bottom right of the canvas to the detail both Abraham and I have missed: it's the ram. I stared at the painting for several minutes before I noticed the animal that will be the son's salvation. In the painting, Abraham's face is surprised at the supernatural presence. Apparently, he has not yet noticed the ram. And I wonder whether he and I have both been blind for the same reason: we are entranced by the son, whose gaping black mouth is an unbroken circle of horror.

\* \* \*

There is one stranger interpretation of the story of Abraham and Isaac on Mount Moriah: some rabbis say that Abraham got it wrong. He misunderstood God. They insist that God never said to *kill* the son but to *prepare* the son for sacrifice, that the act of child sacrifice—Isaac killed in ritual worship of God—had *never entered God's mind* (as in Jeremiah 19:5). Rashi, for example, translates God's initial command to Abraham as "*bring him* [Isaac] *up* as a burnt offering," instead of "*offer him* as a burnt offering." This clarifies God's intention: "[God] did not say, 'slay him,' because the Holy One, blessed be He, did not desire that [Abraham] should slay [Isaac], but [God] told him to bring [Isaac] up to the mountain to *prepare* him as a burnt offering. So when [Abraham] had taken [Isaac] up, God said to him, 'Bring him down.'"[21] Accordingly, Judaism calls this trial "the binding of Isaac," emphasis on *binding*—not the father's deception, not the knife and the firewood, not the child murdered as worship. This story becomes *the tying up*, the scaring the son silly. Abraham was wrong, no other explanation needed.

And though I admit this reading stretches the limits of faithful interpretation, I find I cannot dismiss their theory entirely because I, too, want to smooth out the textual wrinkles. I cannot decide whether my hesitancy to call God cruel is faithful or delusional, a failure of common sense. Humor me? Let's say Abraham *thought* he was following God and missed either the meaning or character of the Speaker. How would Abraham then discover his error? How do we? Note that God does not speak once in the story, but twice. The second time, God speaks to the back row, leaving no room for error. God says, *Stop, do not touch the boy. Stop and lower the knife. Stop this second.* God's return to the narrative, this second speaking, comforts me. As another

Jewish teacher once wrote, "The Holy One of Blessing first places the righteous in doubt and suspense, and then reveals to them the real meaning of the matter."[22]

What is the meaning? To recap: God says to worship, and Abraham climbs the mountain and ties the son to the altar. God says to kill the boy, and Abraham raises the knife. God says to kill, and then God takes it back: do not touch the boy, not a finger. Abraham pauses long enough to sight the substitute, a ram stuck by its curving horns in brush. And Abraham, who had told Isaac that God would provide the animal, *sees an animal provided*. Abraham names the place "the Lord will provide" because the ram arrived (22:14 NIV).

And then God keeps speaking: "Because you have not withheld your son, your only son, I will surely bless you . . . because you have obeyed me" (22:16, 18 NIV).[23] God says, expect more. Now my mercy will never end. All this for the man who raised the knife. For the man who, the rabbis suggest, got it wrong.

* * *

I admit I fear being wrong about God. What if I have received God with confusion instead of clarity? My native Evangelicalism values certainty. Like the scientists of the Enlightenment, we prefer to quantify, measure, sift, and bottle. We value argumentation and decisiveness; we dismiss doubt and paradox. If we could catch God in a net, pin God to a board to collect dust, and then study God from every angle, I suspect we would do it. (Is that the point of this winding book?) Yet I am beginning to suspect that the hike toward God resists a plan. Does any one of us contain the map of spirituality? Wandering may be inevitable.

By the breadth of interpretation of this single story, the Jewish midrash shows me its spaciousness. The midrash represents an entire culture's experience of reading the Old Testament God across time—deeply, reverently, attentively. Yet the midrash is a jumble of opinions and disagreements and half-baked storytelling. The fact of the midrash, its very existence in all its diversity, asserts a belief that God desires to be understood by humans, that the attempt to understand the words attributed to God is worthy. We should at least *try*.

The rabbi Ramban describes both our ignorance of the Bible's meaning and the mercy of God in providing us with flashes of revelation: "We are like those who, though beholding frequent flashes of lightning, still find themselves in the thickest darkness of the light. On some the lightning flashes in rapid succession, and they seem to be in continuous light, and their night is as clear as the day. This was the degree of prophetic excellence attained by the greatest of prophets. By others only once during the whole night is a flash of lightning perceived . . . now it shines and now it vanishes."[24]

Confusion is built into the story, but so is revelation. God, the narrative's ultimate author, means to reveal and to hide Godself from us. Why? Because we humans desire a chase. So, confusion may be a tool used to hold our attention, to keep us chasing down the Being at the story's center. This strange tale suggests that the spiritual pursuit happens individually, between one and his Creator, a moral world of two. God has no grandchildren.[25]

\* \* \*

So, what if you and I are wrong? What if Abraham was? A legend from the midrash offers me comfort. The scene: God and Moses have met, perhaps cross-legged at the top of Mount Sinai, to record the beginnings of humankind. As Moses takes down the dictation that will become Genesis,an urgent question occurs to him: "When [Moses] got to the verse 'And God said: "Let us make Adam"'" (Genesis 1:26), Moses dared to ask, "Master of the universe, why do You give heretics their opportunity? (They will say there are numerous deities)." Moses realizes that the plural will confuse even the most ardent followers of God. So, he asks, why write Genesis that way? God replies, *"Whoever wishes to err, let him err."*[26]

Here, the sages of Judaism make peace with error. We cannot suppose these to be the actual words of God, yet here is an admission from the rabbis that error is inevitable. Yet error is not a matter to fear. These men, so devoted to this text that they spent their lifetimes excavating its depths, picture God as offering a permission slip for exploration.

And why not? God is committed to our total autonomy—as well as to God's own—and so God offers us permission to engage with God's words as we will. Flawed interpretation does not anger, distress, or bother God, though it concerns Moses. Within this legend, God seems to be encouraging us to risk being wrong in pursuit of what is right. Being wrong is not the conclusion; God is.

So, God speaks twice in the story of the binding of Isaac. The first time, only Abraham hears the command; the second, Abraham and Isaac both hear God's speech. Isaac has not heard the voice of God before, and no one would ask for such an initiation as this. But because God speaks to both father and son, the story does not end with Isaac bleeding out. Because God speaks, the father withdraws the knife from the neck of the panting son.

Now, two generations of Abraham's family have met the Deity. Which is to say, religious individualism is another myth of the Enlightenment, because every action done and undone affects the generations after. God has no grandchildren, and God is inherited. Both are true. Isaac will never forget, nor will he let those after him forget: "This story became the powerful message which Isaac transmitted to his son Jacob, and which Jacob transmitted to his sons."[27]

The sons whisper the story to each other, then scrawl and recopy a tale so confounding that you and I still tell it to each other. The retelling is a way of continuing the story. Each generation of parents and children who hear it find themselves wondering about the actions of God, the father, and the son. How might *I* have reacted to the demand, had the word to kill or be killed arrived to me? We assay God's servant. We assay ourselves. We assay God, too. We ask, who among us would be fool enough to obey God? Who among us would climb the mountain, chasing down the flash of light on the horizon? And who could resist?

# 11

# STRANGLEHOLD OF GOD

**"**

*So Jacob was left alone. Then a man wrestled with*
*him until the . . . dawn.*

**—GENESIS 32:24**
*(NET)*

**I USED TO BELIEVE** that following God was simple: a single path, a single meaning, a single truth. One God, one faith, one baptism. The fact of 141 denominations (and counting),[1] with distinctive canons and interpretations all lacquered on top of each other like so many layers of wallpaper, never featured in my imagination of faith. Now, I doubt the old confidence.

I also doubt my uncertainty. What does it say about me if I change my mind about something so essential as the Bible? Am I even *allowed* to change my mind about God? Is this the slippery slope about which I've been warned, the slide away from the presence and favor of God, this God whom I've sought since age four when I laced my fingers and asked for Jesus to come into my heart while settled beneath my Sesame Street comforter? What does it mean to reject the unique and unyielding path, a path without alternatives or side branches? Is it heresy and immorality? Maybe. But I have come to believe my uncertainty and disillusionment is mercy by another name.

I am not the only believer to fear being wrong. Others like me have grown weary of their inherited religion, stale institutions, and strict politics. We fear that changing our minds betrays the Object of Faith. Fear can make us hesitate to discard the old modes—especially when those old modes have become intertwined with people that we love. We fear that our closest relationships will fail when we change.

But our questioning reveals a change has already begun. The moment the doubt occurs to us, we are already different than the moment before. When we invite paradox, curiosity, and empathy to shape us, this very openness, the act of wondering, opens us to mystery.

Certainty was never the game. God is not the God of the enlightened but the foolish. God does not reward the certain but the doubters. Those running away become the sought, the one lost sheep pursued by the shepherd (Matthew 18:12). (Staying home, risks distance of a different kind.)

In fact, the Bible assures us of only one certainty: the search for the ghostly figure of God means loss in this life. Following God means sacrificing either ego—the need to be *certain*—or integrity—the truth that we rarely are. To meet God, Adam and Eve needed to emerge from hiding. Noah needed to push off from dry land. Abraham needed to leave behind his father, culture, and inheritance. Sarah abandoned her fertility goddesses. Hagar wandered into the desert and then returned to slavery. Isaac allowed his wrists to be tied. Every character in Genesis faces a crisis of self and then a reorientation. Their losses are material, psychological, and familial. The only clear gain is God, while all else looks to be lost. They each must decide: will they heed the voice of God or not? Will they risk loss for communion?

In the life of faith, exile is inevitable. But I no longer believe that wandering is an occasion for fear. As French philosopher Simone Weil wrote, "One can never wrestle enough with God if one does so out of a pure regard for truth. . . . If one turns aside from [Christ] to go toward the truth, one will not go far before falling into His arms."[2]

\* \* \*

My favorite patriarch is the last. Abraham's grandson Jacob is famous for his wrestling match with God, and I too resonate with the language of God-wrestling. Over nearly four decades of calling myself a Christian, I have witnessed and experienced crises of abuse, white supremacy, misogyny, greed, violence, and exclusion within the Christian church. I have seen the Bible become a blunt weapon in the hands of American politicians, corrupt institutions, and fallen pastors. And no book has proved more potent than Genesis. Each false reading of Genesis creates a scar in the world.

I am weary and angry at this misuse of this text and of its Centerpiece, the God who made generosity the foundation. Yet what tools do I have to protest this deception? How do I deny and discredit those who make God's name vile in the world, a means of torture rather than blessing? And if God has really created and sustained the cosmos, then God must be in part to blame for not holding God's namesake to account. So, how do we demand a reckoning? You cannot put a cloud in a chokehold.

But Jacob did. Jacob rolled in the dirt with God. Jacob refused to yield until God gave a blessing, reversing the curse on his life. The image of God and humanity dropping to the ground to resolve our differences is romantic, surrealist, mythic. Yet the fight cost Jacob in physical agony. Even protest results in pain. So, I find that neither my reality nor Jacob's is so easily resolved.

*   *   *

On the night of God's visitation, Jacob is camping in the desert. When the sun rises, he plans to meet the twin brother who hates him. Jacob's family-of-origin is so fraught that he fears the next morning will be his last. Jacob fears his brother will murder him, a repeat of Cain and Abel. For decades, Jacob has managed to outrun his brother's grudge. In their earlier life together, Jacob cheated Esau; Esau's rage is reasonable. But now Jacob is returning, obeying a word from God to reckon with his family-of-origin (Genesis 31:3). God has promised to protect Jacob. But returning home is still not safe.

So, tonight, with the sun setting and Esau's shadow looming, Jacob sends his wives, children, servants, animals, and possessions ahead of him, and he calls on God for help, performing a ritual prayer before he stretches out in the sand with a rock for a pillow. Perhaps Jacob drifts off. But then, a nameless, faceless man comes upon Jacob, and the man picks a fight. Jacob has developed a habit of running from danger. But he does not flee. Instead, Jacob yanks, twists, punches. And Jacob does not relent, not even when the fighter calls uncle, not even when the fighter dislocates Jacob's hip. Why does Jacob resolve to see this fight to the end? And who is the foe that inspires such determination?

The rabbis have their theories, like always. The unknown fighter could be Esau himself, Jacob's avenging twin, who has launched a stealthy attack to catch his brother unaware (32:11). Or, if not the brother, then maybe an emissary of Esau, a warm-up. Or perhaps the opponent comes from the spiritual realm—Esau's guardian angel or the messenger Gabriel or Samael, the midrashic Satan—sent to humble the erring Jacob. Or perhaps the match occurs in Jacob's dream, and the fighter is a Freudian manifestation of Jacob himself, his "inner demons" come alive.[3] Yet Jacob's theory is the most arresting: Jacob says the man he fought was God in the flesh.

And I tend to believe him, because Jacob has met God before. Years before, during Jacob's original flight away from his father's tent, Jacob napped and dreamed of a ladder that stretched from the sand to the sky. Angels traveled up and down the rungs, and at the top, Jacob saw God (28:10–17). Then, as Jacob wondered at this sight, God spoke a blessing reminiscent of the call of Abraham in chapter 12. To the grandson of Abraham, God says, "I am with you and will watch over you wherever you go, and I will bring you back to this land. I will not leave you until I have done what I have promised you" (28:15 NIV). And Jacob called that place "Bethel," meaning God's dwelling place.

This time, nearly twenty years later, Jacob hopes for another encounter. So, alone in the desert once again, he summons the Deity in prayer: "Save me, I pray, from the hand of my brother Esau, for I am afraid" (32:11 NIV). And God returns. This second visit exceeds Jacob's expectations, because the Deity who had once sat atop the ladder, this time rends the sky, descends, and enters material reality. Jacob can see and touch and smell this representative of God.

But the Presence is not benign. Even though God comes bearing promises—including a new name for the "heel-grabber" Jacob—the Presence also disables the man. The match between God (or the angel?) and Jacob is violent. One rabbi, Radak, wrote, "Jacob wrestled with him (who?) so intensely that a cloud of dust enveloped them while they were struggling."[4] Then, after an all-night scuffle, God wrenches Jacob's right hip out of joint. This detail is disconcerting because a record of pain moves the story from the plane of dreams to reality. Radak again:

> If you prefer, you may understand this story as . . . a figment of [Jacob's] imagination, a dream, [as in Joshua 5:13, Judges 6:11, Genesis 18–19]. . . . However, the difficulty with such an interpretation in our example is the physical contact not only described in the narrative, but the evidence of an injury sustained by [Jacob] which could hardly have resulted from some hallucinatory encounter. It is difficult to reconcile the Torah's historical note that in commemoration of [Jacob's] injury the Jewish people do not eat the organ of an animal that corresponds to the one which was injured in [Jacob's] body during that encounter.[5]

To me, the note about the patriarch's injury reads like an entry out of an ancient medical journal: "Jacob's hip was touched near the tendon," so "to this day the Israelites do not eat the tendon attached to the socket of the hip" (32:32 NIV).[6] Other Talmudic texts clarify that this is "the prohibition of eating the sciatic nerve," a kosher principle to this day.[7] How do we make sense of the unlikelihood of a flesh and blood tussle with God and Jacob's limp? It could be a myth. But what if it isn't?

* * *

Once we believed that we understood the universe. But astronomer Vera Rubin proved us wrong.

Rubin's obsession with the sky developed in elementary school. As a ten-year-old in the 1930s, she spent her nights staring at the sky above her bed. By age twelve, she was memorizing the paths of that evening's batch of meteorites and celestial bodies so that, in the morning, she could record their journeys in her astronomy notebook. Her mother would often beg her not to "spend the whole night with your head out the window"—or else she feared her daughter would have never slept.[8]

In graduate school, Rubin focused her studies on the movements of galaxies. She wondered, could the path of an entire collection of stars, planets, and suns be measured? Did a galaxy, or a whole system of galaxies, move predictably as a unit as they drifted through the universe? Scientists had assumed that the magnetic pull at the center of any galaxy—the gravity generated by the sun and the planets that spun around it—would decrease by its outer edge. Meaning that whatever orbited at the outermost edge of a galaxy would move more slowly than the stars at the center. Rubin, however, did not take this for granted. She wanted to test whether these assumptions could be proved true.

Her research continued jerkily over the years. As she studied the sky, she earned a master's degree and a PhD, she married and became the mother of four children, and she launched an astronomy career in Washington, DC. Meanwhile, she charted and calculated and puzzled over the motion of two hundred different galaxies—every chart she could get her hands on.

Finally, in the 1970s, she settled it: the stars at the edges of a star system did not drag behind the others. An entire galaxy, from center to edges, moved as one. The whole galaxy was flat with equal energy, governed by a universal speed limit that made all the planets and bodies within a galaxy travel in unison.[9] Our assumption had proved faulty.

What did it mean? Others before her had hypothesized that an unknown force could be stringing together the individual bodies like Velcro, sticking nearby stars to nearby planets; now, Rubin had proved it. An invisible *something* had to be filling the gaps in the universe. That invisible *something* provided universal boundary lines and held the whole together.[10] That invisible *something* kept universes in stasis, and though we could not see it, that invisible *something* was real and measurable. Just like that, Vera Rubin had discovered dark matter.

And Rubin's discovery was only the beginning of astronomers' unknowing of the universe. What we know has shrunk since her data proved that we could not see the majority of what made up the sky. Now, scientists understand that most of our galaxy is *dark*—as in, *dark* matter and *dark* energy. Our eyes can perceive only 5 percent of the cosmos; the remainder is void of light.[11] One NASA official, commenting upon these gaps in our knowledge, said, "More is unknown than is known."[12]

In an interview, Rubin agreed: "I still believe there may be many really fundamental things about the universe that we don't know. I think our ignorance is probably greater than our knowledge." This is what drew her to the field of astronomy in the first place, she said. "It was the wonder of it all. Here were all these things that I didn't know about, and how could you possibly live on this Earth and not want to study these things? When I first started, I didn't know what a star was. It was just all mysterious."[13]

The unknown continues to pile up: quarks, gravitons, quantum entanglement, four-dimensional spacetime, black holes, string theory. The most profound questions of our cosmos remain unanswered and unanswerable.[14]

Yet though Rubin's unseen particles kicked it off, their darkness is not truly invisible. Our retinas cannot make out their shapes because dark matter does not not contain or reflect light, but we can still measure and encounter dark matter by its effects. The bending at the edge of a black hole, the uniform speed of planets in a system, the force of gravity, radio waves, and thermal energy all point us in the right direction. They provide the evidence that we're asking the right questions.

\* \* \*

Like dark matter, the presence of God does not always deign to be verified. Sometimes, what we call supernatural has a clear material presence that can be measured, even if it cannot be wholly explained by the measurement. When a person prays in a lab, an MRI can measure the activity of their brain, a report that reads like a star map.[15] But can this record truly quantify the experience? Can it explain the quality of prayer that keeps a person returning to the quiet to recite words to an invisible Deity? An MRI tracks reality—what is happening and perhaps even *how* it's happening—but it cannot illuminate what it means. We may line up the facts neatly, and still, understanding evades us.

In the past, Christians decided that whatever we could not understand could be explained by the active interference of God: God filled the gaps. Yet this God that caulks the gaps in our knowledge only works until we discover the logic behind the unknown. Why does a brick that falls from a high tower drop to the ground and not float into the sky? That is not God's arm, but gravity. The problem is, if we've depended on a God of gaps, then we no longer need God when the answers arrive. More compelling is the both-and. Why can't the force of gravity be *both* God's active and contemporaneous work *and* an autonomous law of our natural order? Why can't a thing have two causes, mystery and measure, a two-sided explanation?

Theology offers us a two-sided concept of God that blends the lines between the material and the mystical. Sometimes we call this concurrence of the supernatural and the physical a sacrament—as in the Eastern Orthodox belief that the bread and wine of communion transmute into the real, measurable flesh and blood of Christ each time worshipers receive the elements. Sacraments are the holy objects that straddle the supernatural and material planes.

However, holy entrances—supernatural presences donning bodies—that is called *theophany*. When I consider the story of the patriarch who rolls in the dirt with God, theophany is the explanation that makes sense to me. The Genesis narrator insists the presence is material and not a hallucination. Do I trust the narrator or not? I could call these characters crazy, the narrator a liar, and the narrative of Genesis naive. I could name this myth, pure fiction. It may be. But reading a story requires a kind of submission from a reader, a release of your own judgment and an acceptance of the author's reality, however distinct from your own. I am not the storyteller; I am only receiving the words on the page. Thus far, the characters of Genesis act like people act. Wild events have happened, some measurable, and others whose mechanics remain unknown. The genre of the Jacob account is history, as emphasized by the note for why, historically, Jews have refrained from eating a meat animal's sciatic nerve.

I do not presume that I can settle the matter of whether the story of Jacob's nighttime wrestling is fact or fiction. In fact, I refuse to pick one explanation over the other. Doubt and trust *both* instruct us. What if we could practice letting both perspectives loose within us, to release our imaginations from the boundaries of pure naturalism and to accept what is set down on the page? I do not know if anyone could settle the question, really. After all, I have come to understand faith as essentially unsettling, not in opposition to uncertainty, but tested and strengthened by it.

Thomas Merton once wrote, "[The Bible] will remain curiously alien to us if we do not make contact, by living commitment, with the challenging word that is addressed to us, the word that is, in the expression of James (1:21), 'planted in us as a living seed.'"[16] A seed does not live in a hermetic seal. It breathes, cracks open amid piles of leaves on the forest's rotting floor, swelling before its center shoots upward, a green stem seeking light. A seed is not one thing, but many, shaped by the DNA of the plant that came before, and fed by the DNA of fallen bodies. Decomposition is not so different from resurrection.

\* \* \*

The story of God, according to Dr. James H. Cone, resembles the complexity of the living, dying, resurrecting seed. Cone reads the crucifixion of Christ as the story of an innocent victim executed at the hands of oppressors, a mirror image of those Black Americans who died by lynching in the American South during Reconstruction and Jim Crow. In fact, Black Americans, in their experience of overwhelming suffering—first kidnapped, then brutally enslaved, then controlled and dehumanized and murdered and incarcerated—have found companionship with the patriarch who fights with God.

Cone writes, "As Jacob, the God-wrestler, received a new name to reflect his new self, black people's struggle with God in white America also left a deep and lasting wound. Yet they too expressed their hope for a new life in God. This faith empowered blacks to wrestle with trouble as Jacob wrestled with his divine opponent, refusing to let go until he was 'blessed' with meaning and purpose. [They] wrestle[d] with God about the deeply felt contradictions that slavery created for faith. [And their] faith achieved its authenticity only by questioning God."[17] As Jacob did, African Americans stared down the agonizing silence of God. Not all kept religion. But many challenged God violently, and that altercation led to resilient faith.

Jacob—like enslaved African Americans and their descendants—found that making meaning so often occurs when we answer the question of our identity. And identity does not come cheap.

For Jacob to receive the blessing of God, God required him to leave behind his former identity as the secondborn son, abandoning his life within his parents' tent and escaping his brother's dominance. Avivah Gottlieb Zornberg explains that God's reorientation of Jacob began when he first left home in Genesis 28:10–22. This allowed "a movement away, a detachment from previous identities and fixities. [Jacob needed to] wrench himself away from parents and promised land. [But while] Abraham began his journey in response to God's word, in Jacob's case, God is silent, and the very terms in which God blesses him, in the dream at Beth-El, are expansive and even violent in their resonance. The word *u-faratzta* ('You shall spread out,' Genesis 28:14) [has] explosive, even destructive implications."[18] The former identity has fragmented in the palm of the Creator, and Jacob must rebuild away from home over two decades. Yet to become Israel, Jacob must reckon with his past. He must return. And when he returns, his identity shifts again via a violent second reorientation.

God goads the patriarch into steadfastness: *do not let go*. The wrestling match, the effort of pulling the Divine to earth in sweat and dust and desire, is how God redefines Jacob. That night, Jacob's wrestling partner realizes that "he could not overpower" Jacob (32:25 NIV), and so Jacob's foe renames him Israel "because you have struggled with God and with humans and have overcome" (32:28 NIV). Over those hours, Jacob has changed. By the fight's conclusion, Jacob is not the same. The new man who will not let God go becomes the father of a hundred generations because *he has seen God and lived*. In that single word—"Israel," meaning, *he has seen God*—centuries unroll. Those centuries include us. We bear the legacy of the man, Israel, and his blessing is ours, too.

And we, too, limp. The injury, the weakening, prepares Jacob to see God. Pain is revelation. As James Baldwin wrote, "This past, the Negro's past, this endless struggle to achieve and reveal and confirm a human identity, yet contains for all its horror, something very beautiful. I do not mean to be sentimental about suffering—but people who cannot suffer can never grow up, can never discover who they are."[19] No one can pin God to dirt and leave unchanged. Jacob has passed through the shadow of death, has escaped by pure stubbornness, and by it, he becomes a new man. Jacob begins again.

\* \* \*

Jacob passed through fire. So did Ron DiFrancesco, the last man to escape the Twin Towers on 9/11. An investment broker, DiFrancesco worked on the eighty-fourth floor of the South Tower on the day of the terrorist attack. He stood at the windows beside his co-workers as they witnessed the crash of the first hijacked plane into the North Tower. He watched the explosion, the flames, smoke, and glass raining onto the sidewalks below; people leaping from windows into thin air; the commotion of the whirring ambulances, police cars, and fire trucks waiting on the street.

Then a friend called, warning him to get out of the building. He was in the hallway, waiting for the elevator to arrive when the second plane hit his building.[20] The building swayed on impact—seven feet to the left, seven to the right. Ron also toppled, debris showering onto his back. The trading floor where he'd stood only moments before now gaped, sliced open by an airplane wing.

He followed a crowd of bankers to the closest staircase. Some headed up, figuring rescue might happen from the air. But Ron descended, level by level, guided by the stair rail. The lower he descended, the hotter it became. The building was burning. Smoke filled the stairwells, so thick that he could not see more than a few steps ahead.

Then, at the eightieth floor, he encountered an obstacle: the nose of United Airlines Flight 175. The concrete walls of the stairwell had collapsed around it, and people were collapsing, too, a dozen New

Yorkers sprawled on the floor, choking, confused, unconscious. No one seemed able to circumvent the debris of the plane. Ron himself sank to the floor, on the verge of blacking out. He might have collapsed like the others. He might have died there and then. Except he heard a voice.

"Ron, get up." Male, audible, commanding. No person in the stairwell had spoken, and yet a voice urged him to stand. Ron felt himself hauled onto his feet, forward, and down into a crack in the crumbling wall. Then he was beyond the plane, and once again, descending. His invisible guide led him through one story, two, four stories of flames. Now shielding his face with his forearms, now running, now covering his scorched throat with his free hand, the banker finally reached clear air: floor seventy-six. His guide had vanished, but he no longer needed him. His mind had cleared, and he knew what to do.

Ron sprinted down dozens of flights. Above, floors were pancaking, entire stories flattening under the weight of unsupported concrete. Each time a floor crashed onto the one below, the building rumbled ominously. Firefighters passed him in the stairwell, on the way up to search for survivors, but he hardly noticed. He was descending two stairs at a time. Then, he saw an open door, and through it, the sidewalk, pedestrians, flashing lights, sky. He barreled forward, lungs burning. And as he leapt toward the opening, he heard a crash behind. In his peripheral vision, he saw that he was being chased by fire.

He awoke in a hospital bed. His wife sat nearby, her eyes puffy. That's when he learned that only four people who had been on the South Tower floors above the plane's collision point had survived. He had been the last to escape. Despite a broken bone in his spine and burns that covered three-quarters of his body—including his eyes, from which his contacts had to be surgically removed, having been "melted to his eyes"—he had made it out alive.[21]

Only later did he tell anyone about the guide who had led him beyond the obstruction at the eightieth floor. The guide, he knew, was responsible for his rescue. The guide had been an encourager, a helper, a presence, so, to Ron DiFrancesco, he could only explain his guide as his guardian angel.

* * *

Ron DiFrancesco's story is not as unusual as you might think. Sir Ernest Shackleton first recorded the phenomenon of a "survival helper" during his British expedition to the Antarctic from 1914 to 1916.[22] He and a crew of twenty-eight had sought to map the southern pole of our planet; instead, the mission failed. Their ship stuck fast in ice; they ran out of food; sickness, starvation, and cold threatened. So, Shackleton and a few others sought rescue for the group. In a twenty-foot sailboat, they embarked on a risky eight-hundred-mile trip across the Southern Ocean to request help from a remote island of whalers on South Georgia. Once they landed, Shackleton and two of his team, Frank Worsley and Tom Crean, crossed an interior mountain range on foot to reach the settled part of the island, a thirty-six-hour hike that they completed with waning rations and minimal gear to shield them from freezing. They barely stopped for rest, instead opting to complete the journey as quickly as possible. They traversed crevasses, walked along glaciers, and balanced on narrow ledges edged by cliffs. They endured fog, snow blindness, gale winds, frostbite, hunger, sleeplessness. At last, the party of three heard a steam whistle, and they realized they had reached the opposite shore. Rescue was near.

Shackleton's account of his crew's dramatic survival story interested the reading public greatly. Yet later researchers found themselves captivated more by an offhand note of Shackleton's, where he wrote, "When I look back at . . . that long and racking march of thirty-six hours over the unnamed mountains and glaciers of South Georgia it seemed to me often that we were four, not three."[23]

Apparently, during Shackleton, Worsley, and Crean's crossing of the central mountain range of South Georgia, Shackleton had experienced the feeling of guiding presence leading them to safety. In fact, all three of the hikers had. Upon reaching the opposite shore,

Shackleton recounted how one of his men admitted, "Boss, I had a curious feeling on the march that there was another person with us." And the other two confessed the same. Three hikers had felt like four, and the fourth alongside had offered comfort and direction; nearing their own doom, they had felt accompanied.

Psychologists later named this experience the third man syndrome.[24] As it turned out, these hauntings did not appear only on snowy mountainsides, or only to those in mortal danger. The third man has shown himself to the shipwrecked too, as in the case of the lost-at-sea sailor who floated on a raft for weeks in the straits of Malacca. He reported, "I'd had the strange feeling that someone was with me, watching over me, keeping me safe from harm. It was as if there were sometimes three people on the raft, not two." Even after his fellow sailor had been eaten by a shark, the feeling persisted. He hypothesized, "Perhaps it was my mother's prayers for me in Finland. Maybe this strong bond between us came to my mental rescue at this time."[25]

So, what does explain the phenomenon of the third, the one who joins us beyond our peripheral vision? The syndrome is *not* psychosis, despite its similarities to hallucination. Neurologist MacDonald Critchley defined the syndrome as being closer to the experience of a *delusion*, writing, "Usually the feeling merely entails the *belief* that there is 'someone' in the vicinity . . . an intangible feeling 'as if' one were not alone."[26] In other words, the third man is not seen as a hallucination would be, only felt and *believed* to be present.

Some scientists have reproduced the feeling in a lab. A gentle zap of electricity to the brain—the temporal-parietal junction, which defines the sense of our physical self—causes subjects to report the feeling of a body near theirs. The feeling resembles the presence of a hand hovering an inch above the thigh.[27]

Journalist John Geiger, who wrote the seminal work on the syndrome, collected stories from around the globe of those who have experienced the mysterious sensation of presence. His reporting discovered that the third man shares similarities with many other unexplained psychological phenomena such as the common experience of bereaved widows and widowers who report visitations of their deceased partner.[28] Other similar experiences include voice hearing, as in schizophrenia; visions and out-of-body experiences during sleep paralysis; the amputee's sensation of the phantom limb; and a child's invention of an imaginary friend. Researchers have even drawn lines between this syndrome and the strange, delusionary behavior of sleep-deprived postpartum mothers called "baby-in-bed," during which "the presence of a baby in the bed is strongly felt and, although the infant may be sleeping peacefully in a crib nearby, often results in the mother frantically searching for it in the bedding."[29]

Ultimately, Geiger concludes that any attempt to box the experience of the friendly, invisible guide will fail because any explanation is "causal in nature; they do not explain [the third man's] origins or where the power comes from."[30]

So, what does the third want from us? According to those who feel it, the third man directs, consoles, joins. The third man is a presence of love, wisdom, trust. The third man does not ensure safety, but can help us survive. Those who have felt the presence identified first by Shackleton and later by DiFrancesco have called it by other names: my guardian angel, a watcher, a guide, an accompanier, an invisible ally, an unseen companion, a close presence, a second self, a fourth man. To my ear, each name given by a human in trouble conjures the great beyond more evocatively than the ten-dollar words of bonafide theologians. As Shackleton wrote, he and his fellow travelers felt that a description of their journey across South Georgia would not be complete without naming this presence, which he called "a subject very near to our hearts." How can a hallucination reside "very near to the heart"? Shackleton himself feels the impossibility of putting the intangible into words: "One feels 'the dearth of human words, the roughness of mortal speech.'"[31] But if you know, you know.

* * *

One question about the third patriarch, Jacob, still lingers: I wonder, why does God attend so closely to the younger brother while ignoring the older? To understand Esau, we must turn to the second patriarch: the father of Jacob and Esau, the son of Abraham, Isaac. Despite being the miracle baby, Isaac largely recedes from the Genesis narrative after the drama of the binding. An event like that would have shifted anyone's view of God. Yes, God rescued Isaac, but how would a young boy metabolize the fact that his father had raised the knife? That God had commanded his death in the first place?

In Genesis 31:42, Jacob refers to God as "the God of Abraham and the Fear of Isaac" (NIV), an answer of sorts, although the JPS translation clarifies that the Hebrew word translated as "fear" (Heb. *paḥad*) is "uncertain."[32] (Rashi translates the word as "dread," which I suspect fits the psychology of Isaac.[33]) If we see Abraham's actions as demonstrating attachment to God—at least enough attachment to consider sacrificing his son for love of the Deity—then Isaac seems to suffer religious PTSD. Isaac certainly does not trust God. But even setting aside the mountaintop experience, Isaac still has a dysfunctional family system with which to reckon, generational traumas passed down from father to son, including the complex relationships he has with his mother, his half brother, and the surrogate.

Considering Isaac's history, it does not seem a stretch to suppose that Isaac could have passed mistrust of God to his firstborn son, Esau. Esau, the man with whom Jacob dreads meeting after his rest on the desert floor, the man from whom he has run for so many years, the man he fears more than any other.

What do we know of Esau? Jacob's twin brother does not hold court with God in the biblical narrative, not once. This leads the rabbis to rule negatively on the firstborn's character. The rabbis compare Esau unfavorably to Nimrod, as each are described as a "mighty hunter."[34] One legend directly blames Isaac for the firstborn's God-resistance, saying that God struck Isaac blind late in life because Isaac had tolerated his oldest son's wickedness under his roof.[35] Yet later in the chapter, Esau welcomes his brother, Jacob, rather than killing him. So perhaps, we've misjudged the man.

And I cannot help wondering the same about Isaac. Might he be a more sympathetic figure than the rabbis suppose? After all, Isaac *does* pray for God to heal his wife's infertility, an act of mercy his own father did not offer his mother, Sarah (Genesis 25:21). God then receives Isaac's prayer, and Rebekah conceives. The pregnancy is reason alone to infer that God's favor rests on the son of Abraham, but in addition, God (an angel?) then prophesies over the family: the two babies wrestling in Rebekah's uterus are twins, two nations. They will war against each other, and the younger will win because God has picked the younger, not the elder, to shoulder the blessing of the grandfather. The younger is greater than the older; the weaker is greater than the strong. God upends the norms of Isaac's culture and builds a nation from the younger son.

Note this pattern: God rejects the firstborn and picks the younger instead. But why does God pick Jacob and not Esau? The rabbis answer with the wisdom of Solomon: "God seeks that which is pursued" (Ecclesiastes 3:15 JPS). Esau, the older, pursues Jacob to kill him. Therefore, whose side will God take? God takes the side of the pursued: the one in danger, the younger, weaker, victimized. These are the chosen of God. The pattern holds throughout the rest of the Scriptures, too. The rabbis say, "God will always seek [to save] the blood of the pursued from the pursuers. He holds the pursuers accountable for their actions, and He grants favor to the pursued. 'For the Lord has chosen Jacob for Himself, Israel as His treasure' (Psalm 135:4)."[36]

Naturally, the midrashic writers saw themselves and their relatives, the sons of Adam and Abraham, as the archetype of *the pursued*, since they were the genetic and cultural relatives of the secondborn. Israel was made up of the children oppressed by Cain, Ishmael, and Esau. In particular, Jacob becomes a stand-in archetype for the nation.

Jacob is their father. In fact, who doesn't relate to Jacob? Americans like to see ourselves as victims and underdogs, even when we are indisputably the oppressor. Yet God is not fooled by any self-delusion: God attends to those at the *true* bottom. God will not forget to humble the strong. To the weak, rejected, and maligned, to the runners and the wanderers, God says, "I am with you and [I] will watch over you wherever you go. I will not leave you until I have done what I have promised you" (Genesis 28:15 NIV). God loves Jacob and hates Esau (Malachi 1:2–3). Why? Because Esau hates Jacob. And God loves those who are hated.

\* \* \*

The Jewish philosopher Abraham Joshua Heschel wrote, "We do not think [God], we are stirred by Him. We can never describe Him, we can only return to Him. We may address ourselves to Him; we cannot comprehend Him. We can sense His presence; we cannot grasp His essence."[37] God is a breath, a cloud, a dream; God is also a bicep pinning Jacob to the dirt. God is a womb, God is a ram, God is a limp. Who is God? Who can say?

And can God shimmy between a few printed pages? I hope the answer is yes. Though this book has attempted to wrestle the Bible to the ground, rather than coming to the conclusion that it's good for nothing, that the book should be dismissed as outmoded or oppressive, I am reenchanted. The Bible, to me, remains a work of art. The Bible has persisted across centuries, held near by Christians of all eras, and I have found a renewed reason to search its pages.

In the end, what has sustained me in my reading is humility. Bible study, for me, means constant repentance. I see that I must constantly be willing to turn around, change my mind, admit that I've taken the wrong meaning from the text, and accept correction. Because I am not God. I am human, an unavoidable ontological fact. Even the words of the Bible are not God, but contain more humanity than my tribe has reckoned. And fragility and changeability are human hallmarks. Yet even in our failures at biblical interpretation, translation, and application, despite our false readings and how the text has turned into a weapon in our hands, *I can still recognize God in the Bible*. For example, the fact that we can discover our errors is proof of mercy. Correction is mercy. Self-awareness is mercy. Sometimes this correction comes by way of the text itself, a careful reinterpretation. Sometimes correction comes through the neighbor reading the text beside us. *But understanding arrives.*

One legend of the Kabbalists, the Jewish heretic mystics, emphasizes how greatly we need our neighbor's interpretation of the Bible.
The legend states that six hundred thousand Jews stood in the shadow
of Mount Sinai on the day God gave Torah to Moses. And on that day,
God allotted each one in the crowd a tiny portion of Torah, the Torah
divided by six hundred thousand. Each could understand that portion
they had received. So, to interpret Torah as a whole, all six hundred
thousand needed to collaborate to piece the fragments together. Only
by including every member of the community in the group project of
interpreting would Torah be complete.[38]

Imagine a living commentary of the Christian Bible that held *every*
reader as an essential interpreter. An interpretative culture like this
would resemble a nervous system, with each nerve speaking to every
other in its unique sensory language for the sake of the body's ongoing survival. Each nerve ending would offer the whole system a new
interpretation of its environment every second, cultivating a dynamic
conversation that would not end until the body did.

This is the methodology of the liberation theologians, who assert
that the Bible's meaning—and by it, our understanding of who and
what God is like—must be rediscovered repeatedly. Each generation
must answer for themselves the questions of existence: Where do humans come from, and where are we going? Why are we here? Why am
I here? What does a single life mean? We travel in loops of conflict,
tragedy, and beauty, requiring the intercession of Divinity and a transcendent story to make meaning of our short, strange lives. Our ancestors may have successfully pinned God down in their era, and still,
the next generation must wrestle God anew. Only in these clouds of
dust will we discover the word God is speaking for today. As Gustavo
Gutiérrez writes, "The only future that theology has, one might say,
is to become the theology of the future."[39] In a sense, this means that
the Bible requires a present-future reading so that the interpreters of
the future can use our flawed theological methodologies to develop
their reinterpretations. Thus, the interpreting repeats.

Struggle is how we unearth the theology of the future. We must
wrestle. And so, in my view, the trend of fixing faulty translation and

the endless work of reinterpretation is a reason to hope rather than to despair. The disagreements, the drag-out fights, the deconversions, deconstructions, doubting, and renovations represent the wrestling that God's people have *always* performed in the spiraling journey of faith. In sweat and blood, we write the theology of the future. So, the Bible will never expire as long as its readers continue to demand God from its pages. The God of mystery, the God of truth, the God of presence: this is who meets us in the pages of the Bible as we return to its words with our questions. The story never ends.

So, as I have embraced my doubts about the book of Genesis, including questions about the creation of the Bible itself, I now wonder, what comes next? As literary theorist Roland Barthes wrote, "A text's unity lies not in its origin but in its destination."[40] Therein lies the meaning of the thing.

\* \* \*

The journey of faith reminds me of the formation of a shell.[41] A shell is built over decades. Slowly, the spiral grows. A sea snail sucks water and minerals through its fleshy tube mouth, and those minerals then curl onto its back, stuck by a glue-like slime that coats the snail's skin. Eventually, these calcify into the rigid structure humans so admire. For its lifetime, the shell shields the snail as it grows. Each year, it furls larger, matching the snail's body as it stretches and expands. And the snail is safe in its shell. Even as the iridescent spiral floats in the swelling current, sometimes settling into the bottom silt, sometimes rolling in the waves, the snail remains encased, protected. On the day the creature expires, the shell, as fragile as a teacup, releases into the waves. Perhaps a passing hermit crab will claim the empty shelter. Or a child combing the beach for buried treasure will hold the home in her palms, wondering. Throughout our species' history, humans have collected these voluptuous coils for their colors, for their shapes, for how they feel beneath our fingertips. But they hold meaning beyond aesthetics.

In fact, a shell is a fractal, a natural pattern that at first appears to be no pattern at all. But a shell is unlike a globe, a cube, or a pyramid.[42] A shell is not an ordinary three-dimensional shape because a biological mechanism *grows* a shell. So, an underlying code also explains why all snails everywhere live within a spiral, and that code is the mathematical pattern of fractals. While most patterns can be replicated in simple geometry, fractals require calculus. A fractal's complexity emerges only at altitude or beneath the lens of a microscope, and it joins other fractals like the multipronged bloom of the wild carrot or the frills of a fern.

The scale of the fractal, in fact, has given me a shorthand for the complexity of the spiritual life: the leaving and returning, the exile and homecoming, the wrestling and holding patterns. Some have seen the coil of the spiritual life as a labyrinth, but I see a fractal.

This is why I believe that Jacob walking away from his wrestling match with a limp matters. In fact, Jacob's limp is the centerpiece of the third patriarch's story. Though Jacob's relatives had only passed along an inheritance of dysfunction and alienation, his sparring had never been with them and their failures; his fight had always been with God. Even before the night of the wrestling match, Jacob had already been provoking the One who rides upon clouds, the Being with the power to slap favor on any creature chosen or the power to withhold blessing. Jacob had been fighting with God his whole life.

Yet God does not reject the third patriarch's anger. God welcomes a head-on collision. And the result of this wrestling match is sight. Like Adam and Eve, Noah, Abraham, and Hagar before him, Jacob's struggle resulted in seeing God face to face. He beheld God and lived to tell the story to us. He was blessed and he survived. But a fight with God also left its mark. Jacob walked away limping.[43]

So, at the last accounting, who is Jacob? Is he remembered for his deception, his cowardice, his poor judgment and selfishness? Or is he known by his limp, the injury that marked him as one who'd met God?

I remember the words of Jackson Pollock, the American midcentury painter. In his lifetime, his work was compared to a kindergartener's finger painting, a tangled head of hair, a bowl of last night's macaroni. Because of the abstraction of his works, Pollock was often asked by interviewers, what does it mean? Why do you paint like this? He told them, "It's just like looking at a bed of flowers. You don't tear your hair out over what it means."[44] He insisted that his work was not chaos but a study in making meaning from no meaning. When scientists analyzed his strokes decades later, they discovered that his work mimicked fractals.[45] The flicks and swirls of paint on canvas appeared to be chaos, but held meaning we could not identify until decades after the artist's death when the science had caught up to his mastery of paint.

We do not demand a flower explain itself. A flower is not a thesis statement. A flower is not even a question. A flower does not speak or lend itself to flattening on the page. Words will never capture the whole of the flower, even when the finest poet sets himself the task. Yet understanding can arrive as we sit in the presence of the blossom.

Like Vera Rubin's dark matter—the invisible stuff that holds together the visible stuff of our universe—or like the presence that dogged Ron DiFrancesco and Ernest Shackleton, the most powerful forces in the cosmos seem prone to vanishing as soon as we lean in for a look. What *can* be measured is power. For example, a black hole is identified by the way light disappears. We cannot see the black hole with our weak eyes, but its presence is felt and measured by the absence of light. To discover a black hole, we add up the lack.

Doubt is easy; we need only to retreat. Faith, on the other hand, is sweat. Faith requires we dodge the uppercut, pin down the flailing arms of the opponent, roll in dust, and yell down our defeat. Faith requires waiting up all night. Only then will we witness the rising sun and, by its light, the face of God.

The shell furls. The flower opens. And there, at the center, the impossible blooms.

# FINAL THOUGHTS

Madeleine L'Engle once wrote, "There are so many preconceptions encrusting our idea of the Father to whom Jesus turned in prayer, in joy, in anguish, that it is almost impossible to remove all the barnacles of tradition and prejudice which have accumulated over the years, and see and hear *El* freshly."[1]

In fact, an entire ocean of muck seems to have settled on the Face of God. For this reason, these words of mine cannot deliver capital-T Truth to you—I know my limits—so instead, I have aimed for astonishment. I have aimed to "pierce the veneer of outside things . . . to see God in his splendors, [to] hear the text that Nature renders, to reach the naked soul of men," as Shackleton wrote at the end of his account of his journey through the Antarctic.[2]

In any way that God has arrived to you in these pages, embrace it. Embrace God not as I have told, but exactly as God has met *you*, through the Scriptures, your own history, your religious tradition's history, your own metaphors. I am not the final word on God. God is. So, I invite you to wrestle. Disagree with me and with the experts. Ask your pastor harder questions. Discover your own questions. And find yourself flabbergasted by the Bible. I can only pray my words have encouraged you not to give up. Because only in your own personal struggle with truth and mystery will the God who transcends the Scriptures arrive, God's very self, the Third Man.

# ACKNOWLEDGMENTS

Books are group projects. I feel great joy in reflecting on each person who has supported me and my writing over the years it took to compose and publish this book. I cannot name them all individually, but those listed below were the most integral to the process. Your work and presence has brought this particular book into being.

Thank you to the Eerdmans team, including the inimitable Lisa Ann Cockrel and Andrew Knapp, James Ernest, William Hearn, Jason Pearson, Kristine Nelson, and Jenny Hoffman, and to the design team for putting up with our opinions. Thanks also to copyeditor Justin Howell for his helpful changes.

John Blase, thank you for your tenacity and encouragement. Thank you also to the rest of the Bindery team (especially Alex Field and Ingrid Beck).

Michael N. McGregor, your injunction to "follow the heat" was prophetic. Thank you to Carla Durand and the Collegeville Institute for the gift of time.

Thank you, Rebecca Randall, for your thoroughness and professionalism in fact-checking the scientific stories in these pages. Lisa Elmers and Tessa Thompson, thank you for enduring the early drafts of this book, which read like a white-walled museum (you were right to request a docent). Rachel Dzugan, thank you for your help in decoding Latin from the Septuagint for chapter two.

Thank you to K. J. and Ryan Ramsey, Sarah Southern, Ashley Ward, Elena Sorensen, Cait West, Sara Billups, Erin Lane, Charlotte Donlon, Johnna Harris, Lore Ferguson, Marcie Alvis Walker, Marla Taviano, Shannon K. Evans, the members of the Redbud Writers

# Acknowledgments

Guild, and *many, many* more writer colleagues for your generosity and consolation over the years. Thank you also to the editors who have helped me refine portions of this text, including Jessica Mesman, Josiah Daniels, Katy Carl, Meaghan Ritchie, and the writers who made up the *The Curator* magazine team alongside me—Chris Davidson, Victoria Perez, John Hawbaker, John Graeber, Jolene Nolte, Abby Perry, David Wright, Shemaiah Gonzalez, and Kate Watson. And thank you, Chip MacGregor, for first plucking my words out of the slush pile.

Thank you also to those non-writer friends who have collaborated with me via your artform of choice, or who have endured winding discussions about the progression of this book project, including Matthew Langford, Steve Slagg, Carin Huebner, Danielle and Josh Williams, Britt Kwan, Kiri White, and the Knippas' small group at Church of the Advent.

To our families near and far, we love you dearly. Hope and Ezekiel, you are my giddy dream, and I love being your mom. Jeremy, you are my home.

I thank God for you all.

# ENDNOTES

*A Note to Former and Current Evangelicals*

1. Other statements followed the original 1978 "The Chicago Statement on Biblical Inerrancy." In 1982, the International Council on Biblical Inerrancy (ICBI) released "The Chicago Statement on Biblical Hermeneutics," and in 1986, they released "The Chicago Statement on Biblical Application." Read the complete statements: "The Chicago Statement on Biblical Inerrancy" (http://tinyurl.com/42p7s9hh), "The Chicago Statement on Biblical Hermeneutics" (http://tinyurl.com/2uump56s), "The Chicago Statement on Biblical Application" (http://tinyurl.com /yf2dc286).

2. The signatories expound, "The word canon, signifying a rule or standard, is a pointer to authority, which means the right to rule and control. Authority in Christianity belongs to God in His revelation, which means, on the one hand, Jesus Christ, the living Word, and, on the other hand, Holy Scripture, the written Word. But the authority of Christ and that of Scripture are one. As our Prophet, Christ testified that Scripture cannot be broken. As our Priest and King, He devoted His earthly life to fulfilling the law and the prophets, even dying in obedience to the words of Messianic prophecy. Thus, as He saw Scripture attesting Him and His authority, so by His own submission to Scripture He attested its authority. As He bowed to His Father's instruction given in His Bible (our Old Testament), so He requires His disciples to do—not, however, in isolation but in conjunction with the apostolic witness to Himself which He undertook to inspire by His gift of the Holy Spirit. So Christians show themselves faithful servants of their Lord by bowing to the divine instruction given

in the prophetic and apostolic writings which together make up our Bible. By authenticating each other's authority, Christ and Scripture coalesce into a single fount of authority. The Biblically-interpreted Christ and the Christ-centered, Christ-proclaiming Bible are from this standpoint one. As from the fact of inspiration we infer that what Scripture says, God says, so from the revealed relation between Jesus Christ and Scripture we may equally declare that what Scripture says, Christ says" ("The Chicago Statement on Biblical Inerrancy with Exposition," International Council on Biblical Inerrancy, Dallas Theological Seminary, October 1978, p. 8).

Though I do not mean to offend, I will be clear about my own take on their conclusion: it's absurd. Because *Jesus Christ is actually God*, I view their interpretation as an attempt to contain the authority that belongs only to God into a book collected by humanity (albeit *inspired* by God, inspiration is by no means *synonymous with Godself*). A book can be *divinely created* and still cannot reasonably be said to *be the same as God*. I see such a statement as veering toward idolatry of the Bible.

3. Rachel Dicker, "Donald Trump Is a 'Baby Christian,' Evangelical Leader Says," *U.S. News & World Report*, June 27, 2016, https://tinyurl.com/4vju96nu.

4. Dr. Curtis Woods, Dr. John Wilsey, Dr. Kevin Jones, Dr. Jarvis Williams, Dr. Matthew J. Hall, and Dr. Gregory Wills, "Report in Slavery and Racism in the History of the Southern Baptist Theological Seminary," 2017, https://tinyurl.com/yjj9bfab.

## On Genesis and Methodology

1. Tremper Longman III, "Who Wrote the Book of Genesis?," *Zondervan Academic Blog*, August 31, 2018, http://tinyurl.com/bpabtd4f.

2. John C. Reeves, "Scriptural Authority in Early Judaism," *Living Traditions of the Bible: Scripture in Jewish, Christian, and Muslim Practice*, ed. James E. Bowley (Saint Louis: Chalice, 1999), 63–84 (italics mine).

3. Avivah Gottlieb Zornberg, *The Beginning of Desire: Reflections on Genesis* (New York: Image Books, 1995), xi–xiii (italics mine).

4. Wilda C. Gafney, *Womanist Midrash: A Reintroduction to the Women of the Torah and the Throne* (Louisville: Westminster John Knox, 2017), 17–19.

5. For a discussion of Genesis's historicity from the perspective of notable Christian scientists, see *BioLogos*'s extensive archive of articles, such as "Is Genesis Real History?," http://tinyurl.com/mrnjfn8b.

*Chapter 01*

1. Avivah Gottlieb Zornberg, *The Murmuring Deep: Reflections on the Biblical Unconscious* (New York: Schocken Books, 2009), xx–xxi.

2. Zornberg, *Murmuring Deep*, xx, xxi.

3. National Institute on Deafness and Other Communication Disorders (NIDCD), "How Do We Hear?," NIDCD Information Clearinghouse, modified March 16, 2022, http://tinyurl.com/yjbfsyay.

4. Geraldine Pinch, *Egyptian Mythology: A Guide to the Gods, Goddesses, and Traditions of Ancient Egypt* (Oxford: Oxford University Press, 2004), 60.

5. Want to hear the most disturbing of the ancient Near Eastern origin myths? Of course, you do: one Egyptian myth describes the creation of the dieties who created the world as being brought into existence by the first diety's masturbation. Says Pinch, "The actual means by which the creator reproduced were sometimes left vague and sometimes described in terms of blunt sexual imagery. Pyramid texts (PT) 527 says that Atum took his penis in his hand and masturbated 'and so were born the two siblings, that is Shu and Tefnut.' In PT 600, Atum-Khepri is said to be the one who spat out Shu and Tefnut. . . . These apparently contradictory statements are clarified in later sources, such as the Bremner-Rhind Papyrus and the Memphite theology. Atum excites his penis with his hand and takes the semen into his mouth. . . . The mouth of the creator acts as a substitute womb. . . . Once the twins had been born, the sexual identity of Atum becomes fixed as a father. A further development was the personification of the hand of Atum as a goddess, thus giving him a sexual partner" (Pinch, *Egyptian Mythology*, 63).

6. Dan Ruetenik and Nan Hauser, "Whale Song: A Grandfather's Legacy," *60 Minutes*, aired October 20, 2013, CBS News, http://tinyurl.com/ycxnwawh.

7. Mark Morrison, "Amateur Radio and the Cosmos, Part 6: Signalling," *CQ VHF*, Fall 2010, 10–16, http://tinyurl.com/3avknwsd.

8. In 1970, *Rolling Stone* magazine reviewer Jon Carroll wrote of Payne and Watlington's album of whale song, "This is a good record, dig? Not just an interesting record, or, God help us, a trippy record. . . . It's especially good for late at night and peaceful, together moments. It stretches your mind to encompass alien art forms. The kids can't dance to it, but they can't dance to Satie either." He compared it to electronic music but "without the sterile, hyper-intelligence trip that much electronic music gets into" (David Rothenberg, *Thousand-Mile Song: Whale Music in a Sea of Sound* [New York: Basic Books, 2008], 18–19).

9. Hal Whitehead and Luke Rendel, *The Cultural Lives of Whales and Dolphins* (Chicago: University of Chicago Press, 2015), 76.

10. Andrew Louth, ed., *Genesis 1–11*, Ancient Christian Commentary on Scripture: Old Testament 1 (Downers Grove, IL: InterVarsity Press, 2001), xlvi.

11. Louth, *Genesis 1–11*, xlii.

12. "What Are the Contents of the Golden Record?," NASA, Jet Propulsion Laboratory at California Institute of Technology, http://tinyurl.com/37yfc683.

13. "How Do Whales Sing?," *BBC Science Focus*, http://tinyurl.com/k4m3fbsj.

14. Michelle E. Fournet, Andy Szabo, and David K. Mellinger, "Repertoire and Classification of Non-song Calls in Southeast Alaskan Humpback Whales (*Megaptera novaeangliae*)," *Journal of Acoustical Society of America* 137, no. 1 (2015): 1–10, http://tinyurl.com/s6k88h42.

15. Cara Giaimo, "In the South Pacific, a Humpback Whale Karaoke Lounge," *New York Times*, September 11, 2019, http://tinyurl.com/yc5yjerj.

16. Alberto Lucas López, Oscar A. Santamariña, and David Rothenberg, "Whale Song Decoded," *National Geographic*, modified April 15, 2021, http://tinyurl.com/3h3xnkk2.

Chapter 02

1. Giovanni B. Caputo, Steven Jay Lynn, and James Houran, "Mirror- and Eye-Gazing: An Integrative Review of Induced Altered and Anoma-

lous Experiences," *Imagination, Cognition and Personality* 40, no. 4 (2020): 418, http://tinyurl.com/54zmxzbn.

2. Orestis Giotakos, "Mirror and Self," *Dialogues in Clinical Neuroscience and Mental Health* 4, no. 4 (2021): 187–95, http://tinyurl.com/3ch89u78.

3. Ira Spar, "The Gods and Goddesses of Canaan," Metropolitan Museum of Art, April 2009, http://tinyurl.com/bdhp8ef2.

4. Stephen L. Herring, "A 'Transubstantiated' Humanity: The Relationship between the Divine Image and the Presence of God in Genesis i 26f," *Vetus Testamentum* 58, no. 4/5 (2008): 483.

5. For a discussion of sexual rites in ancient Near Eastern religion, see Beatrice A. Brooks, "Fertility Cult Functionaries in the Old Testament," *Journal of Biblical Literature* 60, no. 3 (1941): 227–53, http://tinyurl.com/4b 8z9fjz. One selection of Hittite ritual worship demonstrates, "When the army is defeated by an enemy, then the following sacrifice is prepared 'behind' the river: 'behind' the river, a man, a goat, a puppy, and a suckling pig are cut in half. One half is placed on one side, the (other) half on the other. Before it, they make a gate out of white-thorn(?) wood and stretch a cord(?) over it, and in front of the gate they light fires on this side and on that. The troops go through the middle, and when they come to the bank of the river, they sprinkle water over them" (William W. Hallo, "The Context of Scripture: Selections from Ancient Near Eastern Literature," in *The Book of the People*, Brown Judaic Studies 225 [Atlanta: Scholars Press, 2020], 130, http://tinyurl.com/bddmx5e7).

6. Brooks, "Fertility Cult," 230.

7. Hayim Nahman Bialik, Yehoshua hana Ravnitzky, William G. Braude, and David Stern, *The Book of Legends: Sefer Ha-Aggadah: Legends from the Talmud and Midrash* (New York: Schocken Books, 1992), 13:47.

8. In 1:27, the pronouns shift back to singular—"*he* created man in *his* image" (NIV).

9. Ann Gibbons, "One Scientist's Quest for the Origin of Our Species," *Science* 298, no. 5599, November 29, 2002, 1708–11, http://tinyurl.com/28m2j827.

10. Thomas Grillot, "The Ancestor Seeker: An Interview with Michel Brunet," trans. Michael C. Behrent, *Books and Ideas*, May 6, 2016, http://tinyurl.com/4hv2kfre.

11. To learn more about when Genesis was written, see Pete Enns, "When Was Genesis Written and Why Does It Matter?," *BioLogos*, March 25, 2012, http://tinyurl.com/3ke9vtmu.

12. "Genesis," *Encyclopaedia Britannica*, last updated January 5, 2024, http://tinyurl.com/mserkxxp.

13. Erin Wayman, "Sahelanthropus Tchadensis: Ten Years after the Discovery," *Smithsonian Magazine*, July 16, 2012, http://tinyurl.com/mtu3nhe2.

14. Kate Wong, "An Ancestor to Call Our Own," *Scientific American* 288, no. 1, January 1, 2003, 54–63, http://tinyurl.com/4wx7ptjz.

15. Karel van der Toorn, *Scribal Culture and the Making of the Hebrew Bible* (Cambridge: Harvard University Press, 2009), 65.

16. For more discussion on Karl Barth's insistence that Christians should describe God not as "God in three persons" but "God in three ways of being," not three *I*'s with three distinct personalities but a threefold *I*, consider this argument: Wyatt Houtz, "Karl Barth Says the Trinity Is One God in Three Modes of Being (Not Persons)," March 13, 2017, http://tinyurl.com/yckyk7pj.

17. Michael Lerner, *Jewish Renewal: A Path to Healing and Transformation* (New York: Putnam's Sons, 1994), http://tinyurl.com/4ewvn3z5.


*Chapter 03*

1. "Chauvet Cave," Bradshaw Foundation, http://tinyurl.com/yc8emcfz.

2. Jean-Marie Chauvet, Eliette Brunel Deschamps, Christian Hillaire, Jean Clottes, and Paul G. Bahn, *Dawn of Art: The Chauvet Cave (The Oldest Known Paintings in the World)* (London: Abrams, 1996), 40–41.

3. Joshua Hammer, "Finally, the Beauty of France's Chauvet Cave Makes Its Grand Public Debut," *Smithsonian Magazine*, April 2015, http://tinyurl.com/2f3k9m3s.

4. Chauvet et al., *Dawn of Art*, 40–41.

5. Hammer, "Finally, the Beauty."

6. The rabbis assume that Adam was made of dust "gathered from the entire earth," and some tell of an intermediary stage between the forming of man and man's conscious awakening when the man is called a

"golem," also known as "an unarticulated lump," perhaps of clay, "which lay prone from one end of the world to the other." In this stage, Adam saw "each and every righteous man that was to issue from him." Essentially, the theory was predestination: before the man's life begins, he glimpses the entire line of those who belong to God (Bialik et al., *Book of Legends*, 14:50, 15:63–64).

7. Bialik et al., *Book of Legends*, 14:58.

8. Bialik et al., *Book of Legends*, 15:59.

9. Douglas Kindschi, "Coming from the Earth: Humus, Humanity, Humility," *Interfaith Insight*, B01, http://tinyurl.com/2xmw49jr.

10. Richard Rohr, "A Clod of Earth," Center for Action and Contemplation, October 19, 2016, http://tinyurl.com/3n9wsr6e.

11. As an evangelical, I assumed that "alone," in Adam's case, meant single male bachelor. But this does not match the rabbinical understanding that I will explore further in chapter 6.

12. As scholar Avivah Gottlieb Zornberg writes, when God speaks "not good" in Genesis 2:18, the text offers "the first 'God said' that has no direct effect on reality" (Zornberg, *Beginning of Desire*, 14).

13. I cannot overstate the tremendous gift offered by Zornberg's writings. See Zornberg, *Beginning of Desire*, 16.

14. Stephen Eldridge, "Chekhov's Gun," *Encyclopaedia Britannica*, October 4, 2022, http://tinyurl.com/2xhdkwar.

15. Marina Abramović and Milica Zec, "Marina Abramović on Rhythm 0 (1974)," Marina Abramović Institute, August 8, 2013, http://tinyurl.com/52snkd5j.

16. Marina Abramović and Glenn Lowry, "Marina Abramović and ULAY. Rest Energy. 1980," Museum of Modern Art, http://tinyurl.com/mwseprr3.

17. "When the Holy One created Adam, He made him with two fronts; then He sawed him in half and thus gave him two backs. . . . Someone objected: But does not Scripture say, 'And He took one of his ribs (*mitzalotav*)' (Gen. 2:21)? R. Samuel replied: *Mi-tzalotav* may also mean 'his sides,' as in the verse, 'And for the second side (*tzela*) of the Tabernacle' (Exod. 26:20)" (Bialik et al., *Book of Legends*, 15:60).

"Thus Eve was created out of half of Adam's body and not out of a mere rib (Leon Nemoy)" (Bialik et al., *Book of Legends*, 15 n. 7).

18. "5162. Nacham," *Bible Hub*, http://tinyurl.com/2u3d2m3x.

19. "Torah," *Encyclopaedia Britannica*, last updated December 28, 2023, http://tinyurl.com/3xm5smxr.

20. Samuel Sandmel, "The Haggada within Scripture," *Journal of Biblical Literature* 80, no. 2 (1961): 122, http://tinyurl.com/mvcbebr5.

21. Quoted in Joseph Telushkin, *Jewish Literacy: The Most Important Things to Know about the Jewish Religion, Its People, and Its History* (New York: Morrow, 1991), 156.

22. Marlene Winell, *Leaving the Fold: A Guide for Former Fundamentalists and Others Leaving Their Religion* (Berkeley: Apocryphile, 2007), 73, 74, 78, 79.

23. For discussion of James W. Fowler's faith development theory, see Stephen Parker, "Research in Fowler's Faith Development Theory: A Review Article," *Review of Religious Research* 51, no. 3 (2010): 233–52; James W. Fowler, *Stages of Faith* (New York: HarperCollins, 1995).


Chapter 04

1. *The Last Judgment*, Vatican Museum, http://tinyurl.com/24hm963w.

2. Jane Ashby, "Medieval Doom Paintings in Oxfordshire Churches," *Oxford Art Journal* 2, no. 3 (1979): 54, http://tinyurl.com/yc3bvxhz.

3. Ashby records one such reaction of a nineteenth-century observer to a fresco discovered beneath limewash in 1872: "This was the most awful scene which the mind of man could contemplate, caricatured by Papish superstition for the edification of our benighted forefathers!" ("Medieval Doom Paintings," 54).

4. "The Doctrine of Discovery, 1493," Gilder Lehrman Institute of American History, http://tinyurl.com/33cj8r5n. The full text of the doctrine can be read in English translation: http://tinyurl.com/2fp597a9.

5. One practice introduced by the English colonizers in the Americas was meant to encourage associations between indigenous peoples and dangerous wild animals: the practice of scalping the defeated after a battle. Native activist Vine Deloria Jr.—whose work I recommend—

elaborates in his book *Custer Died for Your Sins: An Indian Manifesto* that scalping "confirmed the suspicion that Indians were wild animals to be hunted and skinned." Bounties were set and an Indian scalp became more valuable than beaver, otter, marten, and other animal pelts. Deloria continues, "Notice, for example, the following proclamation:

> Given at the Council Chamber in Boston this third day of November 1755 in the twenty-ninth year of the Reign of our Sovereign Lord George the Second. . . . Whereas the tribe of Penobscot Indians have repeatedly . . . acted contrary to their solemn submission unto his Majesty . . . I have therefore . . . thought it fit to issue this Proclamation and to declare the Penobscot Tribe of Indians to be enemies, rebels and traitors to his Majesty. . . . And I do hereby require his Majesty's subjects of the Province to embrace all opportunities of pursuing, captivating, killing and destroying all and every of the aforesaid Indians. And whereas the General Court of this Province have voted that a bounty . . . be granted and paid out of the Province Treasury . . . : For every scalp of a male Indian brought in as evidence of their being killed as aforesaid, forty pounds. For every scalp of such female Indian or male Indian under the age of twelve years that shall be killed and brought in as evidence of their being killed as aforesaid, twenty pounds.

To be clear: this practice is evil, disgusting, and unconscionable. See Vine Deloria Jr., *Custer Died for Your Sins: An Indian Manifesto* (New York: Macmillan, 1969), 6–7, 30.

6. Bernice Margaret Hamilton, "Francisco de Vitoria: Spanish Theologian," *Encyclopaedia Britannica*, modified August 8, 2023, http://tinyurl.com/yc3zzur4.

7. "Today in History—February 5: Roger Williams, Rhode Island Founder," Library of Congress, http://tinyurl.com/4bwcv29b.

8. The US Supreme Court March 2005 decision, *City of Sherrill, New York v. Oneida Indian Nation of New York*, concerned land rights and the sovereignty of the Oneida Nation. The court's opinion referred to the history of the Doctrine of Discovery. See Dana Lloyd, "City of Sherrill v. Oneida Indian Nation of New York," *Doctrine of Discovery*, October 19, 2022, http://tinyurl.com/5da6wcnx.

9. Bill Chappell, "The Vatican Repudiates 'Doctrine of Discovery,' Which Was Used to Justify Colonialism," NPR, March 20, 2023, http://tinyurl.com/23fhdtk3.

10. "Geologic Formations," National Park Service, last updated March 4, 2019, http://tinyurl.com/4u5hnydx.

11. "Grand Canyon," National Geographic Education, http://tinyurl.com/ym3fp6xt.

12. Louis Ginzberg, *Legends of the Jews*, trans. Henrietta Szold, vols. 1–4 in one volume (London: Global Grey, 2019), 142.

13. For those who feel uncertain whether referring to the haggadah's imaginative rendition is helpful, 1 Peter 3:19–20 confirms that the haggadah was known to Peter because he references it: he says that Christ, after his death, preached to those "imprisoned spirits . . . who were disobedient long ago when God waited patiently in the days of Noah while the ark was being built" (NIV).

14. Perhaps you hear a tinge of shame in the last question ("What have you done?"). But I suggest that God's question offers *the way back* to intimacy. As any Alcoholics Anonymous curriculum will tell you, confession and amend-making is how someone grows and moves forward. So, God's word here is a forceful invitation to confess so that relational repair between God and humanity can occur.

15. Howard Schwartz and Caren Lebel-Fried, *Tree of Souls: The Mythology of Judaism* (Oxford: Oxford University Press, 2004), 71.

16. Schwartz and Lebel-Fried, *Tree of Souls*, 72.

17. Ginzberg, *Legends of the Jews*, 1:147–48.

18. Ginzberg, *Legends of the Jews*, 1:148.

19. Ginzberg, *Legends of the Jews*, 1:148.

Chapter 05

1. Sir Lancelot Charles Lee Brenton, "Brenton's Septuagint Translation," *Bible Hub*, http://tinyurl.com/mr2a564h.

2. Ronald S. Hendel, "Biblical Views: Noah, Enoch and the Flood; The Bible Meets Hollywood," *Biblical Archaeology Review*, July/August

2014, http://tinyurl.com/375jmjzs; Megan Sauter, "Rock Giants in Noah: Can the Book of Enoch Shed Light on Noah the Movie?," *Bible History Daily*, November 17, 2022, http://tinyurl.com/3yp5nktx.

3. Ham's territory has traditionally been considered those regions west and south of the Nile. For a nuanced discussion of the curse of Ham, that harmful and racist interpretation that has plagued this biblical character, see David M. Goldenberg, *The Curse of Ham: Race and Slavery in Early Judaism, Christianity and Islam* (Princeton: Princeton University Press, 2003).

4. "The Latest Biblical Attraction: The Tower of Babel," *Associated Press*, July 11, 2021, http://tinyurl.com/3c2wewcs.

5. Pieter Bruegel the Elder, "The Tower of Babel (1565)," *Art Hive*, http://tinyurl.com/ytkem6tx.

6. Maurits Cornelis Escher, "Tower of Babel (1928)," *Art Hive*, http://tinyurl.com/36k5zmyy.

7. Evgheniya Sidelnikova, "Description of the Artwork, 'Tower of Babel,'" *Art Hive*, http://tinyurl.com/36k5zmyy.

8. Janet Soskice, *The Sisters of Sinai: How Two Lady Adventurers Discovered the Hidden Gospels* (New York: Vintage Books, 2010), 5. Italics mine.

9. Soskice, *Sisters of Sinai*, 5.

10. I do not excuse the theft of cultural artifacts from Middle Eastern sites by Bible hunters, which is objectively wrong and must be amended. Yet not all of these traveling scholars defrauded the countries they explored, or the people they encountered. Some found a way to study ancient artifacts respectfully under the supervision of their owners, seeking mutual benefit from the exchange of knowledge. Fortunately, we now understand that these relics belong in the countries where they originated, and museums and collectors with stolen artifacts face legal and cultural pressure to return whatever they've unrightfully gained. Though the process of returning is ongoing and incomplete, I hope that the guilty will restore these treasures to the nations and people to whom they belong.

11. Randall Price, *Searching for the Original Bible* (Eugene, OR: Harvest House, 2007), 83.

12. The story of the Dead Sea Scrolls can be read in full in Edmund

Wilson, "The Scrolls from the Dead Sea," *New Yorker*, May 6, 1955, https://tinyurl.com/tvzsek37.

13. "The Dead Sea Scrolls," *The Israel Museum*, Jerusalem, accessed February 28, 2024, https://tinyurl.com/38ytdd2n.

14. Flavius Josephus, *The Whole Genuine Works of Flavius Josephus: The Learned and Authentic Jewish Historian and Celebrated Warrior*, trans. William Whiston (Springfield: Thomas, 1809), 1:20, http://tinyurl.com/35wykxc8.

15. In Genesis 11:5, 7, God "comes down" to view the in-progress tower, and God doesn't need to utilize the human ladder to do it, thank you very much. (This is called divine irony.)

16. Daniel Bodi, "The Ziqqurats of Ur and Babylon and the Place Where the Ark Moors after the Flood (The Epic of Gilgameš XI 158)," in *Ur in the Twenty-First Century CE: Proceedings of the 62nd Rencontre Assyriologique Internationale at Philadelphia, July 11–15, 2016*, ed. Grant Frame, Joshua Jeffers, and Holly Pittman (Philadelphia: Penn State University Press, 2021), 171–80, http://tinyurl.com/4r4zum3c.

17. Ginzberg, *Legends of the Jews*, 1:166.

18. Josephus, *Works*, 20, http://tinyurl.com/35wykxc8.

19. Saint Augustine of Hippo, *City of God*, trans. Marcus Dods (New York: Modern Library, 1993), 528, http://tinyurl.com/35h9fsjm.

20. Walter Brueggemann, "The Peculiar Dialect of Faith," *Church Anew*, January 12, 2021, http://tinyurl.com/ynperzsr.

21. Louis Maurice Adolphe Linant de Bellefonds, *Mémoires sur les principaux travaux d'utilité publique, exécutés en Egypte depuis la plus haute antiquité jusqu'à nos jours* (Paris: Bertrand, 1873), 140, http://tinyurl.com/2sc6hper.

22. Linant de Bellefonds, *Mémoires*, 90.

23. Emily A. Haddad, "Digging to India: Modernity, Imperialism, and the Suez Canal," *Victorian Studies* 47, no. 3 (2005): 368, http://tinyurl.com/3z9hy7kx.

24. George Percy Badger, *A Visit to the Isthmus of Suez Canal Work* (London: Smith, Elder, 1862), 14, http://tinyurl.com/yuvbr7ms.

25. Mohamed Hussein Al Sheikh, "The Canal That Killed 130,000 Egyptians," *Raseef*, March 3, 2017, http://tinyurl.com/msanczms.

26. To learn more about the Egyptians who dug the Suez Canal, I suggest starting with Luis Carlos Barragan's article, "The Egyptian Workers Who Were Erased from History," *Egyptian Streets*, September 14, 2018, http://tinyurl.com/436nap7h.

27. Caitlín R. Kiernan, "Fear of the Sky," *Dear Sweet Filthy World*, August 21, 2017, http://tinyurl.com/55fb7v85.

28. "We know of no ancient Mesopotamian figure, mythic or historical, named Nimrod. Thus, scholars have struggled to identify who the biblical authors are describing," writes Dr. Levin. See Yigal Levin, "Nimrod, Mighty Hunter and King—Who Was He?," *TheTorah.com*, 2020, http://tinyurl.com/4pmbjntu.

29. James A. Diamond, "The Human Desire to Be Godlike," *TheTorah .com*, 2022, http://tinyurl.com/4nmnfsk4.

30. While the Hebrew storytellers leave the individual fate of the man, Nimrod, to the imagination, Islamic sources describe the ruler's death, as summarized by Carol Bakhos: "Nimrod dies from a gnat entering his nostril and gnawing on his brain, in some renditions [a torturous death that lasts] for four hundred years" ("Nimrod: The Making of a Nemesis," *TheTorah.com*, 2021, http://tinyurl.com/37mzrc9h).

### Chapter 06

1. "What Is the Point of John Cage's 4'33"?" *BBC Music Magazine*, September 28, 2021, http://tinyurl.com/mrxvwp8k.

2. Kay Larson, "4'33"," *Tricycle Magazine*, 1999, http://tinyurl.com /4wbjfw2n.

3. John Cage, *Silence: Lectures and Writings* (Middletown, CT: Wesleyan University Press, 1973), 7–8, http://tinyurl.com/44cct9t9.

4. Maria Popva, "Paul Goodman on the Nine Kinds of Silence," *Marginalian*, http://tinyurl.com/4h8fddx3.

5. Beth Swarecki, "Babies Learn to Recognize Words in the Womb," *Science*, August 26, 2013, http://tinyurl.com/266e8kxd.

6. Eino Partanen, Teija Kujala, Risto Näätänen, Auli Liitola, Anke Sambeth, and Minna Huotilainen, "Learning-Induced Neural Plasticity of Speech Processing before Birth," *Proceedings of the National Academy of Sciences* 110, no. 37 (2013): 15145–50, http://tinyurl.com/yx9vh93e.

7. Summarized by Sophie McBain, "The Voice in Your Head," *New Statesman*, March 24, 2021, http://tinyurl.com/527fud49.

8. Julian Jaynes, "Consciousness and the Voices of the Mind," Julian Jaynes Society, October 14, 1982, http://tinyurl.com/2skhvp5d.

9. "The Weirdest Torah Theory You Never Heard," *Jewish Journal*, August 29, 2016, http://tinyurl.com/9a5mjehr.

10. "Summary of Evidence for the Bicameral Mind Theory," Julian Jaynes Society, last updated December 14, 2023, http://tinyurl.com/2zwahmax.

11. Christopher Eames, "The Chronological Debate from Adam to Abraham: In Defense of the Masoretic Text," *Armstrong Institute of Biblical Archaeology*, June 27, 2023, https://tinyurl.com/5477rdnw.

12. The Genesis text *does* obliquely refer to moments of communion with God, as in Enoch's case, where twice (Genesis 5:22 and 24) the writers say that he "walked faithfully with God" (NIV), recalling Adam and Eve's walks through the garden of Eden , conversing daily with God. However, the biblical authors do not record these discussions between God and other side characters.

13. Bialik et al., *Book of Legends*, 476, verse 69. Italics mine.

14. Quoted in McBain, "Voice in Your Head."

15. Noah Weiner, "The 'Original' Bible and the Dead Sea Scrolls," *Bible History Daily*, July 27, 2023, http://tinyurl.com/3bz4c5ve.

16. Soskice, *Sisters of Sinai*, 101. All other details of the sisters' lives have been drawn from Soskice's excellent book, which I highly recommend.

17. Soskice, *Sisters of Sinai*, 258.

18. Agnes Smith Lewis, *A Translation of the Four Gospels, from the Syriac of the Sinaitic Palimpsest* (London: Macmillan, 1894), 44, http://tinyurl.com/38jk8dsb.

19. In the introduction to her published translation, Agnes Smith Lewis explains that while several phrases in the first chapter of Matthew

*do* emphasize Joseph's paternity, the text also names Mary a "virgin," who was "found with child of the Holy Ghost." Furthermore, she writes, "The fact that Joseph was troubled about Mary's condition is simply inexplicable if he were the father of Jesus . . . and we can hardly believe that [the disciples] did not investigate the truth of a statement which most of them sealed with suffering and with death. The seclusion in which Eastern women are kept . . . from social intercourse with all members of the other sex who are not of kin to them . . . make it highly improbable that Mary could be guilty of a lapse of virtue without the knowledge of some female companion." The manuscript takes no clear side one way or the other. Instead, the manuscript presents Jesus as *both* Joseph's son and God's son. Even if these textual disagreements are notable between this manuscript and others of the same time and language, Smith asserts that dismissing the virgin birth is nonsensical based on the agreement of other original manuscripts (Lewis, *Translation*, xxiii–xxiv).

20. Agnes Smith Lewis, *Light on the Four Gospels from the Sinai Palimpsests* (London: Williams & Norgate, 1913), 15–17, http://tinyurl. com/39vrfmzy.

21. Ginzberg, *Legends of the Jews*, 172–75.

22. Ginzberg, Legends of the Jews, 178.

23. According to the legend, when Abram is caught by Nimrod, he says in his defense, "I did not do it; it was the largest of the idols who shattered all the rest. Seest thou not that he still has the axe in his hand? And if thou wilt not believe my words, ask him and he will tell thee." No surprise, the king does not appreciate the teen's cheek (Ginzberg, *Legends of the Jews*, 181).

24. The legend continues with Nimrod imprisoning Abram, and then condemning him to death by furnace—all because Abram refuses to worship the king, instead of God. But every time Nimrod's soldiers try to throw the man into the furnace, they burn up instead. So, Nimrod builds a catapult to fling Abram into the furnace. As Abram flies through the air, God extinguishes the fire. Instead of burning, "The logs [in the furnace] burst into buds, and all the different kinds of wood put forth fruit, each tree bearing its own kind. The furnace was transformed into a royal

pleasance (a walled garden), and the angels sat therein with Abraham." What was meant for death becomes abundant life (Ginzberg, *Legends of the Jews*, 182–84).

25. Charles H. Spurgeon, "Abraham's Prompt Obedience to the Call of God [sermon delivered June 27, 1875]," *Blue Letter Bible*, http://tinyurl.com/2bsczuxx.

*Chapter 07*

1. Graham Bell, *Full Fathom 5000: The Expedition of the* HMS Challenger *and the Strange Animals It Found in the Deep Sea* (Oxford: Oxford University Press, 2022).

2. "Azoic, *adj.*," *Oxford English Dictionary*, September 2023, https://doi.org/10.1093/OED/9841599299.

3. Dr. Tina Bishop, Peter Tuddenham, Melissa Ryan, Diana Payne, and Ivar Babb, "Then and Now: The HMS Challenger Expedition and the 'Mountains in the Sea' Expedition," National Oceanic and Atmospheric Administration, US Department of Commerce, modified November 21, 2022, http://tinyurl.com/5edb6bsz.

4. Sir C. Wyville Thomson, John Murray, William C. M'Intosh, and Dr. David C. Bossard, *Report of the Scientific Results of the Voyage of H. M. S. Challenger during the Years of 1873–1876* (Hanover: Dartmouth College, 2004), http://tinyurl.com/5n8skcjp.

5. Erika Jones, "HMS Challenger: A Trailblazer for Modern Ocean Science," Royal Museums Greenwich, http://tinyurl.com/ym9rx555.

6. Sarai is sixty-five when God first appears to Abram in Genesis 12, and she is ninety in Genesis 21 when she finally births Isaac.

7. Genesis Rabbah 45.4: "Why were the matriarchs barren? R. Levi said in R. Shila's name and R. Helbo in R. Johanan's name: Because the Holy One, blessed be He, yearns for their prayers and supplications. Thus it is written, 'O my dove, in the cranny of the rocks, / Hidden by the cliff' (Song of Songs 2:14): Why did I make you barren? In order that, 'Let Me see your face, / Let me hear your voice' (Song of Songs 2:14)." Similarly, Babylonian Talmud Yevamot 64a suggests that the matriarchs and patri-

archs were initially childless "because the Holy One, blessed be He, longs to hear the prayer of the righteous" (Sefaria Community Translation, "Bereshit Rabbah 45:4," *Sefaria*, http://tinyurl.com/25vryadk).

8. Katharine C. Bushnell, *God's Word to Women: One Hundred Bible Studies on Woman's Place in the Church and Home* (Minneapolis: Christians for Biblical Equality, 2003), 14–17.

9. The NIV translates 2:21 as "one of the man's ribs," stating in a footnote, "Or *took part of the man's side*" (*Bible Gateway*, http://tinyurl.com/y5k8j2z3).

10. Bushnell quotes another example from the Mishnah, a conversation between the Rabbi Rav and a woman who came to him to ask for advice. The story goes, "A woman once complained before Rav (a great rabbi) of bad treatment from her husband. He replied: 'What is the difference between thee and a fish, which one may eat either broiled or cooked?'" (Bushnell, *God's Word to Women*, 4).

11. Bushnell, *God's Word to Women*, 17.

12. Bialik et al., *Book of Legends*, 14:50, 15:63–64.

13. Bialik et al., *Book of Legends*, 15:60 and n. 5.

14. Bushnell, *God's Word to Women*, 3.

15. Bushnell, *God's Word to Women*, 3.

16. Dinah's story can be found in Genesis 34, and Bathsheba's story in 2 Samuel 11:1–12:19.

17. Stephanie Lynn Budin, "Fertility and Gender in the Ancient Near East," in *Sex in Antiquity: Exploring Gender and Sexuality in the Ancient World*, ed. Mark Masterson, Nancy Sorkin Rabinowitz, and James Robson (London: Routledge, 2015), 46.

18. "Biblical, comparative ancient Near Eastern, and early rabbinic material all contain examples of infertility treated as a disability or illness." Jeremy Schipper, "Disabling Israelite Leadership: 2 Samuel 6:23 and Other Images of Disability in Deuteronomistic History," in *This Abled Body: Rethinking Disabilities in Biblical Studies*, ed. Sarah J. Melcher and Hector Avalos (Atlanta: Society of Biblical Literature, 2007), 105.

19. Budin, "Fertility and Gender in the Ancient Near East," 45.

20. Anna Goldman-Amirav, "Behold, the LORD Hath Restrained Me

from Bearing," *Reproductive and Genetic Engineering: Journal of International Feminist Analysis* 1, no. 3 (1988): 284, 288–89, http://tinyurl.com/2xwzww9c.

21. The complete account originates in Saint Teresa of Ávila's memoirs, translated from Spanish as follows: "Do not complain, daughter, for it is ever thus that I treat my friends." She replies, "Ah, Lord, it is also on that account that Thou has so few!" See Alice Lady Lovat, *The Life of Saint Teresa Taken from the French of "A Carmelite Nun"* (London: Herbert & Daniel; Saint Louis: Herder, 1912), 548.

The paraphrase of the conversation between Saint Teresa and God comes from Madeleine L'Engle in Leonard S. Marcus, *Listening for Madeleine: A Portrait of Madeleine L'Engle in Many Voices* (New York: Macmillan, 2012), 20.

22. In Israel's later history, rabbis urged a man to pursue *every* avenue possible to grow his family, or else he would be in violation of God's repeated command to "be fruitful and multiply" (Genesis 1:28 NIV). To obey this command, a husband could divorce his wife after a decade of failing to produce an heir together. According to the Jewish law book, the Talmud, he was on the hook for reproducing, not his wife; infertility was the husband's responsibility before God, not his wife's. Ramban writes, "[Ten years] is the established period for a woman who has lived with her husband for ten years without having given birth to children, after which he is bound to take another" (Ramban, "Ramban on Genesis 16:3:3," trans. Charles B. Chavel, *Sefaria*, http://tinyurl.com/5rbh6tbd). Then again, the Talmud also allowed provision for a husband to stay married to the infertile wife whom he loved, defeating the obligation of childbearing.

Regardless of *when* in ancient civilization, a woman who could not produce a child faced dire repercussions. So, Sarai's choice to offer Hagar to Abram is perhaps her only means of fulfilling and preserving her marriage contract—the only one in her power. After ten settled years in Canaan, Sarai offers the enslaved Hagar as a surrogate mother before Abram can suggest an alternative. Sarai hopes that the couple can finally produce an heir through Hagar, thereby saving her honor and perhaps her marriage, too.

23. As John Nelson Darby's translation has it, Sarai says, "Perhaps I

shall be built up through Hagar" (*Bible Gateway*, http://tinyurl.com/2rs jnseu). The rabbis picked up this architectural vocabulary in the original Hebrew, according to Tamar Kadari: "The rabbis deduced . . . that anyone who is childless is like a ruined structure that must be rebuilt" (Tamar Kadari, "Hagar: Midrash and Aggadah," *The Shalvi/Hyman Encyclopedia of Jewish Women*, December 31, 1999, http://tinyurl.com/5b9dhr8w).

24. Goldman-Amirav, "Behold," 286.

25. Sarai eventually seems to notice that Abram has taken no action on her behalf to cure her infertility—no worship of his god, no sacrifice, no prayer. The medieval Jewish commentator Chizkuni summarizes her later complaint to Abram in Genesis 16:5: "May the LORD judge between you and me." He writes, "The substance of Sarai's complaint was that if Abram had prayed not only to have children himself but had included her in his prayer, the whole subject of offering Hagar to him as a concubine would never have arisen" (Rabbi Hezekiah ben Manoah, "Chizkuni, Genesis 16:5," trans. Eliyahu Munk, *Sefaria*, http://tinyurl.com/3kx4v8a8).

26. Catherine Clark Kroeger, "The Legacy of Katherine Bushnell: A Hermeneutic for Women of Faith," *Priscilla Papers* 9, no. 4 (1995), http://tinyurl.com/2bvvk3wv.

27. Benedicta Ward, trans., *The Sayings of the Desert Fathers: The Alphabetical Collection* (Kalamazoo, MI: Cistercian, 1984), 138–39, http://tinyurl. com/4vajyunv.

28. The rabbis assumed that God must have performed a double miracle to bring Isaac into the world. The first restored Sarah's body to its former state of both beauty and reproductive health. The second conceived Isaac in her, the child of promise. See Judith Reesa Baskin, "Infertile Wife in Rabbinic Judaism," *Shalvi/Hyman Encyclopedia of Jewish Women*, December 31, 1999, http://tinyurl.com/3k82t3px. The rabbis also suggested that Sarah's miracles had a contagious effect, which resulted in the healings of others in tandem: "When the matriarch Sarah was remembered [gave birth], many other barren women were remembered with her; many deaf gained their hearing; many blind had their eyes opened, many insane became sane" ("Bereshit Rabbah 53:8," *Sefaria*, http://tinyurl.com/48s5v72b).

Chapter 08

1. Albert T. Clay, "The So-Called Fertile Crescent and Desert Bay," *Journal of the American Oriental Society* 44 (1924): 186, http://tinyurl. com/8semx4nv. A photographic archive of Dr. James H. Breasted's expeditions can be viewed at the Oriental Institute of the University of Chicago (http://tinyurl.com/mrxxufr3).

2. Clay, "So-Called Fertile Crescent," 190.

3. Israel Finkelstein and Dafna Langgut, "Dry Climate in the Middle Bronze I and Its Impact on Settlement Patterns in the Levant and Beyond: New Pollen Evidence," *Journal of Near Eastern Studies* 73, no. 2 (2014): 219–34, http://tinyurl.com/4hnxuf3a.

4. "Part 1—Geography of the Land in Its Setting: The Physical Setting of the Land of the Bible," United Bible Societies, http://tinyurl.com/ ye26p5v6.

5. Sefaria Community Translation, "Bereshit Rabbah 45:4," *Sefaria*, http://tinyurl.com/tdvdkp3n.

6. Ginzberg, *Legends of the Jews*, 1:216.

7. Sarah J. Melcher, "Genesis and Exodus," in *The Bible and Disability: A Commentary*, ed. Mikeal C. Parsons and Amos Yong (Waco, TX: Baylor University Press, 2017), 37.

8. Exodus 1:11–12 reads, "So [the Egyptians] put slave masters over them to *oppress* them with forced labor. . . . But the more they were *oppressed*, the more they multiplied and spread" (NIV; italics mine). "Oppress" translates as the same Hebrew root word, meaning "afflict." See Phyllis Trible, *Texts of Terror: Literary-Feminist Readings of Biblical Narratives* (Philadelphia: Fortress, 1984), 13, http://tinyurl.com/bdf3ur3x.

9. Referring to Hagar running away from the home of Abram and Sarai, womanist theologian Delores S. Williams writes that Hagar becomes "the first female in the Bible to liberate herself from an oppressive power structure" (*Sisters in the Wilderness: The Challenge of Womanist God-Talk* [Maryknoll, NY: Orbis Books, 1993], 19, http://tinyurl.com/mr3n2j8x).

10. Unless otherwise noted, facts about Saint Anthony's life and any direct quotations can be located within the biography by Athanasius of

Alexandria, *Life of Antony*, in *Early Christian Lives*, trans. Carolinne White (London: Penguin, 1998).

11. While no one can point conclusively to Constantine's conversion as the moment that inexorably led to the Crusades and Inquisition, I argue Constantine's Edict of Milan offered the influence, access, and resources necessary to the Christian church for both later atrocities to happen. State exercises gained theological backing that allowed the government and church to collaborate in harmful, even evil ways.

12. Athanasius, *Life of Antony*, in *Early Christian Lives*, 60.

13. White, *Early Christian Lives*, xxx.

14. Mark Sheridan, ed., *Genesis 12–50*, Ancient Christian Commentary on Scripture: Old Testament 2 (Downers Grove, IL: InterVarsity Press, 2002), 45.

15. Sheridan, *Genesis 12–50*, 43.

16. Sheridan, *Genesis 12–50*, 42–43.

17. John E. Murray, "2. The Semantics of *Hermeneuein*," in *Introduction to Philosophical Hermeneutics* (New Haven: Yale University Press, 1994), 20–23, http://tinyurl.com/4t4x5y43.

18. These translation errors are significant and worthy of close study. Primarily, biblical errors in translation concern the prejudices of modern translators who alter the meaning of texts to satisfy their own biases. Many scholars address these errors thoroughly, so I will leave the necessary work of reinterpretation to those more qualified. Thank you to all who do this necessary work correcting what has been broken. One of my personal heroes in this field is Katharine Bushnell. Kristin Kobes Du Mez has written this scholar's biography: *A New Gospel for Women: Katharine Bushnell and the Challenge of Christian Feminism* (Oxford: Oxford University Press, 2015).

19. Kwok Pui-Lan, "Racism and Ethnocentrism in Feminist Biblical Interpretation," *A Feminist Introduction*, vol. 1 of *Searching the Scriptures*, ed. Elisabeth Schüssler Fiorenza (New York: Crossroad, 1993), 103, http://tinyurl.com/bdhkn2ac.

20. Pui-Lan, "Racism and Ethnocentrism," 103.

21. I want to say strongly that slavery in every form is evil and that

those who enslave others oppose God. God. In America, and particularly within the white American church, we of European descent have perpetuated slavery in the past and continue to uphold white supremacy in subtle and overt ways to this day. The ongoing denigration of Black and Brown bodies still happens in our country and is unacceptable. This dehumanization is a hateful extension of the system of slavery that must be eradicated from American society and from the American Christian church in its entirety if we desire to live according to the way of Christ. I cannot recommend strongly enough that leaders of our congregations repent of any past or present cooperation with white supremacy, both as individuals and as communities, and that we all seek, in humility, ways to offer tangible reparations to Black communities in the United States. Reparations offers one way we can enact Christ's radical call to reconciliation.

22. Howard Thurman, *Jesus and the Disinherited* (Boston: Beacon, 1996), 39.

23. Thurman, *Jesus and the Disinherited*, 20.

24. "Judith Scott at the Museum of Everything," *The Culture Show*, BBC, October 20, 2011, http://tinyurl.com/44ukh8pb.

25. "Judith Ann Scott (1943–2005)," American Visionary Art Museum, http://tinyurl.com/2zsamctk.

26. Avigdor Bonchek, "Hagar's Outcry," *Aish*, http://tinyurl.com/2s3cztyj.

27. Sefaria Community Translation, "Bereshit Rabbah 45:10," *Sefaria*, http://tinyurl.com/4v5vu472.

28. Ramban, "Ramban on Genesis 16:6," trans. Charles B. Chavel, *Sefaria*, http://tinyurl.com/mrxx6w9r.

### Chapter 09

1. Tracy Ross, "Tibet Is Still Burning," *Outside*, modified May 12, 2022, http://tinyurl.com/48knfm9t.

2. "Tibet," Freedom House, https://tinyurl.com/mrythh6n.

3. Ross, "Tibet Is Still Burning."

4. Rashi (Rabbi Solomon Ben Isaac), "Rashi on Genesis 18:21:2," trans. M. Rosenbaum and A. M. Silbermann, *Sefaria*, http://tinyurl.com/yw 435sth.

5. "Sanhedrin 109b:9," trans. Adin Even-Israel Steinsaltz, *Sefaria*, http://tinyurl.com/2jm4aatv.

6. Some theologians have *overemphasized* that the judgment against Sodom and Gomorrah was instigated because of a specific sexual perversion of the peoples—that of sodomy. They equate the gang rape in these passages with twenty-first-century discussions of homosexuality within the American church. But many commentators, including Walter Brueggemann (*Genesis*, Interpretation: A Bible Commentary for Teaching and Preaching [Louisville: Westminster John Knox, 1982], 164), see God rebuking these cities for a broader pattern of abuse of the poor, the stranger, and the vulnerable, which included sexual crimes but was not solely defined by them. Our Western, postmodern ideas about sexuality differ dramatically from those of the ancient Near East, as many excellent scholars point out. Read a scholarly overview of a progressive Christian view of these Scriptures at "What Does the Bible Say about Homosexuality?," Human Rights Campaign, http://tinyurl.com/5efetvdz.

In addition, the Scriptures continue to refer to the citizens of these towns with a range of emphasis. For example, Isaiah 3:9 says, "[The wicked] parade their sin like Sodom; they do not hide it" (NIV). Ezekiel 16:49: "'Now this was the sin of your sister Sodom: She and her daughters were arrogant, overfed and unconcerned; they did not help the poor and needy" (NIV). Jude 1:7: "Sodom and Gomorrah and the surrounding towns gave themselves up to sexual immorality and perversion" (NIV). Jesus addresses both the speed and surprise of judgment (which, like the second coming, will be unexpected), and he seems to imply that the sins of these cities were pride and refusing hospitality to the angels. Matthew 10:14–15: "If anyone will not welcome you or listen to your words, leave that home or town and shake the dust off your feet. Truly I tell you, it will be more bearable for Sodom and Gomorrah on the day of judgment than for that town" (NIV). Because of this range of interpretation within the Bible, I conclude that the severity of judgment against these cities does not occur because of a single issue. In particular, it has less to do with homosexuality as we know it and more to do with a culture's wholesale rejection of the Person and ways of God.

7. Rabbi Bachya Ben Asher, "Tur HaArokh, Genesis 19:13:1," trans. Eliyahu Munk, *Sefaria*, http://tinyurl.com/3873rvkw.

8. "Ai Weiwei: Never Sorry," directed by Alison Klayman, 2012, IFC-Films, http://tinyurl.com/yhh68uh2.

9. Ai Weiwei, "The Artwork That Made Me the Most Dangerous Person in China," *Guardian*, February 15, 2018, http://tinyurl.com/myssnhmx.

10. "Chinese Artist Ai Weiwei Describes His 81 Days in Prison—And the Extreme Surveillance, Censorship, and 'Soft Detention' He's Endured Since," *ArtSpace*, December 20, 2018, http://tinyurl.com/3b5733ku.

11. Brueggemann, *Genesis*, 168. Italics mine.

12. For more on this textual correction and how early church fathers interpreted its meaning, see Tim Hegg, "Genesis 18:22 and the Tiqqune Sopherim: Textual, Midrashic, and for What Purpose?," *Torah Resource*, http://tinyurl.com/2p9xsbk7.

13. David E. S. Stein, Carol L. Myers, Adele Berlin, and Ellen Frankel, eds., *The Contemporary Torah: A Gender-Sensitive Adaptation of the JPS Translation* (Philadelphia: Jewish Publication Society, 2006).

14. Typically, biblical scholars consider other genres within the Bible—poems, lyrics, prophecies, apocalyptic writings, etc.—as means of expounding upon the historical movement of God among the Hebrews. The Bible's history texts sit at the center with other writings as illuminations and commentaries on that recorded history. For an overview of the schools of criticism that have developed to study the Bible, see the following in *Encyclopaedia Britannica*: Robert L. Faherty, Emilie T. Sander, Seymour Cain, J. Coert Rylaarsdam, David Flusser, Linwood Fredericksen, Frederick Fyvie Bruce, H. Grady Davis, Robert M. Grant, Nahum M. Sarna, and Krister Stendahl, "Biblical Literature," http://tinyurl.com/55xtpz4a; "Literary Criticism," http://tinyurl.com/489ujade.

15. To say nothing of the literary agents and agencies, publishers, marketing teams, and the vast network involved in the complex production of the publishing industry! So many people make a book!

16. I am grateful to Karel van der Toorn for his work describing the ancient world's society of scribes so cogently in *Scribal Culture and the Making of the Hebrew Bible* (Cambridge: Harvard University Press, 2009).

17. Christopher A. Rollston presents compelling evidence that Moses did not write the Pentateuch, and he does this without mentioning the theory of source criticism ("Who Wrote the Torah according to the Torah?," *TheTorah.com*, 2017, http://tinyurl.com/3vyn3yka).

18. For a summary of the history of authorial criticism of the Bible, I recommend Thomas B. Dozeman, "The Pentateuch," *Oxford Research Encyclopedia of Religion*, June 25, 2018, http://tinyurl.com/55jjhhz5.

19. Van der Toorn, *Scribal Culture*, 5.

20. Van der Toorn, *Scribal Culture*, 6.

21. Asaf Ronel, "DNA Unlocks the Secrets of the Dead Sea Scrolls," *Haaretz*, June 7, 2020, http://tinyurl.com/3at7cxsh.

22. In an interview with the Israeli news site *Haaretz*, one of the study's authors, Mladen Popović, said of the discovery, "We will never know their names. But after seventy years of study [of the Dead Sea Scrolls], this feels as if we can finally shake hands with them through their handwriting." See Ariel David, "Artificial Intelligence Helps Identify Authors of Dead Sea Scrolls," *Haaretz*, April 24, 2021, http://tinyurl.com/bdd6jvyu; M. Popović, M. A. Dhali, L. Schomaker, "Artificial-Intelligence Based Writer Identification Generates New Evidence for the Unknown Scribes of the Dead Sea Scrolls Exemplified by the Great Isaiah Scroll (1QIsaa)," *PLOS ONE* 16, no. 4 (2021): e0249769. http://tinyurl.com/yvykwrns.

23. Rashi (Rabbi Solomon Ben Isaac), "Rashi on Genesis 19:25:1," trans. M. Rosenbaum and A. M. Silbermann, *Sefaria*, http://tinyurl.com/bddmh4yz.

24. Radak (Rabbi David Kimchi), "Radak on Genesis 19:25:1," trans. Eliyahu Munk, *Sefaria*, http://tinyurl.com/yc6srv72.

25. Chizkuni (Rabbi Chizkiyahu ben Manoach), "Chizkuni on Genesis 19:25:2," trans. Eliyahu Munk, *Sefaria*, http://tinyurl.com/2ujn398z.

26. Ted E. Bunch, Malcolm A. LeCompte, A. Victor Adedeji, James H. Wittke, T. David Burleigh, Robert E. Hermes, Charles Mooney, et al., "A Tunguska Sized Airburst Destroyed Tall el-Hammam a Middle

Bronze Age City in the Jordan Valley Near the Dead Sea," *Scientific Reports* 11, 18632 (2021), http://tinyurl.com/2jfy2yrk.

27. "Sodom and Gomorrah: Historicity," *Encyclopaedia Britannica*, last updated January 2, 2023, http://tinyurl.com/b5sbnetm.

28. "Is There Any Life in the Dead Sea?," *Encyclopaedia Britannica*, modified May 28, 2021, http://tinyurl.com/2y7m28yp.

29. God speaks to Abraham about Ishmael's fate: he will survive, and God will also bless him (Genesis 21:12–13). Abraham *still* does not address the issue with Sarah, and Hagar and Ishmael still wander in the desert, nearly expiring. Even though God has blessed Hagar and Ishmael, God does not rescue them from their exile.

*Chapter 10*

1. "Rachel, Donner Lake in the Sierra Nevada," National Weather Service, http://tinyurl.com/kc2jzebe.

2. "Lightning Survivor Story of Glenn," National Weather Service, http://tinyurl.com/5crh5kxm.

3. "Survivor Story: Anita," National Weather Service, http://tinyurl.com/ycxmeh4j.

4. "Medical Aspects of Lightning," National Weather Service, http://tinyurl.com/yz8enkzk.

5. "Survivor Story: Johanna," National Weather Service, http://tinyurl.com/3euc7chp.

6. The timelines of Genesis go fuzzy again as chapters 16 and 21 seem to blend, so no commentator can pinpoint exactly how old Ishmael is when Sarah kicks him and his mother out (21). The text states that Isaac has recently been weaned (which would have occurred between two and four years old in ancient Near Eastern culture). Since Ishmael is thirteen at Isaac's birth, this would make Ishmael a late teen. However, the text also suggests that Ishmael needs to be supported by his mother as they journey away from the tent of Abraham (his mother "places him under a bush"), leading some rabbis to assume the teen is ill. Yet he's also repeatedly called "the boy," leading some commentators to suppose he's

still a child when mother and son are emancipated, rather than a teenager (21:14–16 NIV). Then again, emphasizing his boyhood could have more to do with Ishmael's unmarried state than his age. So, there is no consensus.

7. Dolores S. Williams writes movingly of the story of Hagar, reframing her enslavement narrative: "Hagar, a foreign female slave whose future would ordinarily not advance past slavery, is given hope not only for the survival of her generation but also hope for the possibility of future freedom for her seed. . . . [And] when Hagar and her child were finally cast out of the home of their oppressors [without] . . . proper resources for survival, God provided Hagar with a resource. . . . [Further, God's promise suggests] that Ishmael will be free and a warrior. He will be able to help create and protect the quality of life he and his mother, Hagar, will later develop in the desert." See Williams, *Sisters in the Wilderness*, 4, 6, 22.

8. Søren Kierkegaard, *Fear and Trembling*, trans. Alastair Hannay (New York: Penguin, 2006, 1985), 76, 77.

9. Kierkegaard, *Fear and Trembling*, 77.

10. "10 Striking Facts about Lightning," Met Office, http://tinyurl.com/mszpa8ks.

11. "Earthquake Lights: Study Sheds Light on Mysterious Natural Phenomenon," *Sci News*, January 14, 2014, http://tinyurl.com/3bma25y9.

12. Lin Edwards, "Some UFOs May Be Explained as Ball Lightning," *Phys.org*, December 2, 2010, http://tinyurl.com/3754umc2.

13. Edward Lorenz, "Predictability: Does the Flap of a Butterfly's Wings in Brazil Set Off a Tornado in Texas?," Massachusetts Institute of Technology, Cambridge, Massachusetts: American Association for the Advancement of Science, December 29, 1972, http://tinyurl.com/2tuunwfy.

14. Spencer Weart, "Chaos in the Atmosphere," *Discovery of Global Warming*, May 2023, http://tinyurl.com/yu6jbz36.

15. Sefaria Community Translation, "Bereshit Rabbah 56:4," *Sefaria*, http://tinyurl.com/ycyr9tat.

16. Sefaria Community Translation, "Bereshit Rabbah 56:7," *Sefaria*, http://tinyurl.com/5n8z5hsn.

17. Only one Jewish commentator allows the slightest doubt to enter Isaac's mind: "Isaac assumed that this was to be a symbolic offering. It

was only when Abraham took the knife and marked the place for the cut did he realize that he was actually to be slaughtered." Then Isaac cries for relief, and his prayer calls down the angel, who stops the hand of Abraham. (See Yitzchak Abarbanel, "Abarbanel on Torah, Genesis 22:3," trans. Rabbi Avraham Davis, *Sefaria*, http://tinyurl.com/ywmrhaa3).

18. Sefaria Community Translation, "Bereshit Rabbah 56:8," *Sefaria*, http://tinyurl.com/2pbxbkkp.

19. Daniel Stone, "This Artist Makes Clouds Appear in Unexpected Places," *National Geographic*, March 2019, http://tinyurl.com/4sx4r8py.

20. Hebrews 11:17–19 NIV: "By faith Abraham, when God tested him, offered Isaac as a sacrifice. He who had embraced the promises was about to sacrifice his one and only son, even though God had said to him, 'It is through Isaac that your offspring will be reckoned.' Abraham reasoned that God could even raise the dead, and so in a manner of speaking he did receive Isaac back from death."

21. Rashi (Rabbi Solomon Ben Isaac), "Rashi on Genesis 22:2:4," trans. M. Rosenbaum and A. M. Silbermann, *Sefaria*, http://tinyurl.com/bdhpkrbu.

22. Sefaria Community Translation, "Bereshit Rabbah 55:7," *Sefaria*, http://tinyurl.com/2s3mw44j.

23. I would be remiss if I did not point out the parallels between the language of Isaac as Abraham's "only son" and the references in the New Testament to the "only son" of God, Jesus Christ, as in John 3:16: "For God so loved the world that he gave *his one and only Son*, that whoever believes in him shall not perish but have eternal life" (NIV; italics mine). Surely, the gospel writer John meant to draw our attention to this parallel, by which he seems to suggest that the event between Abraham and his son acts as a prophetic archetype of the sacrifice God makes through the life, death, and resurrection of Jesus Christ, and this theme is, of course, explored at length throughout the rest of the New Testament, especially in the writings of the apostle Paul.

24. Ramban (Moses Maimonides), "Guide for the Perplexed, Introduction, Prefatory Remarks 9–11," trans. M. Friedlander, *Sefaria*, http://tinyurl.com/2xy8jney.

25. This phrase is borrowed, not my own, but I have been unable to correctly attribute it. (I have a hunch it's a Dallas Willard–ism.)
26. Bialik et al., *Book of Legends*, 13:48.
27. Radak (Rabbi David Kimchi), "Radak on Genesis 22:1:1," trans. Eliyahu Munk, *Sefaria*, http://tinyurl.com/2y8za4a3.

*Chapter 11*

1. According to *Church Finder*'s list of American Christian denominations. Some claim that Christianity may have as many as forty-five thousand denominations worldwide. But tallying denominations is difficult, so I imagine somewhere in the hundreds of Christian international denominations seems likelier. See "List of Christian Denominations with Profiles," *Church Finder*, http://tinyurl.com/mrfdzrkd.
2. Simone Weil, *Waiting for God*, trans. Emma Craufurd (New York: Harper & Row, 1973), 69.
3. To learn about the Freudian theory of Jacob wrestling *himself*, listen to this lecture by Rabbi Shmuel Klitsner: "The Strange Episode at the Lodging Place: A New Reading of Shmot 4:18–26," November 29, 2016, Riverdale, NY, audio recording, http://tinyurl.com/44k7969r.
4. Radak (Rabbi David Kimchi), "Radak on Genesis 32:25:1," trans. Eliyahu Munk, *Sefaria*, http://tinyurl.com/ke5ss6yt.
5. Radak, "Genesis 32:26:2," *Sefaria*, http://tinyurl.com/3v63cbu2.
6. One rabbinic interpretation says that the reference to Jacob's "hip," sometimes translated as "the hollow of his thigh," is likely a euphemism for the nearness to a more intimate part—in other words, Jacob's sexual organs. See Rabbi Bachya Ben Asher, "Rabbeinu Bahya, Bereshit 32:25:4," trans. Eliyahu Munk, *Sefaria*, http://tinyurl.com/4n295ys2.
7. Adin Even-Israel Steinsaltz, "Chullin 90a:2," *Sefaria*, http://tinyurl.com/7ny7e5ma.
8. Alan Lightman, "Oral History Interview with Vera Rubin," American Institute of Physics, April 3, 1989, http://tinyurl.com/2s3bhzfe.
9. Sarah Scoles, "How Vera Rubin Confirmed Dark Matter," *Astronomy*, October 4, 2016, http://tinyurl.com/2crbjfrk.

10. Ashley Yeager and David DeVorkin, "Oral History Interview with Vera Rubin," American Institute of Physics, July 20, 2007, http://tinyurl.com/6yy4rea7.

11. Adam Riess, "Dark Matter," *Encyclopaedia Britannica*, last updated December 15, 2023, http://tinyurl.com/3ur995tj.

12. Dana Bolles, "Dark Energy, Dark Matter," NASA, modified July 27, 2023, http://tinyurl.com/5xu4mf7a.

13. Yeager and DeVorkin, "Interview with Vera Rubin."

14. Wikipedia contains a dynamic list of unsolved questions that physicists are in the process of solving *right now*. I recommend reading it when you want to be reminded that the universe is very large and you are very small ("List of Unsolved Problems in Physics," Wikipedia, http://tinyurl.com/yahab7t4).

15. One study that examines prayer alongside neurology is "A Case Series Study of the Neurophysiological Effects of Altered States of Mind during Intense Islamic Prayer," which measured changes in cerebral blood flow within the brain during prayer or meditation. They hypothesized that "the changes in brain activity may be associated with feelings of 'surrender' and 'connectedness with God' described to be experienced during these intense Islamic prayer practices." Physiological changes in the brain, in other words, map to an experience of the supernatural within material and biological reality. See Andrew B. Newberg, Nancy A. Wintering, David B. Yaden, Mark R. Waldman, Janet Reddin, and Abass Alavi, *Journal of Physiology—Paris* 109, nos. 4–6 (2015): 214–20, http://tinyurl.com/297xfwdd.

16. Thomas Merton, *Opening the Bible* (Collegeville, MN: Liturgical Press, 1970), 72.

17. James H. Cone, *The Cross and the Lynching Tree* (Maryknoll, NY: Orbis Books, 2011), 23, 25, 26–27.

18. Zornberg, *Beginning of Desire*, 182, 183, 184.

19. Cone, *Cross and Lynching Tree*, 162.

20. I have pieced together the story of Ron DiFrancesco from multiple sources: Andy J. Semotiuk, "The Last Known Survivor of the South Tower of the 9/11 World Trade Center Attack," *Forbes*, September 12, 2016,

http://tinyurl.com/55xzk9ua; John Geiger, *Third Man Factor: The Secret to Survival in Extreme Environments* (Toronto: Penguin, 2009), http://tinyurl.com/37stpa6f; Mark McCallister, "'I Struggle with It A Lot Still': 20 Years Later, a Canadian Survivor Remembers 9/11," *CityNews*, modified September 10, 2021, http://tinyurl.com/bdf292k8; Marco Grob, "Beyond 9/11: Ron DiFrancesco," *Time*, http://tinyurl.com/mr23vu6w.

21. Grob, "Beyond 9/11."

22. The story of Shackleton's voyage is documented in the British explorer's travelogue: Sir Ernest Shackleton, *South: The Endurance Expedition* (New York: Penguin, 2004).

23. Shackleton, *South*, 204.

24. The "third" in third man (as opposed to Shackleton's "fourth") comes from a few lines of a poem by T. S. Eliot. Inspired by Shackleton's frank confession of an incorporeal guide who led them out of mortal danger, Eliot wrote in "The Waste Land": "Who is the third who walks always beside you? / When I count, there are only you and I together / But when I look ahead up the white road / There is always another one walking beside you / Gliding wrapt in a brown mantle, hooded / I do not know whether a man or a woman / —But who is that on the other side of you?" ("The Waste Land," *Collected Poems: 1909–1962* [London: Faber & Faber, 2020], lines 359–65; repr. Poetry Foundation, http://tinyurl.com/46k8ra39).

Critics have connected Eliot's "third" to the biblical story of the disappearing Christ on the road to Emmaus. As the story goes, two disciples walk for miles beside the resurrected Jesus without ever recognizing him until, suddenly, they do. Then, simultaneous to their recognition, Jesus "disappears from their sight" (Luke 24:31 NIV). Jesus is the third, there and not there, seen and unseen. See Tyler Malone, "The Hearers to Collection: T. S. Eliot's *The Waste Land*," Poetry Foundation, http://tinyurl.com/2s43jhku.

25. Geiger, *Third Man Factor*, 122.

26. MacDonald Critchley, "The Idea of a Presence," *Acta Psychiatrica Scandinavica* 30, no. 57 (1955): 161, http://tinyurl.com/3hb2dtpc.

27. Olaf Blanke, Theodor Landis, Laurent Spinelli, and Margitta

Seeck, "Out-of-Body Experience and Autoscopy of Neurological Origin," *Brain* 127, no. 2 (2004): 243–58; Zoé Dary and Christophe Lopez, "Understanding the Neural Bases of Bodily Self-Consciousness: Recent Achievements and Main Challenges," *Frontiers in Integrative Neuroscience* 17 (2023): http://tinyurl.com/4njppr92.

28. Gillian Bennett and Kate Mary Bennett, "The Presence of the Dead: An Empirical Study," *Mortality* 5, no. 2 (2000): 139–57, http://tinyurl.com/2juxvj8k.

29. Tore Nielsen, "Felt Presence: Paranoid Delusion or Hallucinatory Social Imagery?," *Consciousness and Cognition* 16 (2007): 975–83, http://tinyurl.com/577w4fsr.

30. Geiger, *Third Man Factor*, 18.

31. Shackleton, *South*, 204.

32. "JPS 1985 Footnotes, Genesis 31:6," *Sefaria*, accessed March 7, 2024, https://tinyurl.com/3cu4685c.

33. Rashi, "Rashi on Genesis 31:42:1," *Sefaria*, accessed March 7, 2024, https://tinyurl.com/39vsrt2z.

34. One legend tells how Esau murdered the former king Nimrod to steal his regal clothing. Nimrod's clothes supposedly charmed animals, drastically increasing a hunter's luck, an advantage too tempting for Esau to resist. And these same clothes stolen from Nimrod will also become the disguise Jacob uses to steal Esau's blessing later (the clothes play a significant role in tricking Isaac, as in Genesis 27:11–12, 15–16, 21, 22–23, 27). See Sefaria Community Translation, "Bereshit Rabbah 65:17," *Sefaria*, http://tinyurl.com/pwexw6yt.

The rabbis also considered Esau—and his descendants, the Edomites—to be the progenitors of Rome. For example, in the Genesis Rabbah account, Shem, the son of Noah, delivers the prophecy about the two sons inside of pregnant Rebekah, saying, "Two nations are in thy womb. . . . They, Israel and Rome, are the two nations destined to be hated by all the world. One will exceed the other in strength. First Esau will subjugate the whole world, but in the end Jacob will rule over all" (Ginzberg, *Legends of the Jews*, 1:248). Where Edom is referenced in the Torah (or Rome in the New Testament), biblical writers likely have in mind the story of Esau (as the stronger enemy) and Jacob (the weaker Israel).

35. Sefaria Community Translation, "Bereshit Rabbah 65:7," *Sefaria*, http://tinyurl.com/4dkfu9nz.

36. Jason Rappoport, Joshua Schreier, Michael Siev, and Yaacov Francus, "Kohelet Rabbah 3:15: The Sefaria Midrash Rabbah, 2022," *Sefaria*, http://tinyurl.com/2u7rf77m.

37. Abraham Joshua Heschel, *God in Search of Man: A Philosophy of Judaism* (New York: Harper, 1955), 160.

38. Judith Plaskow, *Standing Again at Sinai: Judaism from a Feminist Perspective* (New York: Harper San Francisco, 1990), 34.

39. Gustavo Gutiérrez, *A Theology of Liberation: History, Politics and Salvation*, trans. Sister Caridad Inda and John Eagleson (Maryknoll, NY: Orbis Books, 1973), 14.

40. Roland Barthes, "The Death of the Author," in *Image, Music, Text* (London: Fontana, 1977), 148, http://tinyurl.com/2jshvacn.

41. Salama Yusuf, "How Do Snails (and Other Molluscs) Create Their Shells?," *Science ABC*, March 2, 2022, http://tinyurl.com/y56xmhtw.

42. "Fractal," *Encyclopaedia Britannica*, last updated January 4, 2024, http://tinyurl.com/yc2evsm4.

43. Phyllis Trible writes, "What Jacob wants, he does not get on his own terms." See Trible, *Texts of Terror*, 7.

44. Helen A. Harrison, "Pollock's Statements: Interpreting His Art in His Own (?) Words" (paper presented at the seventy-first annual Southeastern College Art Conference, Pittsburgh, PA, October 22, 2015), http://tinyurl.com/3pyvhhay.

45. Richard P. Taylor, Branka Spehar, Paul Van Donkelaar, and Caroline M. Hagerhall, "Perceptual and Physiological Responses to Jackson Pollock's Fractals," *Frontiers in Human Neuroscience* 5 (2011), http://tinyurl.com/569rnfdf.

### Final Thoughts

1. Madeleine L'Engle, *The Genesis Trilogy* (Colorado Springs: Waterbrook, 1997), 26.

2. Shackleton, *South*, 200.

# ARTIST'S NOTE

*About the Artist*

Jeremy Grant (b. 1985) is a multidisciplinary artist and designer who works in collage, assemblage, and animation. He has degrees in graphic design and illustration from John Brown University. He lives and works in Denver, Colorado. Follow his artmaking at https://JeremyGrant.art or Instagram @JeremyGrant.art.

*About the Art*

The collages created for this book mimic the spirit of Liz's work. I have created a series of mysterious artifacts that can be revisited as relics. Each reveals itself further with each look and also invites interpretation and commentary on Liz's words.

I have sourced the imagery of these collages from vintage textbooks, *Popular Science*, and *LIFE* magazines from the 1940s, 1950s, and 1960s. The modernist-era optimism presented in these publications presumed that every aspect of life (including religion) could find neat categories. We believed we could understand the world. But every ideology and system experiences the wear and tear of time; we reinterpret and excavate as we age; we question the simplistic stories we've been told. The collages I've made dialogue with this history of reinterpretation. I aim not only to subvert the kitschy atomic-era mindset but also to connect to the ancient and elemental.

I believe collage reinterprets. Collage recontextualizes by collecting seemingly unrelated images and placing them side by side.

Through these surprising associations, collages can spark meaning. Collage can also act as a means of obfuscation, creating ambiguity that makes us question what we see.

To make sense of our daily contexts, each human must dig through many layers of ideologies, systems, and personal and social histories. Sometimes, this means tearing apart all we've known and gluing back a fundamentally altered picture. The spiritual life also contains many rounds of this tearing and reassembling. Yet the goal of these rounds is not destruction but new sight. I hope these collages offer readers a fresh way to see.

# AUTHOR'S NOTE

Continue your journey in Genesis at LizCharlotte.com. There, you'll find resources, including book club questions, recommendations for further reading, and an audio discussion about the book with both the author and visual artist.

# PERMISSIONS

Artworks that accompany each chapter are reproduced from the original collages by Jeremy Grant created to supplement this book. They are published within this book under a limited license agreement. The work may not be photographed, reproduced, or publicly exhibited without express written permission of the artist.

Portions of chapters 1 and 2 were first published in *Christian Century* as "Strange Sounds in Deep Water" in the August 2023 print magazine.

Portions of chapter 2 were first published in *Dappled Things* magazine as "Mirror Image" in the Easter 2022 issue.

Portions of chapter 3 were first published online in *The Curator* magazine as "The Grandmother of Performance Art: Marina Abramović Is Her Own Medium" in 2021.

Portions of chapter 11 were first published online in *The Curator* magazine as "NASA's Abstract Expressionism" in 2014.